MASTERING THE FILM
AND OTHER ESSAYS

MASTERING
THE FILM
AND
OTHER ESSAYS

by Charles Thomas Samuels

Edited by Lawrence Graver

with a Foreword by John Simon

The University of Tennessee Press

Knoxville

Library of Congress Cataloging in Publication Data

Samuels, Charles Thomas, 1936–1974.
  Mastering the film and other essays.

  Includes bibliographical references and index.
  1. Moving-pictures—Collected works. I. Title.
PN1994.S334 1977   791.43   77-642
ISBN 0–87049–209–8

for Erika and Melissa

FOREWORD

Death by his own hand at the age of thirty-eight was, I am sure, the only thing that prevented Charles Thomas Samuels from becoming the most important film critic of our time. For it must be remembered that a critic is a writer who ages differently from, say, a poet or a novelist, from whom he differs hardly if at all in literary prowess. A lyrical poet is apt to be at his height at a very early age, a novelist usually in his early-middle or middle years, whereas a critic is just beginning to get into his own at thirty-eight. For criticism is not primarily a matter of invention or of response to things as they come along, and formulation of the response with brilliant artistry; it is a matter, above all, of prolonged, profound involvement with the art criticized—a continuous savoring, weighing, reflecting upon, comparing and contrasting, and living with, let us say, films; then placing them in the context of other arts and art in general; finally, situating them in life—as a critic must also have found time to live it.

The apprenticeship of a critic, then, is much longer than that of other literary artists, which is not to be construed as a value judgment—an elephant is not superior to man because its gestation is almost thrice as long as a human being's—it is merely a statement of fact. My point is that Samuels' film criticism, like his literary criticism, had every chance of becoming even better than it already was at the time of his death, and that the loss to us is qualitative as well as quantitative. That only four sections of his book on the major directors survive—and those not necessarily in their final form—is for us a deprivation of inestimable magnitude.

Still, like everyone else, a critic must be judged on what he achieved, not on what he might have done. And we are lucky indeed that Samuels left us as much as he did, and that this posthumous collection brings together what was previously scattered or unpublished. There would have been much more of it had Samuels elected to become a full-time film critic, had he not felt that there were too few good movies around, week by week, to keep a fastidious mind regularly occupied. But even if he could have been a full-time film *and* literary critic, he would not have been happy because of his horror of the Big City where such critics must ply their trade, and because he loved teaching too much to give it up for anything.

At Williams College he had an almost ideal set-up. He could teach both English and film, he lived with his wife and two daughters amid delightful surroundings, and he was not so far from New York City but that a mildly enervating drive could provide him with material for one of his quarterly columns for *The American Scholar*. It was on these lightning visits that I most often saw him, our talk sandwiched in, along with a couple of actual sandwiches, between two of his movies, or a movie and a ballet or play. For all his espousal of the careful and deliberate, Samuels was also extremely quick, quickwitted, almost driven. One of the topics that almost never failed to come up was his loathing for megalopolitan life—its unconduciveness to relaxed ratiocination and inducements to literary dog-eat-doggishness. Samuels preferred to write about a film after viewing it several times in succession with his students in a film course, then, upon brisk discussion with them and his wife Nada, writing out of slowly ripening reflection.

He wrote carefully, perhaps even painfully, but the result justified the pains taken. There is a solidity and finality about Samuels' best criticism, a pregnancy and lucidity that many an easier, more fluent writer never arrives at. If his style lacks anything, it is sensuousness and, to a lesser extent, that wittiness Samuels the man possessed in abundance. Whether his writing, becoming more relaxed, would have acquired these features as well, I do not know, but by comparing the earlier and later pieces in this book, the reader may make his own inferences. What is notable in all the writing, besides the good sense and keen insight, is a marvelous absence of fudging, an absolute concision. By this I mean the special grace that knows exactly where lies the line between cryptic overconcentration and flabby overelaboration. And then there was his judicious, idealistic sternness.

Film criticism, being such a new discipline, is still very undisciplined, especially when one considers that film and writing about it have, until very recently, been mainly acts of rebellion or escape: rebellion against the supposedly narrow confines of the so-called higher arts, and escape from harsher realities against which film was presumed to provide a shelter made of glittering fantasies and womblike darkness. Hence much that passes for cinematic criticism to this day is—unless it is mere reviewing—the spinning out of preposterously cloying tributes and the fabrication of outlandishly abstruse theories by people who are really movie fans or buffs—enthusiasts or fantasts who either worship all films or conceive of film criticism as a means of justifying irrelevant cravings. Movies are adored just because they are there, or because they allow free association in the guise of scholarship. Samuels, however, was of a different cast. For him films had to be as good as the very best work in the other arts, and as the best films he had seen in the course of his devoted, intense but critical moviegoing. I suppose I am merely saying that he had standards acquired through learning, teaching, cultivated diversification and, of course, that mysterious thing we call discrimination or perception or, simply, taste.

Samuels the man was, with the one exception noted above, as nearly as possible identical with Samuels the critic. This was greatly to the benefit of the latter. Whatever the man experienced, felt, thought, believed was faithfully and unaffectedly placed at the service of the critic. And Samuels the critic felt as much accountable for Samuels the man as he did for any of his lectures or publications. This, alas, may not have been to the ultimate benefit of the man. Charles (forgive me if I drop the pretense of impersonality and call him as I would have called him when alive) suffered some critical setbacks with his books *Encountering Directors*, savaged by a number of journalistic reviewers, and *The Ambiguity of Henry James*, which endured the fate common to many university press books of passing by almost unnoticed. As a result of this, and certain disappointments with his own behavior that only an ultrasevere critic would have found disconcerting—and in spite of some academic honors that simultaneously came to him—Charles condemned himself to nonexistence.

Let me make it clear; I do not subscribe to the romantic notion that unjust reviews can kill a sensitive literary plant; psychiatry could doubtless find some highly plausible explanations for Charles's suicide. But I do believe that over and above everything he thought he had "killed" others in his reviews and that, not having lived up to his gallantly extravagant and intransigently perfectionist expectations of himself, he had to draw what must have looked like a logical conclusion to his depressed mind. His friend, Leonard Michaels, the short-story writer, put it succinctly and well when he said of Charles's suicide, "It was a mistake." No more, and no less.

His students loved him—this I know at first hand from a good many of them who have written or talked to me about him. They loved him despite his being perhaps the toughest grader on campus, because they knew he cared about them as much as he did about literature and film, to the point of strictness. But Charles had a remarkably gentle severity, one that patiently explained its reasons, could laugh at itself, and never denied a student, filmmaker, or writer another chance. He was eminently capable of spotting something good in the midst of insufficiencies, as witness his treatment of Hitchcock; or of rescuing an unjustly slighted reputation, as witness his treatment of Carol Reed. And he could be fiercely demanding of those he loved best, like Bergman and Bresson. And so it was not only the young, but also distinguished elder colleagues, such as Stanley Kauffmann, who respected his gifts.

What cannot be overstressed is his love for teaching, of which criticism was for him a natural extension. How often he urged me to return to the classroom, and how—affectionately yet forcefully—he would lecture me on what he perceived as the pedagogical errors of my criticism. He certainly had what all good teachers possess: the ability to reprove without condescension, to correct errors without making such correction emerge as a mode of self-promotion, let alone a source of glee. His criticism is, even at its most negative, unfailingly dignified.

But what, one might ask, was the final critical contribution of Charles Thomas Samuels? Did he leave some useful critical tools— a methodology perhaps, or a theory? No, thank goodness. When he was offered Christian Metz's *Film Language* for review by *The New Republic*, he turned it down after scrupulously struggling through it; a "semiotics of the cinema" (as the book is subtitled) was for him not even worth refuting.

What does come out of Samuels' work is what we receive also from our other best critics—James Agee, Otis Ferguson, Robert Warshow (why do they all have to die prematurely?)—the example of a limpid mind working from the best available aesthetic, psychological, philosophical, and social—which is to say humane—criteria. And working in so above-board a manner, with every move open for inspection, that even if you disagree with some of the premises or conclusions, you cannot help learning from the clarity and persuasiveness with which they are set forth. I want to believe that we can learn by watching a master-critic—a teacher—at work, which is the way other skills and disciplines are taught or transmitted to us—by example. But even supposing that we cannot learn from it, there is pure delight in observing a masterly performance.

JOHN SIMON

X

ACKNOWLEDGMENTS

The following essays have been previously published and I am grateful to the editors of the journals in which they appeared for permission to reprint: "Hitchcock," "The Blow-Up: Sorting Things Out," "Puppets: from Z to *Zabriskie Point*," "Bresson's Gentleness," "The Context of *A Clockwork Orange*," "Hyphens of the Self," "How Not to Film a Novel," "Tampering With Reality," in the *American Scholar*; "Bonnie and Clyde" in *Hudson Review*.

I am especially grateful to Robert Bell, Peter Berek, Lynda Bundtzen, Suzanne Graver, John Reichert and Nada Samuels for answering questions and providing valuable criticism; to Nadene Lane and Theoharis C. Theoharis for help in preparing the manuscript; to the Trustees of Williams College for a research grant to defray costs; and to Neil D. Isaacs, special consultant for film books published by The University of Tennessee Press.

L.G.

BIOGRAPHICAL NOTE

CHARLES THOMAS SAMUELS was born on February 20, 1936, in Brooklyn, New York. He was educated at Syracuse University, Ohio State, and the University of California at Berkeley, where he received his Ph.D. in 1961. For thirteen years he was on the English faculty at Williams College. His books include *John Updike* (1969), *A Casebook on Film* (1970), *The Ambiguity of Henry James* (1971), and *Encountering Directors* (1972). His essays and reviews on literature and film appeared in the *Nation, New Republic, New York Times Book Review, Atlantic, Commonweal, Hudson Review, Modern Occasions,* and other journals. From 1970 until 1974 he was film columnist for the *American Scholar.* Among his awards were a Fulbright Lectureship (1964–65), and fellowships from the American Council of Learned Societies (1968) and the National Endowment for the Humanities (1971). He was selected as a Phi Beta Kappa Visiting Scholar in 1973. He died in Williamstown, Massachusetts, on March 13, 1974.

CONTENTS

INTRODUCTION

Charles Thomas Samuels' career as a film critic lasted only seven years and yet in that brief period he produced books, essays, and reviews of such intellectual vigor and variousness that his work should remain of permanent use to people wishing to see films more clearly. Clarity of vision was always his principal goal as a critic, and he was inspired to call his *American Scholar* column "Sightings" because the word refers both to the ability to see and to the instrument used to assist one's aim by guiding the eye. At different places in his writings, Samuels guided the viewer's eye to different things, and it is a testimony to his growth as a critic that one is able to speak of stages in a career so short.

Prompted by an intense polemical impulse, Samuels' earliest essays (on *Blow-Up* and *Bonnie and Clyde*, 1968–69) have the surface verve and high color of bold journalism written in the midst of controversy. Films open in New York, are extravagantly praised or blamed (often in his judgment from shallow perspectives), and he tangles with reviewers in hopes of straightening things out. As a young cultural policeman, he is sometimes brash, high-handed, by turns glib and overly solemn, but there is no mistaking the intelligence or the aesthetic and moral passions that motivate his contentiousness. Trained as a critic of Modernist literature, he was dedicated to standards that valued irony, ambiguity, and formal complexity; beginning his work as a critic of film, he lamented the single-mindedness, frivolity, and lack of discrimination with which films were so often discussed. "Most movie criticism," he once wrote, "is merely inept, without aesthetics, standards of judgment, or critical vocabulary. Between the effusions of the film buffs and the misunderstandings of newspaper reviewers, there is little to choose." Like his favorite novelist, Henry James, Samuels believed that "the essence of moral energy is to survey the whole field," and he often chided other critics for not bringing more to bear on good and bad films: more precise attention to visual sequences and their implications; a more thorough knowledge of a director's *œuvre*; a greater respect for the extraordinary potentialities of the film form itself.

The reviewer-baiting that characterizes these first essays tells us something not only about Samuels' own temperament and perspectives but also about the context in which much film criticism of the late 1960s was written. Film had long been recognized as the dominant serious entertainment form of the period, and older critics such as Dwight Macdonald, Stanley Kauffmann and John Simon had for years been trying to show how at its finest it could be the dominant art form as well. The stakes were high: film criticism mattered because film mattered; large, eager new audiences needed help to see films more intelligently, not encouragement to pursue mindless pleasures. Samuels was one of the few critics born after 1935 to join forces with men whose critical principles were significantly influenced by reading and writing about such Modernists as Conrad, Joyce, Eliot, Stevens, and Faulkner. The weight of literary allusion in the writings of these critics frequently led to the accusation that they were elitist and bookish, haughtily looking only for masterpieces and insensitive to the properties of film as entertainment and as a distinctive new art form.

Anyone, however, who looks closely at "The Blow-Up: Sorting Things Out," will see that Samuels is already in his first essay demonstrating in detail how Antonioni "thinks with his eyes." While wrangling with Andrew Sarris or Pauline Kael, he was also providing fresh illustrations of how a great filmmaker gets his effects, or how effects that may appear masterful in an overly praised work like *Bonnie and Clyde* are merely crafty. "Most films are to be looked at; Antonioni's are to be inspected," he tells us; and he was the first critic to explain the intricate, crucial pattern by which the photographer in *Blow-Up* comes to realize his own blindness and vacuity, thus demonstrating that Antonioni's basic concerns are moral, not metaphysical. Labeling *Bonnie and Clyde* "decayed cabbage leaves smeared with catsup" may have been designed to draw critical blood; but most of the essay is a poised, evidential demonstration of the film's troublesome flaws in logic and consistency. Although Samuels' analyses of visual patterning, montage, and sound became more original and subtle in his later work, his sensitivity to the generic qualities of film was obvious from the start.

Between the writing of the pieces on *Blow-Up* and *Bonnie and Clyde* and the beginning of his work as columnist for the *American Scholar*, Samuels edited the useful *Casebook on Film* (1970) and began teaching film regularly at Williams College. These pedagogical experiences nourished his criticism, and the essays on Hitchcock (1970) and Bresson (1971) are among the finest he ever wrote.

xviii

Hitchcock is something of a test for a critic accused of being excessively literary, for his films offer little insight into character and moral complexity, and their paraphrasable discursive content is thin. What Samuels recognizes and so convincingly celebrates is Hitchcock's genius for the swift, intense evocation of basic emotions in his audience. Contrivance, "contentless virtuosity," characters as "mere containers of stress," the amoral manipulation of a viewer's aggressive impulses and lust for thrills—traits to be deplored in a serious novel or play—are shown to be fruitful ingredients in Hitchcock's original contribution to popular storytelling. To appreciate properly his elegant, suspenseful variations of rhythm and tempo is to understand the power of film to provoke sensuous responses prior to conscious reflection abut meaning and morality. Primitive mastery, perhaps, but in Samuels' argument, essential to a perception of what the medium can so quickly and forcefully do.

In Bresson, Samuels saw mastery of an entirely different and more praiseworthy kind. If Hitchcock works adroitly on a viewer's nerves, Bresson tries to engage his mind and spirit. The entertainer Hitchcock brilliantly exploits plot; the more speculative Bresson discards it to involve us in a drama of interior perception. Although Samuels does not use the illustration for this purpose, his reminder of John Updike's distinction between circumstantial and gnostic suspense helps distinguish Hitchcock's art from Bresson's. There are, for Updike, two kinds of stories, those in which we want to learn "the outcome of an unresolved situation" and those in which we keep hoping that "at any moment an illumination will occur." Hitchcock creates suspense by the ingenious exploitation of secrets based on circumstance; Bresson—as befits a religious artist—pursues mysteries of a deeper, perhaps unfathomable kind.

What those mysteries are and how Bresson gives them original cinematic form is the subject of Samuels' review of *A Gentle Creature*. Like many of his essays on films he admired, this piece displays his gift for demonstrating how close analysis can be a zestful, indeed necessary, part of the comprehension of a complex work of art. *A Gentle Creature*, he argues, suggests that "tragedy can be comprehended as a process while still evading our need to fathom motives and fix blame," yet his own tribute fathoms Bresson's motives and fixes fit praise to the accomplishment. As evidence, one need only look at his explanations of how Bresson makes narrative commentary functional, how he uses asynchronous dialogue and images to reveal the inner life of his characters, or how he reinforces the theme of spiritual aridity by depicting objects, mechanical sounds, and a wedding sequence that is "not assented to but only performed," not a sacrament but the mere "signing of a register."

In many of the other reviews written during the early 1970s, Samuels continued to perform simultaneously as polemicist and explicator, but his sense of both roles and his ability to execute them deepened. As a polemicist, he insisted that films entertain us and interpret our lives, engage our emotions and respect the intricacies of our characters, dramatize our present concerns while linking us to the past and the future. In his aesthetic, a good film is defined by the skill with which it uses the resources of the medium to pursue complex, significant human goals. To demand that each new release offer pleasure and wisdom meant, of course, that few would pass the test; and much of Samuels' reviewing consists of explanations of how films fail and why.

Such demonstrations are worth attending to now partly for their subtlety and incisiveness, but also because they include within them many bright illustrations of what great film art can look like and sometimes does. A demolition job on the empty grotesquery of the *Satyricon* has several fine paragraphs on the mixture of satire and sympathy that gives Fellini's best work its distinctive, original tone. Stanley Kubrick will be scolded for indulging in *2001* his love of gadgets and special effects; not, however, before he is praised for the brilliant exposé in *Dr. Strangelove* of a death culture in perverse love with machines. A dismissal of *Fat City* and *Deliverance* is called "How Not to Film a Novel"; yet the piece ends citing *Diary of a Country Priest, Lady with the Dog, An Outcast of the Islands,* and the work of Truffaut as examples of superb films that have emerged from the pages of fiction.

Because his reviews appeared quarterly in the *American Scholar,* Samuels was usually limited to writing about films that opened in New York during the previous three months. Free, however, from the dreary obligation of coverage, he could choose new works that seemed important in their own right, or for insights they gave about the development of a major director, or the state of film as an art form. With less deadline pressure than the average reviewer, he could hope to construct a thoughtful essay rather than a provisional report. One of the best of such pieces and a useful illustration of his method is "Tampering with Reality," a column about Buñuel, Bergman, and Jan Troell. Beginning with a characteristically brusque dissent from conventional opinion (the prize-winning *Discreet Charm of the*

Bourgeoisie is "silly" and *Cries and Whispers* "hollow"), he moves quickly to a speculation about the uses of fantasy and realism in cinema. Both styles, he insists, have obviously produced masterpieces, but lately there has been a disturbing development in the making of films and in their criticism. Audiences seem to crave only the startling and the exotic; even the finest directors are tempted to rely on technical dazzle and shock effects instead of pursuing intricacies of dramatic presentation or insights into ideas and people. Reviewers faced with films that "carry false messages or none at all, often shift their attention to the envelop." Virtuosity is mistaken for vision.

Ostensibly, *The Discreet Charm of the Bourgeosie* is meant to be a comic exposé of middle-class behavior. Through the careful examination of scenic progressions, Samuels shows that Buñuel's control of his satire is erratic: the use of dreams and bizarre incidents to suggest the illogicality of bourgeois life fails because that life has never been believably created in the first place. The film is little more than a parade of odd episodes, some funny some grim, but most of which contradict or do not relate to the major theme of the film. Similarly, Bergman is also implausible in blending the real and the fantastic. Harriet Anderson's terrifyingly graphic enactment of death in the opening scenes is subverted by the "insulting artifice" of the sumptuously stylish background; and from this point on credibility is continually sacrificed to unmotivated, random sensationalism. Despite its vastly superior execution, *Cries and Whispers* is as ill-conceived as *The Discreet Charm of the Bourgeosie*: "Each film fails to convince us of its theme. *Cries and whispers* implies that the anguish of death differs only from that of life in being terminal. . . . Yet death is recreated with recognizable accuracy whereas life is reduced to a series of attitudinizing speeches and poorly motivated outrages."

As always in his best work, the persuasiveness of Samuels' argument depends on the steady accumulation of sharply perceived details. Yet once again his analysis of failure is preparatory to his celebration of success. In this instance the film to be praised is Jan Troell's *The Emigrants*. Noting that fewer than fifty triple-spaced pages were necessary to record the dialogue of this three-hour-and-ten-minute film, Samuels goes on to provide a sparkling demonstration of how Troell's historical epic "lives in its images" and achieves the uncommon feat of making "gorgeousness discursive."

At the same time that he was writing these vigorous reviews for the *American Scholar* and other magazines, Samuels was working on the two ambitious books he hoped would be his major contribution to the understanding of film. The first was a set of interviews with major directors; the second an extended study offering an aesthetics of the sound, narrative film. As he told a staff member of the National Endowment for the Humanities: "It won't be the last word, but it's a start—and it's obvious that somebody had better start. The best critics writing today are journalists, working under restrictions that prevent their trying something like this." Between 1969 and 1972 he traveled to Rome, Paris, Brussels, Stockholm, London, Los Angeles, and elsewhere, talked with directors, and saw every available film that any serious critic had ever claimed to be important.

The first project resulted in *Encountering Directors* (1972), an often tendentious yet absorbing collection, full of fresh material, that will continue to be a valued source book for anyone writing about the cinema of the period. Having come to each interview with as full a knowledge of the director's work as he could possibly gain in advance, Samuels pressed forward with a set of questions designed to express admiration, elicit information and statements of intent, and break through reticence, evasiveness, or reflexive responses. Sometimes he provoked silence or hostility; more often, he stimulated his subjects to say things about their art that they had rarely expressed in public before. But as he himself was quick to admit:

> I never succeeded to my satisfaction. Despite candor to the point of abrasiveness and enticing expressions of sincere regard, I could neither provoke nor cajole all the confidences I sought . . . . But as Antonioni, Bresson, and others told me, when one tries to capture reality, he often succeeds by failing. What I had not intended to record proves even more interesting than what I planned. Thus, I discovered, while consecutively reading the interviews, that the consistency of my approach threw into high relief differences among my respondents. Comparisons made possible because of the presence of a common denominator themselves measure each sensibility. That is why, after having selected the verb "encounter" to indicate my interviewing style, I made it a present participle to suggest that each talk was part of a process and that none is more complete than the process itself.

Because Samuels died when the second book was only one third complete, it too remains only part of a process. The exact shape of *Mastering the Film* can only be inferred, but the general intention is clear. The notes for the introduction (pp. 3–11) are admittedly fragmentary and would have been rewritten, but they do provide clues to the critical principles on which the selections and argument of the book were to rest. Further clues are, of course, offered by the essays themselves and by *Encountering Directors*.

Samuels' aim in *Mastering the Film* was to offer an aesthetics of the narrative sound cinema through the inductive study of twelve great directors. At the time of his death, he had written four of the essays and left the rough sketch of an introduction. From these pieces, it is possible to reconstruct a tentative table of contents for the entire volume: Introduction; I Carol Reed and the Novelistic Film; II Jean Renoir and the Theatrical Film; III René Clair; IV Alfred Hitchcock: Emotional Rhythm; V Federico Fellini: Juxtaposition; VI Vittorio De Sica; VII Ermanno Olmi; VIII Jean Vigo; IX François Truffaut; X Michelangelo Antonioni; XI Robert Bresson; XII Ingmar Bergman.

Starting with estimable directors whose films were related to the achievements of novelists and playwrights, Samuels planned to move through the varieties of major cinematic art toward the work of men who—in his judgment—had made the most distinctive and significant use of the genre itself. That only four chapters remain is lamentable; but they are suggestive enough to prove how valuable the book would have been. The manuscript essays on Carol Reed, Jean Renoir, and Fellini are in many respects an advance on Samuels' earlier writings about film. Of the four completed chapters printed here, "Hitchcock" appeared in *The American Scholar* (Spring, 1970); but the essays on Reed, Renoir, and Fellini have never been published. Retaining the best features of his journalism, they are less beleaguered, more appealingly expansive, fully argued and authoritative than the work written within the space and time constraints of the magazines.

The authority of these essays is most impressively demonstrated by the sheer number of things Samuels is able to make happen in them. Bright preliminary speculations about the quintessential nature of cinema mix with analyses of single films where essences are given particular density and weight. Inevitably, since the surviving chapters are only a fragment of a book in which much would have been tied together at the close, the theoretical framework is less substantial than the often brilliant accounts of individual films. Readers may judge the ambitious promise of "an aesthetics of the sound, narrative film" as sadly unfulfilled; but they will find in the opening essays some of the most helpful commentary yet written on the achievements of three important European directors.

The unifying theme of Samuels' tribute to Carol Reed is metamorphosis: the diverse ways in which an artist gives borrowed fictional material new life on the screen. Charting Reed's progress toward an increasingly more cinematic conception of storytelling, Samuels shows how many different elements eventually come together in the Englishman's finest films. *The Stars Look Down* is superior to A.J. Cronin's bulky novel because of its concise, powerful scenario, mature conception of characters, and high degree of visual inventiveness; but despite an admirable subtlety, it ends up too much like a novel, too reliant on words. The excellence of *The Fallen Idol* can be located in Reed's inspired modification of the Graham Greene story on which the film is based. Having convinced Greene to center the action in a boy's damaging misperception of the man he admires, Reed was able to explore the relationship between defective vision and the cinematic methods by which it might be dramatized. *The Fallen Idol* illustrates how the camera can begin to create multiple levels of objective and subjective reality; yet in the end, forsaking perception for melodrama, the film becomes a commonplace thriller.

As Samuels continues to describe Reed's progress toward a greater visualization of narrative, his own criticism gains subtlety and comprehensiveness. Just as Reed found memorable images to bring alive someone else's words, so Samuels has his own language to vivify Reed's images. Particularly fine are the observations about Reed's openings, his casting, and his literal and symbolic rendering of physical reality. Samuels' analyses of the first sequences of *Our Man in Havana, An Outcast of the Islands,* and *The Third Man* can serve as model explanations of how directorial economy and fullness of effect can go hand in hand.

In each instance he shows Reed guiding our eyes, engaging our interest, controlling our responses, getting the story going, introducing characters and themes, and establishing visual and aural rhythms—all, as Samuels puts it—on a swift "stream of images" that prefigures the rest of the film. Similarly, the choice of actors is impeccable. Wishing to create intricate reactions to Willems, Harry Lime, and Holly Martins (characters who could at first sight be seen as singular), Reed uses Trevor Howard, Orson Welles, and Joseph Cotten. Howard's raffish charm and physical grace create sympathy for a fallen sensualist who in Conrad's novel is mostly an object of derision. Welles' commanding presence (craftily intensified by a delayed and startling entrance) does not diminish his villainy, but makes him more appealing than the "adenoidal and wooden" Joseph Cotten, whose naïve, boyish good intentions look increasingly blameworthy. About the process by which Reed uses Havana, Sambir, and postwar Vienna to symbolize the varieties of corruption to which his characters are susceptible, Samuels also has shrewd and original things to say.

Samuels' critique also restores to fresh perception scenes in Reed's films that may have settled in the back of our memories: Willems stalking Aissa "in a silence whose void of words measures the unreasoning power of his lust"; Mrs. Fenwick's face at the beginning and the end of *The Stars Look Down*, which tells us so much about her son's moral progress through the middle; the ruined streets of Vienna shot at an angle to intensify our sense of a world off-balance; and the whore and muscleman behind the credits of *Our Man in Havana*, emblems of Cuba's sensuality but also of "the moral meaning latent in the atmosphere"—the relationship between power and corruption. By the end of Samuels' essay, we realize how much of Reed's art we overlooked the first time but will not miss again.

In the proposed second chapter of *Mastering the Film*, Samuels analyzes the many languages—verbal and nonverbal—that Jean Renoir speaks in his films. Faulting the conventional view that Renoir's distinction is "painterly," Samuels argues that the director's talent rests in a modification of theatrical speech rather than in pictorialization. A basic component of *Grand Illusion* and *Rules of the Game* is a spoken style rooted in French theater: expository, rhetorical, aphoristic, urbane; but it is only *one* element. When Renoir brings another more natural, less-studied, low-keyed speech into counterpoint with his theatrical style, the result is a new cinematic language that expresses basic social and biological conflicts in human nature. In this sense, Renoir's best films can be understood as variations on Freud's theme of civilization and its discontents: social life is an essential, highly refined, but inevitably self-corrupting effort to organize the lives of creatures who are anarchic, promiscuous, and separate. In *Rules of the Game* the subtle relationship between theatrical and ordinary language brilliantly expresses "the contrast between stylization and brute nature that is its theme."

Samuels' demonstration of Renoir playing images off against words, "achieving a synthesis not possible in the theater," ends with his explication of the juxtaposed hunt and ballroom scenes—one of the most suggestive pieces of criticism he ever wrote. Here is a sample:

> In truth, the forms that appeared real to the La Chesnaye world kept them from recognizing the equal reality of the madness they were attempting to disguise. During the ball, this madness unmasks itself.

By constructing the scene so as to parallel the hunt, Renoir makes clear that the game leads to murder. But the very elegance that constructed its rules allows La Chesnaye to pass the murder off as an accident. Style—which had been ruptured by truth's unmasking at the ball—reasserts itself, closing over the body of Jurieu. The film ends by taking us back to the tone and manner of its earliest scenes.

Much of Samuels' essay on Renoir is just as perceptive and crisply expressed. There is, for instance, his valuable distinction between dialogue that is cinematic and that which is an evasion of the medium. From *A Day in the Country*, he cites the scene in which characters read aloud the description of a sign we have already seen in closeup. Here the dialogue is functional because it tells us important things about their feelings that could not be conveyed in the theater. On the other hand, Henrietta's speech about her amorphous desires—having no satisfactory visual counterpart—could have been lifted straight out of a play. Most of the dialogue in *Grand Illusion* is superbly cinematic because it exists "less for the information it contains than to exemplify the human separation" that is one of the major themes of the film. Cinematic, too, are the strong multi-lingual scenes in *Grand Illusion*, and Samuels' comment does justice to their artfulness:

> ... since the theater doesn't permit subtitling, a playwright could not cast so much of his dialogue in tongues foreign to his audience without effectively blocking their comprehension. But even in cases like the discussion of brandy, the dialogue becomes an action (hence relatively cinematic) rather than an utterance: the sign of a condition rather than a piece of communication between characters or to the audience. Renoir and coscenarist Charles Spaak had made their story from the phenomenon of people talking at cross purposes because this babble of dialogue is the outer proof of otherwise invisible conflicts of role.

The last of the completed chapters for *Mastering the Film*—"Federico Fellini: Juxtaposition"—may be less original and provocative than the essays on Reed and Renoir, but it has a good many other virtues. In Samuels' view, Fellini achieves his most memorable effects through the accretion of freshly observed details rather than by formal innovation or a profound vision of life. For this reason, he is best served not by elaborate theorizing that would inevitably exaggerate his importance, but by commentary suited to the scale and quality of his achievement. Such criticism—poised, zestful, sensitive

xxvi

to nuance, strongly phrased—can be found in Samuels' discussions of *I Vitteloni, The White Sheik, Variety Lights,* and *8½.* Emerging from the critic's own careful accretion of details is a tribute to a humane satirist whose subject is "man, the bedeviled dreamer," and whose art brings "yearnings to the surface where they may be felt as well as seen."

The ability to feel and to see—passionate discernment—marked much of what Samuels wrote about film. The previously unpublished essays on Reed, Renoir, and Fellini are especially valuable because they (like the earlier pieces on Antonioni, Hitchcock, and Bresson) show Samuels at his most useful as a critic: perceptive frame-by-frame yet suggestive theoretically; strict in his standards of value yet generous, indeed celebratory about the works he admired. Even as one-quarter of an unfinished book, these chapters are a substantial contribution to the criticism of film and a reminder of what might exist had those other eight chapters been written.

PART ONE

MASTERING
THE FILM

NOTES FOR AN INTRODUCTION

THE FILMS from which the following aesthetic was inferred were not seen by a *tabula rasa* but by a person with certain ideas and tastes. Undoubtedly—and even more frequently than I can know—failures of imagination or of humility made me cling to my prior notions, but I tried to let each film modify them. Insofar as I was able, I tried to build my definition of cinema as I went along. There were, however, some antecedent decisions. Since describing the nature of all film seemed too grandiose a project, I first decided to concentrate on sound features, thereby neglecting four categories that any truly comprehensive theory would need to include: silents, documentaries, *cinema pur*, and cartoons.

Although film's basic techniques were developed in the silent era, sound marked a crucial distinction between the forms. Words being incomparably the most expressive of human languages, silent films, even at their best, suffered narrowness of range as a fixed impediment. Lesser talents tried to overcome this by appropriating words, but they succeeded only in blocking the flow of images with titles that, owing to the temporal demand of films, were simple and easy to read. As a result, neither eloquence nor intellect was served. The period's best filmmakers were those who accepted muteness. But mind was sacrificed, and—since we do speak and make noises—so was reality. However much he may have wanted to be realistic, a silent filmmaker was forced to be artificial; however much he may have wanted to be complicated, he was forced—in the strictest meaning of the term—to stay on the surface. Therefore, one need not study the earlier form, for its best features were absorbed by the later. I decided to discuss silents only when they were a stage in careers of those sound directors I have chosen to analyze. Ignoring documentary seems more debatable. Like Siegfried Kracauer, I believe that film is distinguished among the arts by its ability to duplicate the real world. One might therefore argue that documentaries are particularly authentic because they do only what films do best.

This argument is ingenuous on two counts. First, documentaries are "truer" than story-films only in a naïve sense. Like features, they select and arrange details and hence are no less artful. Insofar as they do come closer to "raw reality" they pass outside the realm of aesthetics. Since they purport to deal with facts, they necessarily invoke tests of accuracy and function that features may avoid. Doubtless, this is a distinction of degree rather than kind. A film like *The Bicycle Thief*, for example, would be impossible if its situation could never have occurred in postwar Italy: yet literal exactitude is crucial neither to its effect nor to its general pertinence as a reflection of poverty and social disorder. On the other hand, a documentary on these subjects. *would* have to be verifiable, and its accuracy would be crucial in producing those effects (in this case, presumably reformist) that are always the goal of such a work. Despite the obvious similarity between documentaries and certain kinds of feature films, the difference between the two forms is as great as the difference between films that can choose not to speak and those that lack the choice. In each case the apparent link is formally avoidable.

Like documentary, *cinéma pur* emphasizes one of the medium's essentials. In this case, the essential is even more obviously aesthetic because non-narrative films make visualization an end in itself. Unlike documentary, this form does not push the critic into alien disciplines of response. But in its purity, non-narrative is as unreal as silent film; one form is mute, the other is lobotomized. Shunning story, avant-garde equally banishes mind. Since film, being a form devoted to surface, cannot be literally discursive, it requires the introduction of narrative (hence utterance) to permit thought. A discourse proceeding entirely by means of visual objects is theoretically possible; practically it will almost never occur. The speed of film and our difficulty in understanding a complex of visual signals militate against the possibility. One would have either to slow the film down so as to permit study of each object—which would be technically disjunctive—or simplify the visual field—which would be discursively self-defeating.

In fact, however, most experimental films of this kind do not even seem to care whether they say anything: showing is all. To a degree, this is surely a fundamental goal of cinema. But as an isolated act, looking is psychologically supportable only for brief periods, which is why, lacking any principle of development save visual succession, most non-narrative films are short. They are also usually boring—a fact negatively admitted by the propensity their makers show for relying on pornography or other sensational effects. Like documentary, this form aids feature art by insisting on essentials; and, also,

4

like documentary, it substitutes one essential for all others and thus misses the full richness of which cinema is capable.

No such argument can be made against animated films. Indeed, theoretically, this is the purest of the subdivisions because it gives most freedom to creativity. I may seem here to contradict my earlier acknowledgment that film is the art that duplicates reality. The earlier observation is, strictly speaking, a matter of history rather than logic. To be cinema, it is necessary only that the image *move*; what it consists of—formally speaking—does not matter. Animation and other radically inventive modes have proved faulty in practice; theoretically, they are closer to art than realistic cinematography. Indeed, many avant-garde films may be understood as an attempt to photograph the real world according to an aesthetic of animation. Animated films themselves have remained faithful to narrative. But in this sector freedom to create has historically coincided with freedom from intelligence. I neglect cartoons not because they are poor in artistic potential but because they have been poor in fact.

What I proposed, then, was to infer an aesthetic of the narrative sound film from those directors who seemed to me to demonstrate how it becomes an art. Operative in the preceding sentence is the phrase "seemed to me." This book is not the map of cinema; it is *a* map. Of necessity, the cartographer is also a critic. At every point, then, what I assert is debatable because of accompanying evaluations; but I hope that I can be viably descriptive even when one disagrees with certain manifestations of my taste.

Taste chose the data. I must, therefore, explain my methods of selection because, although this book arose by a process of inference, it is of course the exposition of the result and not the biography of the formulation. Within limits I shall soon declare, I arrived at my definition of film by seeing at least two works by any director I have ever found mentioned with interest or respect. This took several years, including one almost wholly devoted to the task, thanks to a fellowship that freed me from other obligations. Naturally, I made certain errors during my preparation. Sometimes, I must certainly have rejected a director because I coincidentally saw only his lesser films. At other times, I succumbed to the vagaries of distributors who kept me ignorant of artists I should know. (However, since my film-viewing took me to museums as well as to theaters both here and abroad, I more likely missed talents that are brand-new than directors whose work is narrowly distributed.) After my film odyssey was finished, I decided to define cinema by means of the collective efforts of all di-

5

rectors who had made at least two major films and evolved a style that seemed both distinctive and excellent.

At this point, I must confess a serious weakness in my strategy and indicate why I chose, nevertheless, to press on. Truly inductive aesthetics would arise from a consideration of individual films. One obviously gives the most comprehensive and honest answer to the question "what is film art?" by replying "all the films that achieve it." I did not go this route, however, for several reasons. First, one could be more reasonably confident of having seen all the best directors than all the best films. Second, and much more important, since I aspired to generalization, I naturally wanted to restrict, so far as was possible, the number of items from which the generalizations would be built up. Finally, although film is a collaborative art, there are directors who stamp their work with the mark of a single sensibility; because I was working in a discipline so lacking in good precedents, I wanted to imitate aesthetics in the older arts, where, traditionally, works are first subsumed within the histories of practitioners.

Neatness is a necessity rather than a pleasure. By deciding to treat directors rather than individual films, I forfeited the right to discuss some great works or near-great works that I have always wanted to write about. I list some examples here both to give myself the pleasure of citing them and to offer the interested reader more information about my taste than my self-imposed guidelines would otherwise permit. The great films would include (in addition to those mentioned later) the Joseph Heifetz adaptation of Chekhov's *The Lady with the Dog*, Pasolini's *Gospel According to Matthew*, and Pontecorvo's political quasi-newsreel, *The Battle of Algiers*. The other list (some of which I might rate more highly if I could only see them again and check myself), would be much longer. It would include: Autant-Lara's film of Raymond Radiguet's *Devil in the Flesh*; Bellocchio's *China Is Near*; Capra's Hollywood romance, *It Happened One Night*; two small-scale but perfect examples of realism: De Seta's *Bandits of Orgosolo* and Passer's *Intimate Lighting*; the height of Hollywood musicals (*Singin' in the Rain*) and of equally unreal Westerns (*Stagecoach*); Henning Carlsen's film of Hamsun's *Hunger*; the thrillers, *M* and *Knife in the Water*; Philipe deBroca's flawed but exciting tragicomedy, *The Joker*; Wajda's *Ashes and Diamonds* and *Landscape After Battle*; Huston's *The Maltese Falcon*, and many more. I also greatly admire several films by Kurosawa (notably *Seven Samurai*), Ozu's *Tokyo Story*, Ray's *Pather Panchali*, and others that nonetheless leave me feeling deracinated.

6

Nevertheless, one cannot too often recall that even the most personal film is a joint effort. I tried to take account of this fact, despite having committed myself to the analogy between directors and authors. Since this notion is familiar in film criticism mainly through an aberrant version, I want to emphasize my thorough contempt for the so-called auteur theory. Originally propounded by French critics (most of whom were seeking to be filmmakers and thus were the reverse of critically disinterested), the auteur theory is so obviously foolish that only Andrew Sarris and his epigones still cling to it. Most critics, whatever their differences on other issues, are united in their opposition on this one. (For examples from notoriously opposed camps, see "Circles and Squares" in Pauline Kael's *I Lost It at the Movies* and John Simon's introduction to *Movies into Film*.)

Auteurists maintain that directors personalize even the most obvious hackwork through stylistic trademarks. Like almost everything in film criticism, the auteur theory is not so much aesthetics as propaganda for trash. Thus a sort of crypto-auteurist like Manny Farber devotes himself to third-rate Americans, such as Samuel Fuller and Don Siegel, while viciously attacking not only great European directors but those few compatriots—John Huston, for instance—who have tried, occasionally, to break through the commercial restrictions. In allying myself with the belief that directors are like writers, painters, and composers, I do not ignore the quality of their uniqueness or their films.

Most of the currently fashionable names not discussed here will be missed only by auteurists or buffs. Other exclusions are more obviously debatable. I do not expect the following brief remarks to convince anyone that I made the right choices, but—both to avoid the charge of inadvertence and for the insight it may offer into my fundamental affinities—I wish to indicate why I neglected certain directors of note.

In one large area, taste played little part. After a period of viewing films made in the East, I declared myself unfit to deal with them. I rather suspect that the widespread admiration for Akira Kurosawa and Satyajit Ray is entirely well founded. But in neither case am I internally secure about my reactions. From appreciating the work of both directors, I feel myself debarred by a cultural remoteness as determinant as that produced by an alien tongue. In several respects, this is literal. Not every film by foreign directors is available in America or, in English translation, anywhere. Hence, even did I not have to reject Japanese and Indian directors on grounds explained earlier, since I had also determined to see all films by each director mentioned, I would have had to omit Kurosawa, Ray, and others because some of their films were unprocurable. As it is, I should never have been able to write this book without some competence in French and Italian. Fortunately for me, France and Italy have produced the largest number of great directors.

In the case of Kurosawa—and of all the important Japanese directors, with the partial exception of Ozu—I also feel it impossible to judge the acting. Sensing the presence of conventions I can neither identify nor comprehend, I cannot tell how much I am being repelled or fascinated by the unfamiliar. Ray is more accessible, but I often find him boring. With a Western director, I would hold this against the artist; my students have convinced me, however, that I simply know too little of Indian aesthetics to catch the beat. I regret limiting my subject to Occidental measures, but I cannot honestly feel myself competent outside the Western perspective.

My other exclusions are less apologetic. One group simply fails to qualify according to my rules (two major films and an excellent style). Because Marcel Carné directed *Children of Paradise* he will always have a place in the history of film art, but none of his other films even begins to compare with this masterpiece. The same is true for René Clément (*Forbidden Games*), Stanley Kubrick (*Dr. Strangelove*), and Orson Welles (*Citizen Kane*). Other directors have made several important films without developing a style or one that is especially cinematic. This last anomaly is truest of the otherwise impressive and unjustly neglected André Cayatte, who, in films like *We Are All Murderers* and *Justice Is Done* almost domesticated the *pièce à thèse*. Lack of style together with high-class productivity neatly sums up many directors, including the most admired Americans, like Howard Hawks, John Huston, and John Ford (the last of whom has a set of characteristic subjects frequently confused with a style). Other directors of great talent (an example would be Andrzej Wajda), I regretfully eliminated because, although possessing a distinctive style and several impressive efforts, they had failed, in my view, to attain true distinction. But of my missing directors, four should raise eyebrows: Jean-Luc Godard, Alain Renais, Luis Buñuel, and Roberto Rossellini.

Godard is, I feel sure, the most importantly seminal director since D.W. Griffith. Formulas bequeathed successors by the American, the Frenchman relentlessly discarded. As a result, other filmmakers were freed for experiments in tonal mixture, discontinuity, and rhetorical assertion. In Godard's work, however, such qualities are pushed to the point of incoherence by caprice. His latest films serve up an indigestible stew of dogma and formalism, but theme and narrative do not blend even in his early, relatively unmannered and nonideological movies. Always shuttling between literary elements that demand comprehension and cinematic games which block it, these films can be defended on realistic grounds (the world is not easy to figure out either), but only if one believes that art is meant to duplicate human bafflement.

Equally daring as an innovator, and equally unsatisfactory as an artist, is Alain Resnais, whose major achievement is an editing style that represents the flux of memory—with its confusion of tenses and yearning for the subjunctive. Unfortunately, Resnais neither invents nor writes the scenarios on which this technique is lavished, and he has deplorable taste in collaborators. Marguerite Duras's script for *Hiroshima Mon Amour* is portentous and melodramatic; that of Robbe-Grillet for *Last Year at Marienbad* confuses profundity with conundrum; and in *La Guerre Est Finie*, Jorge Semprun displays a sentimental romanticism no less objectionable than his hero's. Like Godard, then—although for different reasons—Resnais is the inventor of a major way of making films rather than a maker of major films. There is less of a division between means and ends in Buñuel and Rossellini than in Godard and Resnais, but in the work of these directors the means are so maladroit that the ends are fatally compromised. Rossellini is called a neorealist, but his films are lurid and melodramatic. *Rome, Open City*, with its warm suffering Italians and sadistic Nazis, verges on propaganda, whereas *Paisan* (an episodic account of American soldiers in Italy) owes more to O. Henry than to the vicissitudes of war. After making a group of even more contrived melodramas in the 1950's, Rossellini later emerged as a documentarist with such widely-admired films as *The Rise to Power of Louis XIV*. Although these are an improvement, they purchase truth at the price of interest, seldom rising above the earnestness of historical pageants.

Buñuel's luridness reflects a mocking sensibility, but it is scarcely more convincing than Rossellini's. Because of technical deficiencies (the acting in his films, for example, is almost always dreadful), Buñuel's sexual preoccupations dwindle into facile shock effects, his so-called blasphemies into pranks. When he is being impishly comic, as in *Simon of the Desert*, he is effective. More often, he makes the error of trying to mix kinks with high sentence. Since his interests owe more to surrealism than to conventional drama, Buñuel would probably have done better had he ignored commercial expectations. At any rate, his films are outrageous only through details; their substance is too trivial to prove disturbing.

The twelve directors I chose seem to me superior in craft and, most often, in human content as well. Their careers are objects of inherent interest. Therefore, I intend *Mastering the Film* to be a critical study of men who warrant one. Nonetheless, each artist also forms a stage in a developing definition of cinema. Hence, I begin with directors who exemplify the ways in which fiction and drama—fundamental ingredients of film—become modified to fit the new form. I then distinguish between two basic goals or modes of film art: realism and evocation. Finally, I treat several directors whose mastery seems to me to establish the highest reaches of the art—till now.

Although I have been at some pains to limit my topic in the interests of feasibility and clarity, there are some involuntary limitations that should also be acknowledged. One of the reasons so few writers have tried to analyze a large collection of films must be the sheer difficulty of seeing them. But this problem pales beside the difficulty of remembering what one has seen. Even viewing on a moviola, which permits you to stop or reverse the film, cannot cope with the form's complexity (dialogue, gesture, lighting, setting, music, characterization, plotting—all coming at you in the same instant of film). Questions of quality aside, film is simply too rich for a critic to get everything. Moreover, film will not stand still. Published scripts cannot do for the film critic what published play scripts or reproductions or disques do for the critics of other arts. And I soon discovered that even extensive notes cannot arm you against the likelihood of committing errors when you try to reconstruct all that went on in a given shot, let alone sequence.

Exacerbating these procedural difficulties is a major problem or strategy. Like music or art critics, film critics must describe their subject in a language radically different from it. Hence, they are likely either to concentrate on those literary elements that are most easily described in words (or, in fact, quoted), thus misrepresenting the form; or, they try to evoke the visual/auditory experiences and risk falling into false analogies, misleading metaphors, or other traps of language that await even the most talented novelist when he seeks to reproduce life (and who, among film critics, commands a novelist's talent?). Moreover, since any film not currently circulating is more distant from the reader than other works of art, the critic must reproduce the work before he analyzes it. Film criticism, therefore, labors under the double burden of having to be descriptive (which takes time and also gifts not necessarily associated with criticism) and descriptive about a form too complex to be accurately or comprehensively described.

Film criticism seems to me to demand the presence of the actual films. But the ardors of this procedure and the impossibility of making any such discussion available beyond its original audience forces one to attempt the impossible: to talk about films in a time and space so distant from that of the object that we seem to be trying to recall a vanished dream.

Because the film critic finds it so hard to double-check himself and because his reader participates in this difficulty, it is tempting to exempt both from those tests of evidence and logic that we apply to other critical discourse. Despite the difficulties, however, we must be as evidential when treating films as we are in discussing the other arts. I mention some of the impediments to close film analysis because my experience of them bids me to seek a sort of provisional mercy. But that is all I seek.

CAROL REED AND THE
NOVELISTIC FILM

THE MEDIUM of sound features is cinematography; its material is literature. Not until we recognize the inescapable presence of novelistic and theatrical elements in film can we consider the form's essence, which consists in their modification. Hence our first task is to recall briefly what the forms have in common before we begin to understand how film art nonetheless differs from the arts of theater and fiction.[1]

Nearly every sound feature photographs people talking and gesturing and to that extent is a filmed play. Dialogue may be minimized, but all the other paraphernalia of theater—actors, physical backgrounds, lighting, costumes, make-up—remain to declare the resemblances between the forms. Nonetheless, the likeness between film and fiction is more inclusive so that I will postpone exemplifying the dramatic roots of film (in the work of Jean Renoir) to the next chapter. We must first concentrate on the essential similarity between fiction and film, letting the link to drama stand, for the moment, as a simply observed fact.

Plays enact stories; novels tell them. In a film even enactment is "told," since no more of the performance is revealed to us than is deliberately captured by the camera. The camera gives film an authorial presence found in fiction but not in drama, and the overtness of its movements, optical effects, etc., allows style to be a vehicle of expression just as it is in prose. Plays can render only what may be spoken or mimed; films, like novels, can render anything available to perception. Description and representation are fundamental to both forms, and although cinema has been weak in expressing abstractions, even that is possible, as can be seen in the films of Bresson and Bergman.

Despite the dialogue they share with plays, most novels and films give no more attention to speech than to the mute items of reality. These, film presents through techniques more vivid but conceptually equivalent to those of language. Just as the formal identity of fiction depends on the existence of narrated description as well as dialogue, so the formal identity of film is dependent on its ability to describe experience through the medium of cinematography as well as to make statements about it in language. A film cannot be good unless it is good as a film.

Yet a good film is good in ways analogous to a good book or play; the experience it renders cinematically must be worth having on grounds not only of form. If the formal identity of film is dependent on converting literary into cinematic expression, its human value is not. As we will eventually see, films do exist that have the same relationship to theater and fiction that water bears to oxygen and hydrogen, but even such masterly combinations refresh us not only by their artful way of mixing literary constituents to produce cinematic experience but by the value of the literary elements that are mixed.

However much a critic may wish to establish purely aesthetic criteria, judgment of works of art that are mimetic must consider the issues of truth and virtue as well as beauty. Film critics cannot be expected to demonstrate greater clarity than their more traditional colleagues in specifying exactly how much content a given work of art must possess to be worthy of their consideration. But if a film critic insists on even a modicum of non-formal interest or value, he must simply ignore the vast majority of films.

Filmmaking is expensive—so expensive that more people are required to pay for it than can ever possess adventurousness equal to their pennies. Since producers need large returns to amortize their investments, they understandably take risks in inverse ratio to cost. Clinging to what has already sold widely and well, they encourage narrative formulas, simplistic characterizations, and banal themes.[2]

Therefore, the vast majority of films come as close to wish-fulfilling best-sellers or emotionally titillating but intellectually soothing melodramas as men talented enough to produce films can debase themselves into making them. Then, an audience used to lies becomes the effective non-conductor of truth. And what the market-place does not murder, the censor mutilates. With most reviewers busily approving the already approved, the rare good film that manages to get past producers, censors, and the mass audience usually suffocates in an "art house" or gets tossed into a vault by some venal distributor. The wonder is not that so few films exist that are formally distinctive and intelligently representational but that such films exist at all.

Among these rare works, the majority is less impressive for formal distinctiveness than for intelligent imitation of life. Such works convert literary into cinematic experience, but their excellence as films results less from the extent of the transformation than from narrative interest, emotional impact, human insight, etc. in the thing transformed. Since such attributes of content are, of course, difficult to quantify, insofar as I seek to praise content in discussions of individual films and directors, I do so on an *ad hoc* basis, rarely attempting comparisons. But whereas fineness of content earned the directors I have chosen entrance into this book, considerations of form have placed them on the ascending scale that is my structure. Fine literary content is, as it were, a common denominator; formal transformation is the variable that causes me to begin with Carol Reed and end with Ingmar Bergman.

A desire to measure formal transformation is apparent even among reviewers. It does not take long for anyone concerned with films to recognize that they are so like plays and novels as to make the medium seem parasitic or otiose unless one discerns the means of specialization. Once the elements of specialization are recognized, we inevitably want to measure different degrees among different representatives of the form. But distinctions cannot be established until one has studied an exemplary range of films. For this reason, I must ask my reader to be patient because my judgment that the literary roots of cinema are less modified by the directors in the early chapters cannot seem plausible until the later chapters are reached. Insofar as I intend to define cinematic art and suggest different intensities of its presence, I must place my examples in a coherent order; but the order of their interrelationships cannot, of course, be fully clear until the end.

We begin our examination, then, with a man who adapts good fiction to the screen with relatively great dependence on literary material rather than cinematic form. This we must do because by far the largest number of films are actually adaptations of pre-existing fiction and the largest number of estimable filmmakers are men who know how to "bring novels to the screen." Such men hold candles of craftsmanship and maturity in the darkness of the flickers, without however lighting up the screen with cinematic innovation. One thinks of men like Claude Autant-Lara, who adapted Raymond Radiguet's *Devil in the Flesh*, or René Clément, who directed the greatest of war films (*Forbidden Games*), of virtually all the best Hollywood directors (Mankiewicz, Stevens, Huston, Wyler, Kubrick), or any of the legion of directors who occasionally finds a literary project good enough to inspire a good film. Each of these men might have served for the one position in this book that wasn't naturally preempted. I chose Carol Reed because he seems to me to have made a larger number of good, essentially novelistic films than the others. Through his methods of adaptation and his general avoidance of melodrama and sentimentality, he serves as a perfect example of cinematic artistry in its least distinctive but fundamental form.

Like most filmmakers who adapt rather than invent and are thus dependent on the luck of finding a "good property," the majority of Reed's work is trivial or deplorable in content—of interest only to a student of film history.[3] Given the right subject, however, Reed shows as well as anyone why the values of a good story may be preserved and even enhanced through filming. He does this by instructing his scenarist to alter the source so as to increase the opportunity to convey information visually rather than through dialogue. Without abandoning narrative conventions of plot, character conflict, and so on, he progressively shifts the emphasis in his films to the more tangible element of setting, attaining in his best work an expressiveness through atmosphere that is aesthetically independent of the scripts that are otherwise the basis for achievement in such novelistic films. In search of maturity of content, he is likely to prove equally cavalier with his sources, not hesitating to change the story wherever this will produce a diminution of melodrama and a greater proximity to the inconclusiveness or ambiguity characteristic of real life.

The latter and, to a lesser extent, the former of these qualities are evident in the first of his successes, *The Stars Look Down* (1939). Based on A.J. Cronin's 600-page novel, this film is, first of all, distinguished by its marvelously concise script. In a clear, swift hundred minutes, scenarist J.C. Williams renders a complicated portrayal of mining as destructive capitalism.

The book concentrates on the lives of two miners' sons and on the owner's scion, Barras, but the film reduces the prominence of the latter so as to point up the paradigmatic contrast between the self-seeking Joe Gowlan and the reformist David Fenwick. Whereas Cronin gives no more attention to a mine disaster than a romantic complication, the film disdains such lending library formulas. By eliminating Cronin's repetitions and banalities, the script tersely analyzes a social machine.

At the beginning, the machine has stopped; literally, for we see the pulleys grind to a halt. David's father has urged the miners to a wild-cat strike. Since he shares his father's ideals, David has meanwhile been studying the law so as to take that route to justice, but his mother, out of a conservatism even deeper than family feeling, opposes both his plans and her husband's agitating.

To the oppressed like Mrs. Fenwick, Joe Gowlan gives a more pertinent demonstration of the uses of native intelligence: he goes to the city to get rich. David follows him there for idealistic reasons, but he eventually shows himself vulnerable enough to urban glamour that he can be seduced by Joe's cast-off girl-friend, Jenny. Drawn into marrying her, David learns that he has sold his soul. In her egotism, her greed, her vulgar idea of success, Jenny represents all the values that David had dedicated himself to opposing. When he is given a chance to plead his case before the Mining Board, word of Jenny's postmarital involvement with Joe discredits Fenwick's purpose in attacking Barras's association with the shady Gowlan. Immediately after this, the mine caves in, and David must acknowledge that he permitted the death of his father and the other workers by allowing himself to be diverted from his goals. At the end of the film, he is leaving home to rededicate himself to the task of obtaining legal redress.

The excellence of the film's content depends on its transformation of the novel's Jenny (a Maugham-like bad girl) into embodied materialism. The book's private and public dramas are thus joined because Jenny represents yet another force necessary to destructive capitalism. Showing courageous disdain for an unwritten law of best-sellers and movies (you must present the entire fate of an important character), this adaptation gives us only so much of Jenny as is relevant to David. When he finally understands that she is fatal to his reformist efforts, he rejects her; despite our investment of interest in her story, Jenny then passes out of the film.

Their last scene together illustrates Reed's admirable avoidance of melodrama. Having just discovered that Jenny has both injured his plans and insulted him with her infidelity, David tells her that they must part. Yet he admits, "I can't blame you for loving Joe any more than I can blame myself for loving you"; *mutatis mutandis*, she is his tragic flaw. In the book, Jenny is a wicked vamp; in the film, she is a weak, covetous simpleton. Such even-handedness in re-conceiving the novel's characters is evident elsewhere in the film. Barras, for example, is changed from a villainous exploiter into a man susceptible to guilt (although it comes too late). Even the protagonists are morally shaded. The miners are depicted as instinctive conservatives, hostile both to David's attempts at reform and to his father's strike. Through David's mother as well as a religious fanatic who hovers around the action, the film shows that retrograde social consciousness thwarts the miners just as much as does the owners' materialism.

Reed's talent operates mainly to encourage conciseness and maturity in the script of *The Stars Look Down* and plausibility in its performance (there are wonderfully convincing portrayals of Mrs. Fenwick, David and Jenny by Nancy Price, Michael Redgrave and Margaret Lockwood). His filmic touches are mainly designed to produce conciseness. Typical is the early montage that establishes the duration of the strike through a pattern of dissolves and tracking shots which focuses on a posted notice. Successive stages of the signs deterioration are represented, as are seasonal changes in the surroundings. No writer could establish the passage of time so succinctly without sacrificing the vividness with which the fact of duration is impressed on us.

One scene in particular shows how well Reed can combine swiftness and authoritativeness in telling his story. Because the strike has gone on so long, the miners exhaust their credit at the local butchershop; yet since the owner is of their class, they feel that he shouldn't be governed solely by the profit motive. Nonetheless, they are both too proud and too beaten down to do more than meekly beg for kinder treatment. Only when the husband of a sick wife is denied the bit of meat she needs does their frustration explode into rage. By cutting among the crowd, Reed analyzes the mass into its motivational components. The instigator merely takes the meat he had asked for, but the others loot the shelves. One man vents his anger rather than appease his want; he is too busy mauling the butcher to take anything. A wide-eyed young boy grabs the advertising placard of a lamb, while his dog busies himself with more pertinent goods. David's father pleads against the vandalism while, outside, the religious fanatic predicts the apocalypse. Soon, literalizing the sermon, the police come, arrest Mr. Fenwick and thereby accomplish what Barras had wished: the end of the strike. Joe Gowlan empties the till, rings up "no sale," saunters past both police and preacher and then, via a dissolve, is seen vaulting into a train compartment occupied by a young, attractive woman. Since the sequence now comes to an abrupt end, only later do we realize that the woman was Jenny.

An even better example of visual story-telling is the image of David's mother peering through the window when he first leaves home. Eloquent in itself, this is made doubly so through its repetition at the end of the film. When David first leaves for Tynecastle, where he hopes to work on the miner's behalf, Mrs. Fenwick is so distraught by his apostasy that she will not even say goodbye, although she does pack some food for his trip. Yet when he exits, and can no longer see her, she comes to the window, while an in-tracking camera reveals her inexpressible love for him. At the end of the film, after the waste of his efforts and the tragic loss of her younger son and husband, she must suffer David's departure a second time. Again, the camera tracks into her as she stands looking after him through the window, but now she smiles with a pride she could never articulate.

This change of expression measures the extent of David's victory in the film. We cannot know how close he will come to his goal, but the small revolution that events have inspired in his mother's view of him may exemplify a future willingness on the part of such people to fight for the cause. Reticently, because this image is both unspoken and indeterminant, the film closes. But this fine naturalizing image only confirms what an M.P. friend had previously told David, "Life's like a wheel. Your turn will come." To that extent, its visual eloquence is compromised, whether by commercial fear that audiences might overlook the unstated or because, even in this stripped-down version, the narrative is so complex that underlining seemed desirable.

Reed's obligation to handle so much narrative material seems, in any case, to have made him restive, as one can see from certain instances of willful visualization. When Michael Redgrave speaks in behalf of mine nationalization before the Debater's Union, a montage of mining and its discontents is superimposed on his forensic climax. Unfortunately, these images either overwhelm his words, whereas the scene is meant to prove him a gripping speaker, or the contrary, in which case, they are superfluous. Later in the film, we have another indication that Reed wanted more chance to be pictorial than his story invited.

After having been abandoned by Joe, Jenny decides that she must marry the available David. Their scene together begins with a dissolve through a rain-spattered windowpane in the room where David is studying. Reflected in the window, Jenny makes her entrance, soon falling on her knees before David and deceitfully telling him that she has rejected Joe. David embraces her in his joy but also speaks of the responsibilities that indicate a long engagement. To this, Jenny responds with effusions about the pleasures of marriage and the marvels of installment-plan buying. Reed's camera then tracks away from the couple so that we are watching two drops sliding along the windowpane. While she wins her point, the drops merge; David, diverted from his path, drowns in sexual absorption. The "objective correlative" is clever, but (being so rare in the film) it also seems, at best, a distraction, at worst, ludicrously obtrusive.

18

The Stars Look Down suffers precisely because of such formal in-
adequacy, despite the excellence of its content and the impressive-
ness of its craftsman-like adaptation. Committed to a complicated
story and subtle portrayal of manifold social forces, it must use
words—the swiftest, most efficient of languages—to make its points
quickly. Richness of content is therefore bought at some cost in visual
impact, as one can notice if he remembers a film like Pabst's *Kam-
meradschaft*. The German work, despite its heavy message about
brotherhood and its socialist rhetoric, is nonetheless more convincing
in showing the physical anguish of coal-mining. *The Stars Look Down*
is more satisfying to the intelligence, but it does not convey so well
the dirt, smell, cold, danger that Pabst's camera dwells on.

Reed's next important film, *The Fallen Idol* (1949) is as conventionally narrative as *The Stars Look Down*. It is also smaller in scope.
Yet, this work illustrates Reed's progress toward a more cinematic
style—like that of Pabst's *Kameradschaft*—which softens the edges
of fictive contrivance and brings to it the immediate force of pre-
verbal experience. Reed accomplished this by persuading his collaborator, Graham Greene, to alter his short story, on which the film is
based.

Greene's "The Basement Room" concerns a boy whose admiration
for the family valet traps him into involvement with the man's adultery. When Baines invites his lover to the house because he thinks
that Mrs. Baines is gone for several days, the outraged woman makes
a surprise appearance, precipitating a quarrel that ends in her death.
Philip, who is an involuntary witness to the crime, refuses to accept
responsibility for his former hero. As Greene's narrator remarks cen-
soriously, "you could almost see the small unformed face hardening
into the deep dilettante selfishness of age." To banish trouble, the
boy consigns Baines to the police.

As cinematic material, this story posed two problems. Its main action (Philip's rejection of adult complications) is not so much an
action as a resistance to action, and Greene states rather than dramatizes this point. Moreover, although "The Basement Room" has
an interesting situation, its meaning arises not from the situation but
from the aftermath. The change that Reed suggested eliminated both
shortcomings.[4]

Reed suggested that Baines should not have murdered the wife
but that Philip, from childish belief in the older man's courage, should
attribute premeditation to what really was an accident. This locates
the action not in Philip's final retreat into childish irresponsibility but

in the whole process whereby innocent misperception becomes a threat. Ironically, Philip puts Baines in jeopardy because he idolizes the man. Baines, who had boasted of killing wild beasts, could certainly kill a mere woman. Since, in her hysterical search for her husband and his paramour, Mrs. Baines had tried to force Philip into collusion, surely Baines would have wished to protect him from the virago. Because he believes that Baines is motivated by courage and friendship, Philip reciprocates with feints and lies that nearly put the valet's head in a noose.

This transformation in plotting gave Greene's story a new, more cinematic subject. *The Fallen Idol* is dominated by images of Philip peering at the adults through bannisters, around corners, and from various distances. These images remind us that the drama is precisely what Philip sees. Then by adroitly cutting between Philip's subjective and our objective views of the action, Reed dramatically establishes that the boy sees with distortion.

A single addition to the short story shows how carefully the film is designed to visualize this psychological reality. Reed gives Philip a pet snake so that he can show us when the boy is not psychologically present during scenes where he is physically a witness. For example, when Philip chances on Baines and the girl in a tea-room, his mental distance from their tête-à-tête is graphically represented by cuts that discover him unconcernedly playing with his snake while we hear the lovers' dialogue on the soundtrack.

Reed's adaptation of "The Basement Room" finds a visual equivalent for fictional point of view, thereby releasing the latent Jamesian power of the original and thus improving the story at the same time that it is made more cinematic. Because camera position can imply the existence of a perceiver, Reed is able to show what Philip does or does not see. Shots succeeding a cut of the onlooking boy illustrate subjective reality; absence of such cuts or of tracking shots that might indicate his movements alert us to the objective status of a scene. Synchronizing of image and dialogue can show that participants in a conversation are the only participants in the scene, whereas asynchronous juxtaposition between dialogue and the mutely observant child recalls his determinant presence. "Reaction shots" (the listener's image or his silently responding face) dramatize the effects of action. All these devices are used by Reed to make Philip's limited consciousness the subject of *The Fallen Idol*.

To understand fully how the objective form of cinema can explore subjectivity, however, we shall have to wait until later chapters that deal with more masterly directors, like Antonioni, Bresson, and Bergman. Although *The Fallen Idol* creates a picture of a child's mind, Reed's allegiance to narrative interest eventually overcomes his interest in using the camera to visualize thinking. Because Philip's idolatry has the ironic effect of hurting Baines, the valet starts to usurp Philip as the center of attention. Then the film becomes a conventional thriller, arousing concern over Baines's fate and shunning those cinematic techniques that make the film less conventional in form than *The Stars Look Down.*[5]

The Fallen Idol measures both Reed's visual artistry and the limits imposed upon it by his commercial devotion to plot. Not for him are those apparently random constructions, composed of unverbalized and anti-dramatic behavior, that we shall come to see as the essence of cinematic mimesis.[6] As a result, Reed never goes all the way in making action equivalent to what is demonstrated rather than discussed. But in his three best films, he reaches a higher level, by depicting atmosphere. This ability to make the physical world motivate his characters and express their significance constitutes his most important exemplification of the art of film. As it happens, the works in question make the point in inverse order to date of filming, so we will have to take them backwards.

Our Man in Havana (1959), the only notable film in what is widely regarded as the disastrous second half of Reed's career, gains most of its interest from Graham Greene's witty adaptation of his own novel and from brilliant and varied performances (by Alec Guinness, Noel Coward, Ernie Kovacs, Ralph Richardson). The story is a send-up of espionage. For reasons that are neither logical nor clear, the British Foreign Office decides to situate an agent in Cuba. It therefore despatches to Havana a Mr. Hawthorne, who must recruit someone to check on local "activities" and to relay home encoded messages by means of a copy of Lamb's Shakespeare and, in an emergency, ink made of bird droppings. Since Havana's police force is ruled by a sadist, Segura, and since other governments have loaded the tropical paradise with too many spies for the available information, Shakespeare and shit aren't the only invitations to ingenuity.

Hawthorne chooses Wormold, an inveterate loser. His marriage has failed, he can't make a living selling vacuum cleaners; only his daughter implies success, which she defines as a horse, a paddock, membership in the Country Club—things Wormold can't afford.

Hence, despite reluctance born of common sense, he signs on with Hawthorne and, when unable to produce the needed data, simply invents it. He "recruits" people from the telephone book or his imagination, creates troop movements, and reports on a horrible new weapon that the Foreign Office doesn't dare suspect is an enlargement of a vacuum cleaner.

As much to bolster their confidence as to facilitate Wormold's activities, his employers send him a secretary and a short-wave expert. Now overwhelmed by his importance, he is forced to earn it through ever more lavish fantasies, else F.O. will cut off his cash (payments to the "underlings") and Milly won't get her horse. The more he lies, the more he is believed—by the foreign spies too, and even Segura. Things get tangled; a man is killed; Wormold himself is nearly murdered and driven to murder. Segura packs him aboard a plane for London. Rewarded by a Foreign Office bent on saving face, Wormold goes off to marry his secretary.

As this summary suggests, Greene's story is full of fine ideas; but it is also weakened by three linked contradictions that crucially limit its effectiveness:

1) We can't feel horrified when characters who have been presented as stylized grotesques suddenly turn real enough to bleed or die.

2) Because we can't be horrified, we aren't convinced that espionage is immoral as well as silly.

3) And because of that, we can't take the final marriage as a tribute to personal values over political chicanery, so it seems a mere happy ending.

This last identity between film and novel shows not only that Reed was wrong to let Greene retain all of his book but that Reed wasn't himself in doing so. As often as possible, he uses scripts with unhappy endings, and in his most famous film (*The Third Man*), he got one despite both producer and scenarist (Greene, *ipse*).[7] Moreover, as we have seen, Reed normally modifies his fictive source.

Internal evidence suggests that Reed dimly perceived the error of his unwonted self-abnegation. Under the credits, we see the silent meeting of a whore and muscleman, for which there is no parallel in the novel. Reed took responsibility for this in our interview, as well he might; for the couple, engaged throughout the film in a silently developing assignation, epitomizes that use of background locations which makes the film more convincing than Greene's novel.[8]

22

Whereas the book is poor in the description of physical settings, the film establishes a Cuba real enough to keep the action from seeming wholly stylized. This, in turn, makes Greene's imposition of moral issues and actual deaths less disruptive than they appear in the novel. Moreover, Reed creates a real Cuba without sacrificing symbolic potential. The credit sequence—which, significantly, lacks Greene's dialogue—shows how this works.

Before the credits, the whore stands on a balcony eating an apple. The muscleman, ogling her, comes forward. They exchange a glance. She descends, throwing him the apple as she passes. He bites. The image freezes. Suddenly, exciting Latin music explodes on the soundtrack and the credits appear. Thus is the couple turned into an emblem not only of Cuba's social characteristics (sensuality, intrigue, easy living) but of the moral meaning latent in its atmosphere (the Fall). Throughout the film, Reed extends this metaphor by having the couple wander through all the outdoor scenes.

Nowhere are they used more brilliantly, however, than at the end of the credits, when they start to move offscreen, the man stalking the woman. From the opposite direction, accompanied by a loud, vulgar, conspicuous mariachi band which, in his professional need of circumspection, he tries to wave aside, dressed impeccably (down to spats and cane) and wearing an expression that is synonymous with *hauteur*, strides Noel Coward, the film's master spy. Reed's camera follows Coward running the gauntlet of importunity, impropriety, and indignity until the image is fixed in our minds, for this man, wearing the look of perfect rectitude, must later be found to incarnate an evil that makes the noise and sensuality of Cuba seem comparatively harmless. Had the rest of the film so perfectly combined the reality of Cuba caught in the location shooting with symbols of absurdity and evil so unobtrusively present in this first scene, it would have been that perfect mixture of stylish comedy and moral pertinence that Greene's story attempts but does not achieve. Only where Reed takes off from his source into visual invention does he show how good a film this might have been.[9] Visual invention, equal in artistry to the fiction it embellishes, is more fully present in the two earlier of Reed's films.

Although *An Outcast of the Islands* (1951) is an adaptation of Joseph Conrad and *The Third Man* (1949) is an original work by Graham Greene, the two scripts have much in common. Each is the story of a charming hedonist whose fundamental egotism turns wicked under the pressure of his environment. The hero of *An Out-cast* is trapped without money or work in a colonial backwater where he falls prey to sensuality; Harry Lime, in *The Third Man,* finds himself amid the ruins of post-war Vienna, where survival demands the cunning of a beast. Each man is befriended by someone less worldly and self-seeking, whom he disillusions and by whom he is, at last, violently rejected. Both films could bear the title of Reed's *Fallen Idol,* but they are more complex works that show the process of disillusionment in its moral and social ramifications and not merely as an event in personal psychology.

Stylistically, these films perfect the mixture of realism and near-allegory, of which only the residue remains in *Our Man in Havana.* Setting is rendered both as physical reality and moral symbolism. Narrative is accomplished in swift, high-pitched scenes, with dialogue spoken at high volume and in staccato rhythms by actors giving larger-than-life performances. Music, played by a single instrument in *The Third Man* and tending in that direction in *Outcast,* is used not only to exacerbate our feelings—as in the average film—but also discursively. The results achieve the same effect of narrative heightening that occurs in the similarly complex medium of opera.

"Operatic" is surely the word for *Outcast,* although the complexity of its plot also creates, in a manner reminiscent of *The Stars Look Down,* a good deal of rhetoric. Nevertheless, Reed had learned in the decade before the later film all that he would ever know about the need to tell a story visually and about the means for doing so.

Conrad's story is almost a re-enactment of the Fall in socio-moral terms. Willems, the hero, is a kind of Satan, charming but irresponsible, who is placed by his benefactor, Captain Lingard, in a position of some importance. When larcenous impulses cause Willems to lose his post, Lingard kindly agrees to take the man to Sambir, a river village with a lucrative economy that is under Lingard's control because only the Captain knows how to navigate through the rocks that crowd its entrance.

Sambir is a pre-lapsarian world, ruled paternalistically by the Captain through his manager, Almayer. Since Almayer lives in hope of amassing a fortune large enough to enable his return to civilization, he is reluctant to let Willems share the work. Involuntarily idled, his sensuality unpurged by labor, Willems then becomes easy prey for an avaricious itinerant tribe that always wanted to wrest control of Sambir from Lingard.

From this point, because he is up against a worse adversary (the schemer, Babalatchi), Willems begins to seem comparatively sympathetic; less a Satan than an Adam with a particularly large tendency to sin. Like Adam, Willems falls through a woman. Then, re-enacting the primal story, he betrays his benefactor, becomes a moral savage, and opens paradise to strife. Cast out of Sambir for his pains, he now possesses the woman for whom he sinned, but by this time Aissa hates him as much as does Lingard.

William Fairchild, the scenarist, tightens up Conrad's plot by eliminating everything unrelated to Willems' downfall. In a manner recalling the script of *The Stars Look Down*, a sprawling story is narrowly channeled. More clearly than in the earlier film, concentration and economy are characteristic of Reed's direction. The opening minutes show how economically the film is edited and staged.

An Outcast fades in with the image of someone announcing the arrival of Captain Lingard and then tracks across the dock area, following bales as they are transported from hand to hand by native bearers. When the shot reaches a native pulling the rope of a large flapping fan near a sign indicating the name of Willems' employer, we simultaneously hear the word, "scoundrel." By flapping through the cut, into Hudig's office, the fan keeps up the rhythm set by the original tracking shot and thus makes the shift seem less abrupt. Because the fan moves both in the direction of the original camera track *and* against it, the eye is appropriately arrested during the action.

Hudig is dispatching an underling to fire Willems. Since the underling is portrayed (by Wilfrid Hyde-Whyte) as unctuous and gloating, we immediately feel sympathy for Willems, by a default of admiration that increases as Hyde-Whyte, twirling an absurdly oversized parasol, canters out of the office. This we see through the window behind Hudig's desk, for Reed does not move his camera, relying instead on the receding image of Hyde-Whyte's parasol to inform us of his destination and to increase the absurdity of his impression on us.

Our eye, which had been taken from right to left by the tracking shot, and then been kept static in the office, moves from right to left again—this time, however, voluntarily—as it follows Hyde-Whyte. Then when he enters the club where Willems is playing billiards, the cut comes at precisely the moment that he collapses his parasol. Reed combines editing and staging so as to set up a visual rhythm (there is no music in the scene) that "covers" the functional exposition at the same time that (like marching tempi) it controls our emotional response—in this case, favorable to Willems.

Admiration is increased by our first view of Trevor Howard, decked out in an elegant suit, arching himself with cat-like grace over the billiard table and juggling the game, a cigar and witty repartee with unfailing style. Our awe is furthered when Willems dances through swinging doors on his way to see Hudig, thus setting up—beautifully—a motion counter to that which we have thus far been following.

On his way, Willems stops to exchange some words with Lingard, who, by this time, has docked. Stichomythic dialogue (in which we are told all we need to know about the two men's former relationship as well as initial facts about Sambir) and reverse cutting maintain the scene's rhythm. Recalling the to and fro of Hudig's fan, the shots of Willems are all taken from the ship's perspective, thus showing him as a rocking figure. This prepares us for the climax not only through reference to the fan but by visually effacing the earlier image of Willems as a solid, domineering presence. Thus, after gracefully dodging his waiting wife, whom he puts off with insouciant rudeness as he literally twirls out of her grasp, and after waltzing down the street more sinuously than Hyde-Whyte but in a similar bit of staging, when Willems appears at Hudig's on a dissolve timed to the words, "Get out," we are not wholly surprised.

The sequence had set up a rhythm to which Hudig's expostulation bears the satisfying relationship of a necessary chord. The marvel of it all is how much exposition and characterization are floated on its stream of images and also how brilliantly it prefigures the film. Repeatedly, we will accept such an invitation to feel wonder but then dismay at Willems, until the latter overwhelms all identification with the man. At that moment, both for audience and Lingard, Willems is cast out.

Since the cause of Willems' moral collapse is his total subjugation to lust, nothing is so crucial to the film's success as the decision Reed made about representing Willems' tempters. In one important particular, Conrad's writing compromises his novel's brilliant conception. Intending, as always, to make his native characters embodiments of pure libido, Conrad nonetheless tries to make them anthropologically realistic. The result is a patois worthy of Edgar Rice Burroughs. Instead, Reed decided to keep all the natives except Babalatchi from speaking English and Aissa from speaking at all.[10] The substitution of idiomatic but unvernacular dialogue for Babalatchi's Conradian pidgin English makes the man more dignified and plausibly menacing (an effect enhanced by the icy control with which George Colouris delivers his lines), while the muting of Aissa turns her into a purely physical presence, more terrifying than her prototype, because she joins passion to inscrutability. Willems stalks Aissa in a silence whose void of words measures the unreasoning power of his lust, and Reed fills the void with sounds and images that create an infernal machine.

With Aissa's first entrance, a rhythm of inevitability is established. Drums accompany her appearance at Almayer's outpost, where Reed holds the camera on Willems while Almayer deals with her father and Babalatchi. Cuts to the latter show us that Babalatchi notices the fixation from which he may profit. But Babalatchi is not the only vehicle for Willems' entrapment.

Recalling similarly objectifying additions in *Our Man in Havana* (the whore and muscleman for Cuba) and *The Fallen Idol* (Philip's snake for his innocent self-absorption), Reed creates for *An Outcast* a silent representation of tropical seductiveness. When Willems first arrives in Sambir, whose people jubilantly greet Lingard, he is virtually ignored by all save an androgynous-looking boy in the crowd. Then, throughout the film, Reed uses this figure of sybaritic emasculation to guide Willems toward Aissa and to comment visually on their affair. At the dock, the boy smiles sympathetically at Willems' isolation from the love shown Lingard. Later, he entices the man through the river community. But when he sees the result of his efforts, he shows a grief that we are meant to share. A kind of savage cupid, the boy ultimately becomes the sign of censure.

Nor is the boy Willems' only censorious witness. Frequent reaction shots of Almayer's wife and anonymous native inhabitants of Sambir provide silent commentary on Willems' deterioration, thereby also establishing the personal debacle as what it turns out to inspire: the collapse of an entire community. This equation between Willems' and Sambir's fates gives the sordid personal drama some of the ennobling effect of tragedy. But the specific enactment of his temptation is more akin to ritual, with heavy dependence on music and dance.

Accompanied by the accelerandos of Brian Easdale's score (with its implacable drums), presided over by the dreadful Babalatchi, who glares down at Willems from his piling-elevated hut, a series of short scenes pictures the progress of Willems' erotic obsession. It is hardly fanciful to describe this great sequence as the ballet within the opera; ultimately, it becomes a literal dance into darkness.

Driven to Aissa by the combined force of her appeal and his own boredom, Willems stalks off through the mass of dancers assembled by Almayer to perform at his daughter's birthday. Besides providing

27

a tumultuous beginning for the seduction scene, Willems' wild-eyed disruption of the dancers prefigures his ruin or order and richness in Sambir, of which the dancers are expressions. But Willems is off to a dance of his own.

It begins when the boy takes him to a lagoon, at the end of which Aissa waits beneath a hut. The drums that were played for Almayer's dancers and that accompanied Willems in his frenzied rowing are now overwhelmed by a slow series of symphonic crescendos, each fuller than the last. To their rhythm, Willems advances on Aissa, while the camera tracking from his perspective, identifies us with his feelings. Willems attains the girl, but she barely moves her head, while her eyes reflect both expectancy and her sense of power. Then Willems moves around her and begins walking backward to the darkest corner, beckoning her on and only looking behind him occasionally to see how much further he must go. Now the camera becomes Aissa advancing on him, as she observes the destination of his lust. Reaching him, she stops. He advances, she retreats. They circle each other. He moves her on. When Aissa reaches the corner, Willems walks about her while she stands tensely, wondering when he will make some move. By elongating this moment, by choreographing it, by surrounding it with sinister shadows, Reed makes the embrace into the entire yielding of a soul that Conrad required but lacked the courage even to describe. With his back to us, Willems now embraces Aissa, whose eyes blaze over his shoulder like those of a demon, while her hand moves upward to clutch him. Then we dissolve into a scene of Almayer's wife putting up the bed in which Willems will no longer sleep. The exile is complete.

When next we see the lovers, they are installed like monarchs on rattan thrones, but already Willems seems degraded. A crowd of jabbering children mock their tryst; when he tries to send them away, they spit at him. Terribly, Willems' lust needs privacy no more than love. "Why do you put that stuff on your hair," he sneers at the uncomprehending Aissa, "it stinks!"

Now that Willems is caught, Babalatchi springs the trap. Calling Aissa from Willems' side, the schemer whispers something into her ear, while the camera tracks in on her nodded assent and the music reaches an even greater crescendo than in the seduction scene. The sequel is a second search for Aissa, more pathetic than the first, for Willems has become desperate to regain lost pleasure. But Aissa has been instructed not to return until Willems betrays Lingard's navigational secret to Babalatchi and then, adding brutality to treachery, initiates a raid on Almayer.

This scene, the most violent in Reed's films, displays the total brutalization of Willems. Binding Almayer into a hammock, he cruelly forces his enemy to swing over spears and flames. The natives scream; their faces, reflecting the fire, hideously grin at us. Reed mounts one camera in the hammock with Almayer, thereby turning the melee into a sinister blur when the hammock swings to and fro. Suddenly, Aissa runs to Willems, wearing a look of triumphant viciousness that he also assumes. Like two devils, they glare at Almayer and at us until Babalatchi enters, announcing that the tribe's chief had uttered a dying curse at Aissa for failing to attend him. Since she did this because Willems had selfishly neglected to tell her of her father's condition, the end of their affair is now in sight. Although Aissa is left behind, when, betrayed in its turn by the unscrupulous trader to whom they sold Lingard's secret, the tribe departs, Aissa's hatred is her only connection to Willems.

Up to and including this scene, Reed's inventions or illustrations give an immediacy and force to what in Conrad often becomes an unfortunate piling up of adjectives. The last scene is the film's greatest example of the contribution made by cinematic actuality.

Regarding Willems' treason as a moral mystery that must be solved, Lingard sets off to confront his protégé. What he finds is neither the dandified charmer of the early scenes nor the open-shirted sensualist of the middle, but a scrofulous failure whom Trevor Howard makes into a mass of twitching enervation. The erect bearing and *basso profundo* voice of Ralph Richardson (as Lingard) also contribute to the effect of operatic intensity. So does the setting: a desolate mountainside under a lowering sky, with the sound of distant thunder. "I wonder where in perdition I found you," Lingard intones, "You are not a human being that may be destroyed or forgiven. You are a bitter thought . . . You are my shame." Have pity, the outcast cries, for someone already self-condemned; "it isn't what I've done that shames me; it's the reason." "You've been possessed by a devil," Lingard agrees. "Yes," Willems replies, his face a mixture of amazement and disgust, "isn't it pretty."

Now the thunder increases; Lingard hurls a last curse at Willems and prepares to depart. Willems follows, threatening to shoot; but Lingard walks off, judging his betrayer by not disdaining even to look back at him. Rain starts to fall. Reed's camera cuts back and forth between the men, promising an explosion to match the elemental uproar, but instead revealing the profundity of Willems' impotence. Lingard sails off. Aissa runs to Willems, shrieking at him to shoot; but all he can do is crawl away to his hut, there to look after the stiff bearing of Lingard while the departing man condemns him to total banishment. Aissa comes to the hut and sits outside. As the music reaches its final chord, she puts her head down over her crossed arms; a figure of magnificence, now rain-soaked and defeated. Relentlessly, the film has moved to this last image of waste.

Willems and Aissa have been brought to this by their abandonment to pleasure and gain, their betrayal of Lingard's ethics. On the personal level, they enact what the film shows in its setting: the wilderness that awaits anyone who gives himself to uncivilized sensuality. What words can only evoke, the film makes us see. Pages of explanation are replaced by the single image of Willems stalking Aissa through a labyrinth of swaying bridges in her river village or losing his way, in pursuit of her, through its baffling system of canals. And only the spectacle of Trevor Howard's good looks, animal grace, and charm can so draw us to Willems that we feel desolated by his fate. In the novel, on the other hand, the words with which Conrad chronicles Willems' decline cannot free themselves from condemnation and thus encourage a moral distance that drains the story of power.

Improving on Conrad, as it does, *An Outcast of the Islands* is by far Reed's richest film. Yet the complexity of its plot requires several essentially theatrical scenes that are not without cost. Reed wisely takes these at a fast tempo so as to maintain an accelerating rhythm, but that makes it difficult to follow all the twists in the intrigue. Moreover, because of their speed, these scenes work against the active, wordless, and temporally extended passages in which we watch what is happening to Willems. The former are addressed to our comprehension; the latter operate more directly on our senses and feelings: as a result, the tension strongly produced by certain scenes is sometimes dissipated in others. Brilliant as it is, *Outcast* shows that immediacy, sensory vividness, emotional build-up—cinema's particular qualities in story-telling—are sometimes ill-served by too complicated a story.

Novels are frequently said to translate easily to the screen only insofar as their excellence inheres in plotting and characterization rather than style; and good prose, saturated in verbal and mental reality, is surely difficult to transform into the vocabulary of things

30

seen. But film equivalents for style can be found; plot is the more fundamental challenge.

The same instinct that sends most filmmakers to fiction, where they can exploit both narrative ideas and the familiarity of a tested product, inspires a conventional running time of about an hour and a half. Insofar as a given plot is too complicated to be clarified quickly, most filmmakers will resort to discussion rather than enactment, either producing an even more serious instance of opposing modes than one finds in *Outcast* or a species of theatrical film in which explanation replaces embodiment. Novelistic cinema is cinema in which plot predominates, in which the chief goal is satisfactory fulfillment of narrative expectations. In novelistic cinema, then (which is to say in most movies), formal artistry depends on management of plot. A conventional fiction film may be less beautiful, intellectually resonant, rich in implication, etc. than its source if it finds no visual equivalent to a writer's style; it can hardly be a film at all (save in the nature of its existence) unless it devises ways to enact or visually render a story.

No film of Reed's does this more successfully than *The Third Man*. Indeed, it would be hard to find another film by anyone that managed to tell so gripping and interesting a tale with such a clever use of the medium. Conceived by Graham Greene directly for the screen, with Reed's fullest collaboration in all stages of its preparation, *The Third Man* exemplifies what I believe to be the essence of art in novelistic, conventional filmmaking.

To its ultimate benefit, *The Third Man* is conventional in more than one way. Like the average film, it creates character and theme mainly through words; but because its plot belongs to the thriller genre, action predominates. The results of one convention improve the results of the other; dialogue and characters lift the film above mere action at the same time that generic conventions restrain wordiness and provide ample occasion for visual expression.

The Third Man is a mystery laid in occupied Vienna immediately after World War II. Holly Martins, an American writer of pulp Westerns, comes to the city in order to work with his old friend. Told that Harry Lime has just been killed in an auto accident, he determines to uncover the circumstances; but, in so doing, he is forced to concede what the British Military Police had told him: Lime was a vicious racketeer. During his search, he meets and falls in love with Harry's Czech mistress. Then when Lime turns up alive and the British offer to grant Anna immunity from deportation if Martins will help apprehend Lime, he agrees to betray his friend. The result is a chase that climaxes in Martins gunning Lime down.

Despite these adventure story formulas, Greene's characters are conceived to dramatize serious moral issues. Martins is an innocent, who knows violence only through his imagination. Before meeting Major Calloway, he had probably never seen a cop, although he writes about "lawmen." Similarly, although he had long known of Lime's contempt for legality, he had always passed this off as a gift for fixing things. The bravado he displays by taking the investigation into his own hands is more than the standard daring of a thriller hero: it is abysmal innocence about corruption, American ignorance of the manifold enticements to vice offered by war-ruined Vienna. Calloway repeatedly notes that Martins' judgments spring from the pulp fiction world that has formed his sensibility, but Holly never gets the point. Nor does he understand what one of Lime's cronies means by telling him that everyone in Vienna is involved in the rackets and that he should drop the search because, it might turn up something, "well, discreditable to Harry." The very innocence that keeps Martins from conceiving of such a possibility causes him to overreact when he learns that it is true. After Calloway shows him the dossier on Lime but before he has discovered that his friend only feigned death to escape punishment, the disillusioned innocent asserts, "Whoever killed him, it was justice. Maybe I'd have killed him myself."

As the script makes clear, Harry and Holly are alter egos, the former an acerbic realization of the latter's boyish love of daring.[11] No more than Holly has Harry grown up. But, as Anna says about Lime: "The world grew up around him . . . and buried him." What Holly and the audience must learn is that the charming rogue with a talent for fixing things becomes a villain when transported from the world of dates and exam cribs to Vienna, where survival takes extreme forms. Albeit willfully, Lime remains as ignorant as Martins of what it signifies to have to scratch amidst the rubble. Rather, he takes license from the international immorality that has produced these ruins to perpetrate his lesser crimes. "In these days, old man," he tells his anguished pal, "nobody thinks in terms of human beings. Governments don't, so why should we? They talk of the people and the proletariat, and I talk of the mugs . . . They have their five year plans and so have I." For Lime, the great categories remain pals and girls. In trouble because of his criminal activities, he still thinks he can fix things, so he offers to "cut [Martins] in" and grants him proprietary rights over Anna, not foreseeing that the very boy's code that underlies these proposals will, in Holly, lead to murder.

The climax, even though Holly is ordered to shoot by the police, is a murder.[12] Calloway had originally appealed to Martins' love for Anna, thus allying self-interest to the man's righteous indignation and impelling Holly to turn against the friend who had been the most interesting thing in his life. But, as Anna says, "a man doesn't alter because you find out more." Love has its own duties, no less crucial than the more public obligations of justice, in whose behalf, as Martins conceives it, he is willing to sin against friendship. "I don't want to see Harry," Anna insists, "but he's in me. I wouldn't do a thing to harm him." Thus, when Martins returns to the cemetery where "Harry" was buried at the beginning of the film, and, after seeing the act truly take place, waits for Anna to join him, she walks on by.

More than just an exhilarating reversal of cliché expectations takes place in this famous finale. Gone along with the conventional couple walking off to a happier future is the no less conventional belief that a deed exists within one moral purview. From the point of view of Vienna's need to return honorably to the family of nations, Lime must be punished for his bad example of profiteering; from the point of view of more intimate relations—the bedrock even of society—Harry stands beyond punishment. As Anna implies, the rule of love forbids that he be brought down by a friend. With her European comprehension of life's complexity, Anna represents a mature compassion that neither man can match; neither Harry, with his proud view of Anna as a possession earned by cleverness, nor Holly for whom she was a prize due his moral superiority. Although a melodrama, *The Third Man* holds the melodramatic viewpoint up to question and soberly demonstrates that nothing is simple. Conventional on the surface, both in style and genre, Graham Greene's script is one of the most searching and mature in the history of commercial filmmaking.

Significantly, Greene was willing to compromise this maturity when producer David Selznick argued that it would be bad box-office for the boy not to get the girl.[13] One needn't seek evidence, however, to prove that Reed is responsible for the conception as well as the execution of *The Third Man* since the latter is achievement enough. I want now to inspect its artistry because, as I have said, it exemplifies the way in which cinematic techniques make a film great even when the greatness is based on a prior narrative invention. In the interest of clarity, despite the obvious fact that such techniques merge and cooperate in the actual work, I will discuss them under separate headings:

Since setting motivates the action of *The Third Man*, Reed makes the film convincing through the pains he takes to establish the reality of a ruined Vienna—of streets heaped with rubble and of once grand houses where a new emptiness causes voices to echo through the corridors. When a taxi taking Holly to a lecture careens wildly through the almost deserted city, Reed intercuts shots of astonished onlookers, their eyes expressing a fearfulness that forbids the satisfaction of curiosity. Well they might be fearful in this place where police of four countries harass you, take you away from your home in the middle of the night, move about with impunity, even, as we see, in the pleasure sanctuary of a nightclub. In this club, Reed frames Kurtz, one of Lime's confederates, playing a violin for the lone customers— so that we see him near a fat, ugly woman who listens superciliously to the music that she will not even pay the compliment of realizing is too romantic for her. How low Vienna has sunk we also realize when, Holly, trying to drown his disillusionment in liquor, is peered at by a veritable army of expectant whores. Such details make us comprehend both why the Viennese have become pitiable and how vicious Harry is for adding to their pain.[14]

At the same time that Reed actualizes Vienna, he turns it almost into a symbol of the stealth and inhumanity imposed on the citizens by war. Most of the action occurs at night, within mists that enhance the ominous mystery of squares paved with glistening cobblestones on which the foot falls in a clatter and men are seen mostly as shadows looming across broken walls or have become bodiless voices echoing through the vacant landscape. Continually we witness a disturbing mixture of established beauty and current decay. Conspiracies are hatched under magnificent statues, treacheries are uncovered amidst baroque splendor, a doctor tells lies while surrounded by antiques and crucifixes. Everything, however innocent or beautiful, is shot at an angle, so as to enforce our sense of a world off-balance.

Nowhere is the suggestive use of setting more important than in the film's two best scenes: Holly's only meeting with Harry and the final sewer chase. Appropriately, the confrontation between these superannuated boys takes place in an amusement park, their colloquy on a ferris wheel. Holly's discovery of what his friend is really like is timed to the wheel's ascent; when their cabin reaches the top, Martins understands that Lime is capable of hurling him from it. Their subsequent descent is the dramatization of a figure of speech, as is their return to hard earth. Similarly poetic is the decision that Harry be brought to bay in the sewers, where man's filth runs on beneath the notice of the city's inhabitants but, as one of the characters notes, the fouled waters lead "right to the Blue Danube." Indeed, for reasons I shall soon take up, the association of Harry and the sewers does service for the dirty subterfuge we are not actually permitted to see.

CINEMATIC CONSTRUCTION

Under this heading come all the techniques that make *The Third Man* exciting, that create involvement and expectancy. No fades impede the story's progress; Reed always cuts or dissolves from one scene to another, thus prohibiting relaxation. For the same reason, he shoots most conversations in extremely tight close-ups, as if to warn us that the slightest grimace might be telling.

Then, of course, there is the famous zither score used to join diverse scenes, to quicken our pulses, to create climaxes quickly and wordlessly, as when during Martins' first talk with Anna, her admission that she has often wondered about the anomalies of the accident sets off a chord. In other scenes the very absence of music creates anxiety, tells us that what we are about to hear is important enough to require a silent background.

Speed and concentration hold us and make us alert. The opening minutes show how adroitly *The Third Man* grips its audience. After an initial commentary added to please the producer, the film starts with a train pulling into the station with Joseph Cotten (Holly) leaning out in anticipation of being met. But Harry Lime, who had offered him a job and promised to meet him, hasn't come, as we learn in three exchanges with an M.P. Then we dissolve from this scene and its zither music to Cotten entering and climbing the stairs of an apartment building. The music now becomes joyful singing, thereby continuing the thrust of the previous scene but changing its style into one more natural. Cotten rings the bell of Lime's flat, but a voice calls out in German that nobody is there. A series of reverse cuts and ten lines are all that is necessary to inform us that Lime was just killed and is to be buried. We track Cotten's face as it registers an astonishment that we surely share, the music resumes, and we slowly dissolve to the cemetery. Barely three minutes are required to set up the plot, which a combination of visual and auditory elements makes as shocking to us as to Holly.[15]

Occasionally, Reed compresses action through montage, achieving intensity by the sudden rush. Thus after Martins meets the mysterious Popescu, Reed dissolves through three shots of Lime's confederates leaving their homes to end at a four-man meeting on a bridge. As the music that unites these cuts reaches a crescendo, Reed moves to an extreme high-angle shot that frustrates our interest in seeing who the other man is and implies that we ought to. In another mood, Martins' disillusioning contact with Lime's dossier is constructed as a series of dissolves joined by ascending chords and dominated by the image of magnification (through various optical instruments needed to facilitate decoding, etc.), which is appropriate because Martins is, for the first time, *seeing* the enormities of Lime's behavior.

Sometimes the speedy exposition has more to do with character than plot. When the M.P.'s come to search Anna's apartment, Reed stages the scene so as to present simultaneous planes of action: in the background, Holly is telling the police that there was a third man at Lime's accident, while in the foreground Anna is anxiously asking them if they must have the love letters from Harry that they have taken as evidence. Besides quickening the tempo, this simultaneous action dramatizes the distinction between Anna's interests and those of Martins, a distinction that, in his zeal for uncovering the crime, he doesn't recognize until she literally goes her own way at the end.

STAGING

In one scene such doubling of action is combined with revelation of character through gesture—a feature of Reed's staging that allows him to create meaning without dialogue. When Anna and Martins go into Harry's apartment to question the porter who saw the accident, as the investigation transpires in the living room, Anna moves into Harry's bedroom, sits near a vanity table and absent-mindedly reaches into its drawer for a comb. A few moments later when she sits on the bed to take a phone call, she just as absent-mindedly reaches for a backgammon piece in a box on the night table and casually throws the dice while she talks. These details (the mistress's comb that is all she leaves in her lover's apartment and the game near the bed) establish the precise degree of her involvement in Harry's life and the essence of his appeal to her at the same time that they remind us how distant Martins is from both.

36

Reed depends on our alertness to such visual details throughout the film: so that we may become suspicious in the funeral scene when Winkel (Harry's doctor), on seeing Martins, becomes so distressed that it takes a gesture from Kurtz to remind him to lay the wreath he is carrying; so that we may understand how accurate Kurtz was when he said that everyone is a racketeer in Vienna from his simple gesture, moments later, while he and Martins are out walking, of stepping off the sidewalk to let a policeman pass through; so that we may understand that Martins realizes the men are in cahoots when he comes to question Winkel and sees by the presence of Kurtz's dachsund in Winkel's apartment that the man must be hiding there.

The film's most brilliant examples of non-verbal characterization control our responses to Lime. The point of *The Third Man* requires that we acknowledge Lime's viciousness but find him more attractive than Martins. This Reed accomplishes, first of all, through the brilliant stroke of casting as Lime the charismatic Orson Welles and as Holly the adenoidal and wooden Joseph Cotten, but also through the staging of Lime's scenes beginning with Martins' discovery that he is still alive.[16]

When Martins comes to Anna's apartment from the night club, on her bed is a cat which refuses to play with the string around some flowers that Martins had brought her. "He only liked Harry,"[17] she says, thereby establishing the cat as analogous to her, since she too will not respond. As they talk, the camera tracks through a nearby window to show us the square outside, in which an anonymous figure stands. Then there is a cut to the animal coming around the corner and walking in time to zither notes. With the camera at the pet's level, we watch its slow movement toward a pair of shoes protruding from a doorway. Then as it cranes its neck up to look at the man, the zither plucks out its movement only to break into a series of chords as it curls up on the shoes.

Reed now cuts back to the apartment, where, without music, the couple concludes their conversation. In reverse shots of Martins and Anna, Reed continually brings the camera closer, as if to signal a growing rapprochement, but the final close-up reveals a tear trailing down Anna's face as eloquent testimonial to her grieving involvement in Harry and her utter unconcern for his friend. At this point, the scene changes to show Martins walking in the square—once again, with music on the soundtrack. Seeing the cat curled in the doorway, Holly calls out to the shrouded figure, but only after his cry irritates a neighbor into putting on a light is he able to see who the man is. As

Welles flashes his famous wry smile, the camera tracks in to show in his face what the preceding scene makes us regard as a proud assertion of unsuspected vitality—not only because he is still alive but because he has remained alive for Anna.

Martins now begins to go toward Harry, but a suddenly arriving jeep nearly runs him down (ironically recalling Harry's presumed fate). When the jeep passes, Harry is gone. Martins, who had seen a shadow on a wall and heard footsteps, winds up in an empty square, not sure whether he has found Harry or a ghost.

Our thrill in discovering that Lime lives—achieved by acting, staging and scoring—also contributes to the sense of Harry as a nearly fabulous presence that can appear or vanish at will (only later do we learn his secret: a kiosk with a staircase that goes underground). We are meant to feel the attraction that works on the cat, on Anna, and on Martins himself. Not for nothing has Holly's life become a virtual dependence on his friend's—until the moment when he understands the moral excess into which unbridled selfishness can lead you.

Harry is no mere villain, however, which is why the film, as I have said, never shows the effects of his crime.[18] Sinner though he be, Harry appears before us as a figure of charm and ultimately as a victim. The appeal which the film creates turns into active sympathy at the end so as to permit the moral complication that is the goal of the story. More than an obligatory display of climactic chase thrills, the great sewer sequence is an extension of Harry's ambiguity.

Caught in a trap, Lime has, as always, recourse to the sewers, but this time "police pour down every available manhole," sirens scream at us as at Harry. Previously the audience and Martins experienced Vienna as a city of shadows and unidentifiable voices; now it is Harry who is afflicted by shadows and echoes that keep him from knowing the position of his assailants. Admiration for Harry is evoked along with pity. How resourceful he is, we think, to elude so many for so long. He is clever enough to know how to sidestep through a cascade; the police have ropes and equipment to help them. These images of a resourceful man hunted and outnumbered have, of course, a greater impact on us than the crimes we have heard about but never seen. Then when Reed's camera trains on the tight close-up of a wounded Harry's agonized efforts to climb out of the sewers we become totally identified with the prey rather than the police. What we take away from this sequence is the famous image of Lime's fingers stretching through the street-level grate in a last frustrated enactment of his powerful will to live and the face of Joseph Cotten agonized and hesitant before the final cut and the echoing gunshot. When Anna rejects Martins in the next scene, the memory of these poignant images fills us with something like satisfaction.

The pleasure we derive from Anna's rejection of Martins is inseparable from the thrill created by Reed's technical audacity. After being driven by Calloway from Harry's burial—this time, actually accomplished—Holly asks to be deposited at the side of the road where he leans against a decrepit old cart waiting for Anna to reach him. Reed sets his camera up for a stable shot just slightly ahead of Cotten. In the distance, between two rows of trees denuded by autumn, with a few last leaves falling to the pavement, Valli (Anna) walks, her eyes, utterly devoid of feeling, staring straight ahead. The dreariness of the vista is enhanced by grainy photography and by the zither score that has now become associated with death and deterioration. Surely, Holly will be able to bring life out of this death, we think, surely Anna will listen to the word he has announced the intention of speaking, we say to ourselves as, for what seems ages, the lone figure comes toward us and him. The very camera position predicts a stop, an effective destination. But no, Anna walks and walks, past Holly and then right out of the frame. Then, for another long period, Reed holds the shot while Holly slowly lights up a cigarette, throws the match aside, and the zither plucks out "that's that!" In a single stroke Reed both ends Greene's story with full fidelity to its inner logic and shows how film language can create a powerful climax.

This scene exemplifies the minimal definition of film art. As content, it is artful because it opts for truth to theme and characters rather than audience-gratifying conclusiveness for the plot. The majority of conventional films try to have firm closure (even if unhappy), but, as Carol Reed says, "A picture should end as it has to . . . . [nothing] in life ends 'right.' "[19] Formally, the last scene of *The Third Man* is artful because it opts for action and cinematography rather than words.

But at the same time that this film exemplifies the achievement of what I have called novelistic cinema, it also defines the limitations. Something lies beyond: cinema in which story, characters and theme are not so much captured through the resources of filmmaking as they are created by them. *The Third Man* comes close to this ideal because it impresses much of its material directly on our feelings and senses. We have only to recall the sewer chase, whose climax is the mingled look of supplication and acceptance on Orson Welles's face and the reluctant but resigned face of Joseph Cotten that is held in a long close-up before the camera cuts away from the murder. By such combinations of what we are made to see and forbidden from seeing does the film communicate.

However, if we consider the film's other big scene, we note that visual imagery is subsidiary to dialogue in *The Third Man*. Since Graham Greene's writing for the ferris wheel scene is excellent, there is no reason to deplore the fact that without such verbal revelations about character and moral conflict the subsequent sewer chase would be figuratively as well as literally mute, but we must recognize that this is so.

Because novelistic cinema emphasizes plot, dialogue must always be its primary language. Even a director like Reed, who adds resourceful use of ambience, cannot become much more than the playwright's servant. Almost everything Reed shows either objectifies or validates Greene's literary inventions. What we must see is how a director can, instead, "write" with film.

Reed's example permits us to formulate certain axioms about novelistic cinema:

1) Novelistic cinema represents the extension of drama through the use of commentative settings. Even when, as in *Outcast* and *The Third Man*, ambience may be said to motivate plot or, as increasingly happens when we move from *The Stars Look Down* to *The Third Man*, a plot is communicated through wordless behavior, dialogue still conveys essential information. In novelistic cinema, visualization points up or underscores; but character, plot and theme still live essentially in the lines.

2) Since a novelistic film is essentially a play enhanced by descriptive passages, its soul, as Aristotle noted long ago about drama, is its plot. Since, further, a novelistic or conventional film observes fairly rigid restrictions on length, insofar as its plot has many twists it will depend on language to expedite communication. The more complex the plot, the greater the temptation to rely on dialogue rather than action or setting or anything else that can speak without words.

3) Hence novelistic cinema is drawn toward theatricalism by virtue of the very element (plot) that endears fiction to most filmmakers who look toward the novel for material.

Even if all this is accepted, does it follow that dramatistic (dialogue-centered) film is deplorable? Need one commit himself to the assumption that words are anti-cinematic? Isn't this contention both too narrow and too negligent of certain kinds of film?

I have already argued in the introduction against the simple equation of film art with wordlessness. Thus, so far from regarding silent film as quintessential, I have argued that the form is both artificial and meager. Furthermore, no discerning viewer of films like *Smiles of a Summer Night* or *Children of Paradise* can simply disdain words. But words may be shown to cooperate or compete with images. If they compete or assume a principal role, we are back with the achievement of theater, whether distributed on film or in the flesh. The truth that words are the common denominator among fiction, drama and film implies the further truth that each form establishes its integrity and distinction from the others because of the special ways in which it uses words. To this truth we must now turn.

JEAN RENOIR AND THE
THEATRICAL FILM

An Outcast of the Islands and *The Third Man* resourcefully communicate through ambience and action; nonetheless, they must alternate visual description with explanatory speech. Not until Babalatchi talks to Lingard's rival about annexing Sambir are we shown Willems silently pursuing Aissa; Harry Lime glamorously materializes *after* Holly and Anna discuss him. Pictures alone can seldom create even a plot, as silent films proved. Soon after they went beyond the addition of one bandit and one sheriff to imply a chase they had to spell out causality with titles. Much of the dialogue in sound films might be considered titles spoken.

If visualization rarely suffices to clarify plot, even less often can it establish theme. Although we can see the bewitchment that drives Willems, the moral significance of his behavior depends on consequences of which we must be told. Panning around ruined Vienna, the camera can suggest what drove Harry to crime, but the meaning of this experience can only be understood from Anna's line: "He never grew up. The world grew up around him, that's all—and buried him."

Ambience, action, even (to a limited extent) verbal style (as in off-angle shots in *The Third Man* that are like portentous figures of speech): all these can be rendered visually. It takes an extraordinary filmmaker, however, to find cinematic equivalents for the explanations and interpretations so fundamental to writing. Thus, most directors exploit theatricalism, which makes it possible to say anything one wants by putting it in the mouth of a character. Novelistic directors achieve occasional moments of independent creation by picturing things; just as often, they operate at the lower level of their theatrical counterparts, whose main job is helping actors to perform a pre-existing text.

Of the cinema's two roots—fiction and drama—the latter more nearly resists hybridization. The director who describes with pictures is an offshoot of the novelist, but his medium is obviously distinctive; one who arranges gestures and intonations to enhance a playwright's words finds himself grafted to another's stem. Therefore, those who film with continuous reliance on dialogue usually assert their independence from theater by "opening out," since viewers are quick to accept the cinematic discreteness of anything that could not be staged. But "filmed theater" can't be avoided by occasional moves out-of-doors. Words must interpenetrate with the visuals so that we don't feel we are merely hearing a text within an actual rather than a painted set. Novelistic films define themselves aesthetically because they contain visual description; theatrical films, which rely more heavily on dialogue and acting, must modify their dramatic borrowings or they become a recording medium rather than an art.

The best films of Jean Renoir show how this is done. Like most filmmakers who came to prominence during the first decade of sound production, Renoir emphasizes dialogue, even though he had made eight silent films during the twenties. André Bazin is surely right to "admit" that "while [Renoir's] silent films foreshadowed what was to come, there is no comparison between even the best of the silents and the worst of the sound films. Unlike René Clair, who perfected his style in 1927 with *The Italian Straw Hat* and confirmed it with *Les Deux Timides*, Renoir is decidedly a sound director."[1] Clair, who cares little for reality and designs films principally to control the viewer's emotions, relies on physical movement and editing; Renoir is essentially a realist whose ideal of duplicating the world is impossible without sound.

Attempting to define Renoir's talent, critics commonly stress the eye for nature he is held to have inherited from his painter father, but "naturalism" in a wider sense comes nearer the mark. That Renoir's excellence is based on a modification of theatrical techniques rather than on pictorialization is evident in the very film that admirers of Jean-the-son-of-Auguste are so fond of citing.[2]

As its title indicates, *A Day in the Country* (1936) takes place entirely out-of-doors and seems therefore to be cinematic simply by virtue of its setting. Yet the film isn't about the countryside but rather responses to it, and these are constantly put into words. The subject invited Renoir's camera to lend mute nature a voice and to capture the delight taken in a family outing simply by showing his characters at play. Instead, *A Day in the Country* is full of talk even when it needn't have been. Occasionally, Renoir is even less cinematic (i.e., descriptive) and more theatrical than his source.

With a minimum of interpretation or dialogue, Maupassant's story describes the sojourn of an ironmonger and his family, who are comically determined to get all they can out of a pleasure indulged in no more than once a year. Choosing Poulain's hotel-restaurant be-

43

cause it has swings and a view, they decide to lunch on the grass rather than at the tables so as to be able to enjoy the unfamiliar surroundings. Excited by the fresh air, food and drink, they begin to lose their city tightness. When two young blades offer their skiffs for an outing on the river, the mother and daughter, Henriette, gladly agree. The couples row off separately to small islands where both women (allowing for the differences of age and experience) are pleasurably seduced. Afterwards, Henriette feels let down by her experience, but all concerned part company politely, without a scene. Two months later—signalled by an ellipsis in the text—Henri, the daughter's one-time lover, spots the sign "Dufour, Ironmonger," while walking on the Rue des Martyrs. Inside, he learns that the girl married the shop assistant and that the mother is ripe once again for adultery:

> "'Remember us to him—don't forget—and tell him to drop in if he's passing this way.' And she added with a fiery blush: 'Tell him I'd love to see him again!'"

A year later, Henri visits the island, meets Henriette and her husband, and tells them that he often returns nostalgically to this spot. The story ends:

> ". . . she looked him straight in the eyes and said: 'I think of it, too, every night.'
> 'Come along, my dear,' interrupted her husband with a yawn, 'I think it's time we were moving.'"

Except for eliminating the scene between Henri and Mme. Dufour in the latter's shop,[3] and bringing the young men on earlier, the film follows the story faithfully, using every incident and the original dialogue. However, Renoir multiplied the latter by a factor of more than ten and made the characters speak even when they could have been silent.

For example, Henriette, whose susceptibility to Henri begins as an enthusiasm for nature, is shown rhapsodizing over a caterpillar. To convey her emotion, Renoir could have intercut the animal and her response, ending with shots in which she plays with it and perhaps exclaims over her prize. Instead he puts a long speech in her mouth as accompaniment to the action:

> ". . . How wonderful the country is! Under every blade of grass, there's a heap of things moving, living—naturally. Everytime you set foot down you miss killing some of them!"[4]

On she goes, conversing with her mother about the possibility that animals feel as humans do and ending with an eloquent outburst:

"... do you feel a sort of tenderness for the grass, the water, the trees. ... A sort of vague longing, isn't it? It catches you here, rises, almost makes you want to cry. Tell me mama, did you feel it when you were young?"

Not only does Renoir invent such unneeded and literary speech; occasionally he ignores an opportunity suggested in Maupassant about how to impress us visually with the appeal that nature must exercise for shop-bound Parisians. Before they reach Père Poulain's Inn, the Dufours travel through a stretch of bare, ugly country:

At intervals an outcrop of factory chimneys rose from the barren soil, the only crop that grew on this sour land, where the spring breeze wafted the scent of crude and shale oil, mixed with even more unpleasant smells. At last they crossed the Seine a second time, waxing lyrical over the view from the bridge. The river was one dazzling sheet of light; mist drawn up by the sun was rising from it, and they were all conscious of a feeling of placid content and refreshment, as at last they breathed a bracing, purer air, not fouled with the black smoke of the factories or the smells of the sewage farms.[5]

This passage, with its vivid detail and suggestive transition, quickly establishes the thrilling relief inspired by the landscape and simultaneously warns us that the country isn't all fresh air and grass. Before it shows us why the Dufours will be excited, it signals an eventual disappointment. Yet Renoir doesn't film it (perhaps his locations lacked the indicated contrast), so he must depend on dialogue to establish the Dufours' sense of escape. Yet even though Renoir didn't photograph Maupassant's illustration of encroaching industrialism, his fidelity impels him to allude to the passage. Thus Henri tells Rodolphe that since the factory was built the fishes taste of oil, and Poulain, who wants to feed them to the cats, is advised that the Dufours should get them because they won't sense the taint. A final sign of the film's verbal emphasis (although we know this to have been caused by Renoir's inability to complete shooting) is the intertitle before the last scene that replaces Maupassant's asterisk-ellipsis. Despite all the talk, however, the film isn't stagey. Henriette's theatrical speech about her "vague longing" is an exception to the cinematic appositeness of the rest of Renoir's dialogue.

In *The Third Man*, when Anna explains the relationship between

Harry's immaturity and the effect Vienna had on it, she is explaining something not evident in the action. In *An Outcast of the Islands* when Lingard finally dubs Willems his "sin," he is asserting a relationship that had not been dramatized. These are instances of inherently creative dialogue, speech that establishes otherwise unmanifested meanings. We are trained by the theater to believe that people speak in language so speculative or analytic because in the theater, save for occasional and usually complementary gestures,[6] everything we learn comes to us through speech. But in film, which has so many resources for non-verbal communication, abstracting dialogue is formally evasive and often sounds artificial. In Reed's best films the artifice is expedient because we have seen so much that needs to be explained, and permissible because what we have seen is, though real, partly stylized. Nonetheless, Reed has such an instinct for the essential actuality of cinema that he "covers" a speech like Lingard's with natural signs of tumult that complement the human rage.

By contrast, *A Day in the Country* is a realistic film in which nothing is explained wholly through dialogue. That there is so much talk establishes the film as theatrical rather than documentary. But the language is handled according to a documentary rather than a theatrical aesthetic. To use a fine term coined by Michael Roemer in another connection, it is "symptomatic" dialogue.[7]

"Symptomatic" dialogue is speech as part of human behavior. Although sometimes symptomatic, theatrical dialogue is more often expository, interpretive, or propositional; it fills in background, externalizes emotion, or presents ideas. Probably no film lacks examples of such speech (like Henriette's about her "vague longing"), but insofar as screen dialogue is theatrically constituted rather than symptomatic it places action and visualization in wrongly subordinate roles. Why show something that has been well stated?

That speech normally upstages action was, of course, contended by most early analysts of film, who therefore believed that sound increased audience appeal at too high an aesthetic price. But when speech becomes a sign, like gesture, rather than a statement of what would otherwise remain invisible, it completes the illusion of reality that is film's principal achievement. As we will later see, non-theatrical films achieve this illusion with a minimum of dialogue, but more copious speech need not prove subversive so long as it is properly handled.

The very superfluousness of much of Renoir's dialogue in *A Day in the Country* is precisely what makes it cinematic. For example, at the beginning of the film, Renoir tells us something of the Dufour family's desires by using a traveling shot that includes the restaurant sign with promises of swings and fresh fish. At the same time, we hear the offscreen voices of the family registering what the sign tells them, ending in a speech in which Mme. Dufour actually reads the inscription. Such dialogue has a meaning that is independent of the words; it does not exist to provide information, since we can read the sign for ourselves. Rather, it signals the delight with which the characters perceive what is visually rendered to the audience. Even a line like Henriette's offscreen "We're going to have fun," turns out to be one of several expressions of expectancy doubled by behavior, as we see when the Dufour carriage pulls up to its destination.

In contrast, Henriette's speech about her "vague longings" has insufficient visual counterpart and, to that extent, represents an evasion of the medium. Other externalizations of feeling are more cinematic because their meanings would be mistaken without their visual accompaniments. For example, after Mme. Dufour has met and clearly been affected by the handsome young men, the following dialogue occurs between the family and Madame, who is suddenly annoyed by the assistant's hiccups:

MME. DUFOUR: Monsieur Dufour, make Anatole be quiet or I shall have a nervous attack.

HENRIETTE: Calm yourself, mama, they're going to make him drink a glass of water.

M. DUFOUR: A glass of water, my dear? But they only have wine.

MME. DUFOUR: Oh! If you were a man! You'd know how to find water!

Unassuaged longing is what troubles Mme. Dufour, who is now aware of the poor figure her husband cuts alongside Henri and Rodolphe. Yet we don't learn that from what she says but from the way that she says it and from the subsequent moment in which Henriette calms her mother by scratching her back.

When Renoir's dialogue is neither natural accompaniment for the action nor obliquely representational, as in the previous case, it reflects the setting. Thus Rodolphe and Henri constantly employ fishing terminology when discussing seduction; and references to a storm, which actually breaks toward the end of the film, allude to the likelihood of erotic explosions. By such means, the dialogue is tied to what we see and is not felt as an independent mode of communication.

We are, of course, dealing here with a modification of theatrical

speech rather than with a radically different kind. Technical modification, in place of innovation, is what makes films like those of Carol
Reed or Jean Renoir clearly literary in essence. Even the sewer chase
from *The Third Man*, which is more apparently distinct from literary
practice because of its non-verbal medium, is not wholly unlike certain kinds of theatrical spectacle. As Nicholas Vardac has shown in
his important book, *Stage to Screen: Theatrical Method from Garrick
to Griffith*,[8] so far from inventing a language of spectacle, cinema can
be regarded as an extension of means already employed by certain
stage directors of the late nineteenth and early twentieth centuries.
Even more obviously, symptomatic dialogue is not peculiar to the
screen. Modern drama is, to a large degree, distinguished from drama
in previous periods through its development of more symptomatic,
less rhetorical speech.

Among the more naturalistically inclined of modern playwrights,
there are also precedents for the sort of "plotlessness" one encounters
in both Maupassant's and Renoir's country outing. Thus, it would be
overstating the difference between stage and screen to assert that
plays are more complexly plotted than films. But, Aristotle was surely
right to claim that plot is the soul of drama, and film is drawn toward
theatricalism by too complex a plot since plot complications make it
expedient to rely on explicatory dialogue. Consequently, plays *may*
choose to be relatively plotless if they want to seem realistic; films
must, at least, de-emphasize plot, whether or not they seek to simulate
reality, just in order to avoid becoming dialogue centered, and thus
too much like plays.

In novelistic films, like those of Reed, theatricalism is disguised by
a wealth of wordless communication, but in theatrical films, where
characters are almost always talking, action is rarely available to
establish the work's formal identity. Hence such films must avoid explicatory dialogue and, because plot encourages explication, must
avoid plot. (We will qualify this in discussing *Rules of the Game*.)
Maupassant's "slice-of-life" story is uneventful enough to discourage
explicatory dialogue and this fact helps to make Renoir's speech
sound natural or real, untheatrical or uncontrived.

In part, the uneventfulness is expressed by the brevity that the film
shares with the story (it is barely 40 minutes long). Renoir, however,
goes further than Maupassant to deemphasize plot; he refuses to satisfy implied narrative expectations.

Renoir's chief revision of Maupassant is his elaboration of the
characters of Rodolphe and Henri. Present from the Dufours' arrival,

as they are not in Maupassant, the two young men are also provided with copious dialogue invented for the film. Much of it concerns the ethics of seduction. Thus Henri admonishes Rodolphe against following Henriette lest he "give her a child," to which the heedless friend answers, "Oh. If one is going to make a child every time he amuses himself a little . . . the world would become overpopulated!" Such talk prepares the audience for a banal "seduced and abandoned" story, but, retrospectively, we can see that it exists to make us understand that life is more casually ironic than a careful novelist. By chance, Henri rather than Rodolphe goes off with the girl, and nothing much happens. Not events but an emotion is the result of the day's outing. Henri doesn't impregnate Henriette; rather, their casual coupling infects both with gradually developing nostalgia.[9]

Appropriately enough, the film achieves its climax through greater reliance on images than words. The camera becomes the principal means of communication, now that feelings have become too intense to be verbally expressed. Henri and Henriette embrace, Renoir moves in for a magnified close-up that is complemented by a crescendo in Joseph Kosma's score; then the camera tracks back rapidly across the river on which the lovers had sailed to their pleasure but whose waters, suggestively, are now pierced by rain. The poignant aftermath, in the brief last scene, is expressed not only through words ("I come here often. You know my fondest memories are of this place." "I think of it every night.") but by three powerful images: Henriette's distraught and yearning face, Henri disconsolately smoking a cigarette, and Henriette rowing her doltish husband back to shore.

Dominated by non-verbal techniques (the objective correlative of the fretted river, as well as the framing, music, and gestures), these images are rare in the manner of their eloquence and thus fittingly climactic. Elsewhere, the excellence of A Day in the Country is due entirely to the dialogue and acting.

Negative proof that Renoir's talent is essentially theatrical rather than cinematographic is provided by his other famous excursion into the countryside, Picnic on the Grass (1959). Setting is even more important in the later film, which is an explicit celebration of nature, and nature is more lavishly photographed here because of Renoir's new command of color. Indeed, one frame from this film, showing the leading lady bathing nude in a river, has become the obligatory illustration for those who locate Renoir's genius in his eye. Nonetheless, Picnic on the Grass is a failure, admired only by those for whom Renoir never errs, whereas A Day in the Country is widely and properly regarded as one of his successes.[10] The difference is what Renoir has conceived for filming, not the manner in which he films it.

Picnic heavy-handedly asserts that science is unnatural. Its hero Alexis is a biologist, apostle of artificial insemination, and candidate for the presidency of Europe. He plans to marry his German cousin— a superannuated girl scout, the death of whose fiancé made her turn to athletics and public service to replace her lost opportunity for more intimate sport. Having chosen a picnic in a ruined temple of Diana as the place to announce his engagement, the professor unwittingly surrenders to a magical shepherd, who raises a storm that turns the guests into nymphs and satyrs, and sends Alexis to the bathing nude. The superiority of natural insemination thus dawns on him, and, after numerous complications, he marries his luscious peasant.

Tendentious and sophomoric, the film pits caricatured sophisticates against real peasants and thus reduces its thesis to an incompatability of styles.[11] As played by Paul Meurisse, Alexis is also a simpering fool, who couldn't organize a laboratory much less a continent. Adding over-explicit rhetoric to the self-canceling characterization, Renoir makes Alexis say things like "Passion exists, but therapeutic means can render it inoffensive. It can be cured like the common cold," and "Perhaps happiness is submitting to the natural order."[12]

Almost nothing of the film's theme is portrayed through action. The fantasy storm, on which the plot turns, is relevant neither to nature nor science. Moreover, it is badly staged; one can almost see the wind machines. And what should be the visual high point is a major gaff. Off go Alexis and Nanette into the bushes, while, to represent what they are doing there, Renoir cuts to a montage of waving grass, moving water, and, at the climax, raging rapids. Only after closing in on a tremulous dandelion does he allow the lovers to re-enter the frame. Such obvious punning might work as a deliberately ludicrous blatancy; but the plot and the lyrical musical accompaniment make it clear that Renoir doesn't mean us to laugh.[13]

Taken together, *A Day in the Country* and *Picnic on the Grass* show how little Renoir's success is due to visualizing nature or to staging non-verbal action, how much it comes from natural speech and realistic behavior. Only the latter film's peasants have any of the credibility of the earlier characters, and even they seem to come out of Marcel Pagnol rather than life. That *Picnic*, an original, should seem more derivative than *Day*, an adaptation, is a sign of its intense artificiality. Propositional as well as mimetic, the film is more ambitious than its shorter predecessor, but Renoir states rather than dramatizes his ideas. That they aren't good ones to begin with is, of course, the chief reason for the film's failure. But for our purposes, the more notable causes are the rhetorical dialogue that replaces action and the fantasy/staginess that contradicts the moments of realism.

One of Renoir's two great films is even more ideological than *Picnic on the Grass*, but *Grand Illusion* does create a believable story and characters in behalf of an avowedly doctrinaire intention.[14] Moreover, it does so despite an even greater reliance on speech than is true of *A Day in the Country* and a higher proportion of assertive rather than obviously symptomatic dialogue.

In plot, a prison break film and thematically pacifist, *Grand Illusion* is scarcely to be described by either designation. Suspense about the break is minimized. Instead Renoir illustrates social forces that divide men, cause wars, and produce inevitable resistance. Escape becomes not only escape from a literal prison camp but from what it embodies: hostilities engendered by nationalism, class and race. As the title indicates, perfect human fraternity is a grand illusion because ties that bind simultaneously exclude. Two of the principal characters escape from prison into neutral territory, but only on the way to a geo-political unit where enmity will once more assert its power in human affairs.[15]

In effect, the plot of this film holds our attention in order to express thematic meaning. But whereas, for example, *The Third Man* alternates moments of action with statements of theme, Renoir subverts his plot in the very act of dramatizing it, throwing us onto the dialogue by a kind of default.

First, Renoir de-emphasizes the prison break plot by showing the inmates as less occupied with wanting to escape than with wishing for or enjoying food, longing for women but getting only men in drag, etc. They trade stories about home, comment on the attractions of Holland, busy themselves with the show that turns some of them into ersatz women: many things besides imprisonment.[16] When the topic of escape comes up, the prisoners can't even agree on a motive. *Grand Illusion* knows that real men aren't so single-minded as characters in a movie and that real events don't follow a script.

The escape plan is hatched by accident, in a scene less important for the plot than as a comment on contemporary history. The Czarina sends her imprisoned subjects a shipment of books, causing them to set fire vengefully to so irrelevant a gift. From this, Boeldieu infers the need of a diversion to permit Rosenthal and Maréchal to flee, but more significant is the gift's example of fatal incomprehension by the Russian monarchy and its analogy in Rauffenstein's haughty disdain for his common prisoners. Both the immediate flight and the worldwide escape from the burdens of aristocratic oppression are facilitated through ill-advised superciliousness.

An even better example of Renoir's interest in social documentation rather than plot occurs in the penultimate escape attempt by the French prisoners. Having been foiled in their tunnel excavations and, as a consequence, finding themselves even more formidably locked up in a remote castle, Maréchal and his cronies have been making a rope with which to descend from the ramparts. German captors enter their room, forcing them to hide the rope, and Boeldieu, recognizing the folly of their choice of a bed for concealment, places the dangerous object in an outside gutter. While the Germans are rifling the quarters, von Rauffenstein enters to order that Boeldieu not be disturbed. "Give me your word of honour that there is nothing inside the room which is against regulations," von Rauffenstein asks of Boeldieu, who, after complying, wonders why the commandant didn't request assurance from the others. Take "the word of a Rosenthal . . . or a Maréchal!" (p. 69), his fellow aristocrat exclaims.

Not the search itself, which is staged too perfunctorily to create suspense, but this exchange dominates the scene. We aren't meant to worry so much about the rope as to savor the irony that von Rauffenstein expects a scrupulous answer from a fellow aristocrat, even though he is French, but is sure that a Jew or commoner would lie. And, after a fashion, von Rauffenstein is right, for it takes someone of Boeldieu's refinement to stand on such technical veracity: there is nothing *inside* the room.

Scenes that don't contain such thematic irony are almost tossed off. For example, during the tunnel excavation, the Actor is supposed to be protected by his fellow prisoners who are to keep one eye out for guards and the other on a cup attached to a string he will pull if suffocating. After a diversion that turns the soldiers away from the cup, Renoir cuts to show it falling unnoticed on a bed, but that is all he does to inspire anxiety. Even a novice could work his audience over with editing and music more successfully than Renoir does. Equally maladroit is the scene where Maréchal, thrown into solitary for flaunting camp rules, manages to escape from a sentry by simply pushing the man down when he enters his cell. Such signs of bad staging in scenes of strenuous action happen to reflect a common weakness in most of Renoir's films, but here—albeit negatively—they aid the deemphasis of plot that is so crucial to the *Grand Illusion*'s seriousness and realism.[17] Were *Grand Illusion* a film of action rather than theme, the careless staging would be deplorable. As it stands, the resulting casualness makes this prison camp seem imperfectly oppressive, and hence more plausible than those we are accustomed to in conventional films.

Instead of the merely physical story of pain and victory that is the normal escape movie, *Grand Illusion* is a sociological documentary. The opening makes this clear. We begin at the officers' mess of a French air squadron, where Maréchal, who is listening nostalgically to a popular record, is interrupted by the spit-and-polish Boeldieu. From this we move to the other side's mess hall, where the entering Rauffenstein informs us that he has just shot down the Frenchman's plane. Thus quickly setting up the situation, the sequence concentrates on an identity between locales that suggests how arbitrary is the clash between their inhabitants; where nothing is obviously distinctive we wonder what can cause the French and Germans to war against each other.

Immediately thereafter, Renoir presents a scene of believably inconsequential table talk that nonetheless reiterates the foregoing theme. As the Frenchmen eat alongside their captors, Rauffenstein bends toward Boeldieu, inquiring in French about the latter's cousin and then switching into English, as does Boeldieu, after the link has been established. Panning a bit, Renoir shows a German officer asking Maréchal why he doesn't eat and kindly cutting the Frenchman's food when he learns that Maréchal's fasting is caused by the disablement of his broken arm. "You speak French well," the Frenchman says while the German performs the courtesy. "I once worked at Gnome, in Lyon," the latter replies. "No joking!," Maréchal blurts out happily, "Me too, I'm a mechanic!" (pp. 17–18). Suddenly, a German soldier enters with a wreath for the French killed in military action; all stand at respectful attention; Rauffenstein pronounces a blessing, and eating resumes. But there is immediately a second interruption; the military police arrive to take away the prisoners.

Meaning is conveyed here by conversation as an event rather than through the dialogue's statements. What we learn as Maréchal talks to the German soldier, for example, is the simultaneous existence in any encounter of role-affinities as well as distinctions. The specific details make little difference because we won't see this soldier again and Maréchal's previous profession plays no part in the action. Renoir means us to notice that men who share the same profession and who once even worked in the same place can become enemies simply by the accident of being nationals of different countries. But if they even speak each other's language, we are meant to ask, how can they kill each other? More clamorously, this question is raised by the talk of Rauffenstein and Boeldieu, which moves into a language that transcends differences in nationality, as does their aristocrats' world of shared friends and values.

Renoir's dialogue doesn't state these questions; it inspires them. As Siegfried Kracauer puts it, the multilinguism of the soundtrack "materializes language"; that is draws attention to the medium, regardless of its content[18] and thus, effectively, makes us scrutinize language, not passively receive information from it. In one of his best scenes, Renoir dramatizes this fact of language as an object by showing it as a material barrier between Maréchal, who knows a hole has been dug, and the English soldiers who are taking over the Frenchman's cell but cannot comprehend the tip he wishes to leave them with.

Most of the film's dialogue exists less for the information it contains than to exemplify human separation. Rosenthal, who receives gourmet shipments from his rich relatives, provides his cellmates with a feast. While they eat, Boeldieu congratulates him on the quality of his brandy. "It's the barman at Fouquet's who sent it to me in a bottle of mouthwash," his host replies. "Fouquet's," an inmate wonders, so Rosenthal explains to his interlocutor, a schoolmaster, "Yes . . . a bar on the Champs-Elysées." To which the man returns, "When I used to go to Paris, I'd eat my meals at my brother-in-law's . . . It's much cheaper than a restaurant" (p. 29). This exchange tells us of class distinctions that put one man out of phase with another just as dangerously as distinctions of nationality.

In manifesting the latter barrier, the film's multilinguism is obviously cinematic because, since theater doesn't permit subtitling, a playwright could not cast so much of his dialogue in tongues foreign to his audience without effectively blocking their comprehension. But even in cases like the discussion of brandy, the dialogue becomes an action (hence relatively cinematic) rather than an utterance: the sign of a condition rather than a piece of communication between characters or to the audience. Renoir and co-scenarist Charles Spaak had made their story from the phenomenon of people talking at cross-purposes because this babble of dialogue is the outer proof of otherwise invisible conflicts in role.[19]

The depth of these conflicts is established after the men have escaped. In their separate peace, Maréchal and the German war widow,

Elsa, show that love conquers language barriers. But even when Maréchal and Elsa are most intimate, Renoir reminds us that nationality isn't the only wall between people. While the couple and Rosenthal admire the crèche that Elsa has made for her daughter, "Oh, the Virgin Mary!," she exclaims, quite moved, "And baby Jesus," Rosenthal interjects good-humoredly, "my blood brother!" Complete escape is impossible; beyond the prison there is the force it embodies, and beyond the love that can unite French and German is the hatred that can set French Catholic against French Jew.

Yet although Renoir is aware that roles divide, he also knows they can unite. Boeldieu, who condescends to Frenchmen with whom he would hardly consort in peacetime, ultimately sacrifices himself to save them because of a code of duty made operative by war. Cutting across this bond is the natural brotherhood of the aristocracy that makes Rauffenstein care more for Boeldieu than for his own country and leads to the touching scene in which he apologizes for not having merely wounded his "enemy," as he intended.

Among the non-aristocrats, the suffering caused by war takes the place of international elegance in forging community. This is most apparent in the final scene, where Maréchal's anti-Semitism might have caused him to leave Rosenthal behind did not the latter's wounds make him seem more French and in need of help than Jewish and worthy of execration.[20] With terrible and complex irony, *Grand Illusion* shows that war and peace are not strictly distinguishable, for the brutal state inspires comradeship that the normal regime often precludes.

Nothing so clearly dramatizes the film's relentless ambiguity than the famous theater scene in which the prisoners, who have been allowed to entertain themselves and their captors, affront the latter's kindness by bursting into the *Marseillaise* when word comes that the French have retaken Douaumont. Unlike the suspense scenes, this sequence is carefully edited to rouse the spectator.

Immediately before the show began, we had learned that Douaumont was in German hands, but the French decide to show the Germans that morale is unaffected—thereby thrilling the native audience intended for the film and anyone else who admires pluck. As the show transpires, Renoir cuts back and forth between the stage and the spectators so as to increase admiration for the French prisoners' heroism and the German captors' complacency. However, when the Actor asks all to sing a popular song, even the Germans temporarily join the international fraternity of pleasure-seekers. Now comes a

55

cut of Rosenthal reading a newspaper and signalling to Maréchal, who bursts onstage with news that Douaumont is once again French. The German spectators' frozen astonishment pleases our sense of partisanship, which is raised to fever pitch by the stirring rendition of the *Marseillaise*. While the Germans storm out angrily, we are transported by what seems a victory in fact as well as emotion. Immediately Renoir dissolves to the capture and incarceration of Maréchal and from this to the soldiers reading a placard announcing that the Germans have retaken Douaumont.

Through action, editing, and ironic repetition, this intensely cinematic scene shows the senselessness of nationalist feelings. Moreover, it implicates the viewer by making him acknowledge that he too was carried away by a thrill that counted for nothing. Yet this irony is subsumed within the contradictory fact that patriotism causes the protagonists to escape. By such means does Renoir keep us off balance, thereby acknowledging the truth that no aspect of life permits a single response.

Stylistically, the film is equally rich, obtaining a higher truthfulness by mixing verisimilitude with theatricalism. Siegfried Kracauer has argued that the literally theatrical show scene helps to make the rest of the film seem more realistic by contrast;[21] but, as I have shown, this itself is perhaps the film's most realistic and cinematically constructed episode.

The relation between theatricalism and naturalness is better displayed by the acting, which deliberately joins the stagey performances of von Stroheim (Rauffenstein) and Pierre Fresney (Boeldieu) to that of roles performed in a near monotone, by actors almost swallowing their lines and using minimal gestures. Jean Gabin (Maréchal), for example, says most of what he needs merely by eyes that seem to look at nothing and to place everything they do see beneath the necessity of fear. The combination works because Rauffenstein and Boeldieu belong to a separate world. So perfect is their joint maintenance of this artificial medium that they enable Renoir—as he rarely can—to create an effective instance of visual symbolism. As we have seen, the director's eye tends toward the blatant in such moments; in *Grand Illusion* the blatancy of the characters excuses him. When, after Boeldieu dies, Rauffenstein cuts the one flower he had been able to cultivate in the bleak stockade, we accept the grandiose gesture as appropriate to a man who resists chaos through deliberateness in style.[22]

This tendency toward stylization in von Rauffenstein (and Boeldieu) also permits the film to include rhetorical dialogue without seeming artificial, since these men naturally express themselves in formal speech. What would be the author's thematic blatancy when issuing from the mouths of other characters becomes "symptomatic dialogue" in their cases. Both men are living out a drama that is more rhetorical and stylized than the one in which we find them. They—not the show scene—are the theatrical elements that heighten the reality of the rest of the film through contrast. In *Grand Illusion* Renoir has it both ways. He uses real locations, natural acting, and anti-rhetorical dialogue to obtain a cinematic illustration of his theme. At the same time, he includes characters originating and performed in the opposite style.

Renoir usually attempts to have it both ways rather than to de-theatricalize (as in all of *A Day in the Country* and parts of *Grand Illusion*). The former's "symptomatic dialogue" is scarcely more common in Renoir's work than the latter's "materialization" of language, and none of his other films moves so far away from plotting. Normally, his scripts are full of theatrical contrivance and dialogue, though he frequently plays against them with real locations and casual performances. Sometimes, this combination achieves a measure of success.[23] More often, the real settings only point up the artificiality of what takes place in them and the actors seem incompetent, not unstylized.[24]

Yet, as *Grand Illusion* shows, artificiality can enter a film without destroying realism so long as it seems to arise from the subject. When Renoir turns his antagonists in *Picnic on the Grass* into caricatures, he loses credibility because the rest of the film exists in a world, as we know from experience, that sets greater limits even on folly. But von Rauffensteins and Boeldieus do exist in the real world, so their stylization doesn't seem falsely imposed. In *Rules of the Game* (1939) Renoir goes even further in making artifice part of a realistic style. He chooses a world in which eloquence and formal behavior are normal and is thus able to seem naturalistic despite contrivances in plotting and theatricality in speech.

Rules is modeled on Musset's *Les caprices de Marianne*, a typically bitter-sweet stylization about amorous vagaries. Renoir appropriates Musset's subject and approximates his artificial plot. The film commences with a sort of prologue in which we meet the lover (Jurieu) and the older friend (Octave) who will, as in Musset, guide him to his lady love. Next there are expository scenes that introduce the woman, her husband and the husband's mistress (a complication added by Renoir). All the principals then arrive at the Marquis' chateau, where the woman contrives to relieve her husband's embarrassment at Jurieu's impulsive declaration of love. What may be regarded as Acts IV and V comprise the subsequent hunt and masked ball.

These later events, for which there are no parallels in Renoir's source, reflect his specific intention. Whereas Musset focuses exclusively on interpersonal relations, Renoir relates them to mores. This adds to the film's theatricalism (character conflict rendered through speech) a novelistic emphasis on social reality that, in turn, leads to cinematic exploitation of ambience and action. The result is as much a combination of theater and cinema as of individual emotions and social forms. The artistic mix, as we will see, perfectly expresses the mix of forces that Renoir wishes to explore.

Structurally, the film is theatrical. The beginning is blatant exposition: a radio announcer tells us who André Jurieu is; Jurieu then appears to announce his love for Christine; Christine is introduced and joined by her husband, who phones his mistress; the mistress answers from an apartment, where a friend tells us all we need to know about the married couple's background. Classically, the main plot is imitated by a subplot, in which servants are shown aping their masters. Turning points in both plots are contrived: during the hunting scene, Christine chances to be given a pair of binoculars that she accidentally trains on Robert at the precise moment that he is kissing Geneviève, so she discovers that her husband has a mistress; Schumacher comes upon his wife, Lisette, and the poacher, Marceau, at an equally revealing moment. Since the plot is meant to end in violence, we are constantly forewarned of such a possibility; when Marceau is first caught poaching by Schumacher, the gamekeeper threatens him; during the hunt scene, Octave warns Jurieu that the hunters might mistake them for quarry; later in the same scene, the General tells of a friend who blew his own thigh off; and Schumacher explicitly threatens to shoot Marceau for poaching not only on the boss's rabbits but on his own wife. All this contrasts sharply with the narrative technique of *Grand Illusion*, in which scenes are related thematically rather than causally, progress in the plot is brought about by chance, and action is de-emphasized.

Also more artificial is this film's dialogue, which, though frequently symptomatic, is even more often expository. Having a larger number of Boeldieus and Rauffensteins among the characters, Renoir lets them comment regularly on the action. Christine wonders "what is natural nowadays?" (p. 31), Geneviève quotes a definition of love "in society" as "the exchange of two fantasies and the coming together of two epidermises" (pp. 38–39); and Octave reminds Jurieu that Christine is "a woman of the world . . . and that particular world, it has rules—very stiff ones" (p. 42).[25] Because he is played by Renoir himself and figures in the story as a surrogate director of the events,[26] Octave often offers such comprehensive explanations. Most famously, he asserts that it is wrong "to search . . . for what's good, and what's bad. Because you see, on this earth, there is one thing which is terrible and that is that everyone has their own good reasons" (p. 53). The prevalence of such dialogue in *Rules of the Game* explains Alain Resnais' discovery that the "soundtrack recorded on my tape recorder . . . stands up even without the picture."[27]

This fact places Renoir's film within the vast majority of movies that are effectively "photoplays;" but in this case whatever visual elements there are exist to subvert the theatrical self-sufficiency of plot, dialogue and acting. Renoir wants to show how a highly formal society deals with primordial impulses, so he pits formalities of talk and gesture against a range of physical disruptions.

Occasionally, Renoir has declared a more topical intention (to expose "the malady which was afflicting my contemporaries),"[28] and one speech supports this characterization of the film (when Christine laments having been married for three years to a man who was deceiving her, Octave replies, "Listen, Christine, that's a sign of the times, too. We're in a period when everyone tells lies: pharmacists' handbills, Governments, the radio, the cinema, the newspapers . . . So how could you expect us poor individuals not to lie as well" [p. 155]). But nothing else pertains to this subject; and, in any case, Renoir has not dramatized a temporary condition. Although accurately rendered, the society of the film is shown only in that aspect of its behavior that timelessly links it to all societies: attempts at maintaining fidelity against the force of lust or, put in words closer to those used by the characters, attempts to experience friendship and trust despite the essentially impersonal desire that underlies sexual relations.

The universality of Renoir's theme is explicitly broached in a talk between Robert, Marquis de La Chesnaye, and Marceau, just before both go to do battle with their rivals:

> ROBERT: The Moslems are the only ones who've shown the slightest sense in this notorious question of relationships between women and men.

MARCEAU: Well!

ROBERT: Bah! In the end, they're built the same way as us!

MARCEAU: You said it . . .

ROBERT: There's always one woman they like best.

MARCEAU: Yes . . .

ROBERT: But they don't think that just because of that they have to throw others out . . . and make them suffer.

MARCEAU: Of course not!

ROBERT: Me, I don't want to hurt anyone. Especially not women. . . . It's the drama of my life.

(p. 122)

These are the rules of the game. One loves, yet one wants other women. To have more than one without causing pain requires the elaborate forms and duplicities of civilized society. Representing a less advanced class, Marceau, as he admits, is heedless of anything except working his will, in behalf of which aim he urges on Robert the effectiveness of giving a girl a good time. But as Robert says, he lacks talent for so simple an expedient. Too delicate to pursue women as Marceau does, he gives as much pain as pleasure, thereby breaking the very rules that he most wishes to uphold.

Still, the pain had always been moderate, until Robert frivolously invited Marceau's amoral animality into his own highly deliberated world. Marceau is thereby enabled to chase Lisette, which antagonizes Schumacher, who relieves his fury by shooting the man he thinks is yet another of her suitors—Octave. But by accident Jurieu is dressed in Octave's coat, so the wrong man is killed.

In a sense, however, Jurieu is not the wrong man. He too had been guilty of an infraction of the rules, like Marceau with his animality or Octave with his unthinking attempts to meddle in his friends' lives. Because André's plan to take Christine away asserts a right to exclusive possession, he cannot be included in the game. Thus it was wrong for Octave to urge Robert to invite him to the chateau and as foolish an act for Robert to commit as the inviting of Marceau. The latter's bluntness is no more a threat to the La Chesnaye world than is Jurieu's romanticism. Both are excesses threatening rules designed to combine variety and fidelity with peace. As such, both uncover the latent danger in the game. Like any compound of volatile elements, the La Chesnaye world can easily explode. Marceau and Jurieu set the charge.

This they do by exposing the fact that the La Chesnaye world *is* playing a game, which—though admirable in its elegance and moral in its resistance to pain—is a lie, hence potentially dangerous. Ironically, the lie is unmasked when the characters assume literal disguises that are more self-declaring than their everyday dress. Christine becomes the Tyrolean girl that her Austrian heritage and sentimentality make her; Genevieve, the predatory mistress, puts on a gypsy's scarves and bangles; Octave encases himself in the skin of a bear, from which cute but subhuman disguise he finds it as difficult to extricate himself as from the real personality that it symbolizes; the male guests appear as hunters; and Jurieu and Robert, the rivals for Christine, reveal an underlying similarity by refusing to wear costumes.

Or rather, Jurieu begins with one added to the black trousers of his tuxedo but quickly resumes formal dress. This uncovers a surprising degree of formality in the impulsive man, and the formality helps to cause his death. For all his antagonism to the La Chesnaye world, Jurieu—unlike Marceau—is only partly its antithesis (the romantic aviator who literally soars above society). When Christine declares her love and begs him to take her away, he protests that he must first tell La Chesnaye, "because it's the done thing" (p. 128). Insisting to the distraught woman that "there are certain rules, after all!" (p. 128), Jurieu produces the delay that makes Christine run off with Octave, forces Jurieu to chase her, and permits Schumacher to make his fatal error. Jurieu's punctilio conforms to a code different from Robert's, but it reveals him as a social creature. Being civilized, he balances lust against responsibility. However, since the former is the latter's implacable enemy, his attempt—like that of Robert—is foredoomed. That the pain he receives was intended for another only underlines the essential anonymity that lust confers.

Anonymity subsumes even the women who, unlike the men, prefer the personal uniqueness affirmed by love. When Geneviève, who had always been content to play the "other woman" finally asserts her claims to being the only one, she becomes simply an impediment that Robert must lock up. Christine, who had tried to follow her husband's libertine example by going off with St. Aubin, immediately pledges undying love when Jurieu interrupts this assignation and then pledges the same love for Octave when Jurieu temporarily defects. At the end, Schumacher mistakes her for Lisette, just as he mistakes Jurieu for Octave, but there is as much underlying truth in the error about her as in the more fatal mistake about André. Through her search for romance, she has become nearly as promiscuous as her maid; the latter's cloak that she puts over her costume is, in the moral sense, only a further disrobing.[29]

Therefore, Christine must, at the end of the film, clothe her nakedness in the rules. Jackie, the young girl who was truly in love with Jurieu, goes to pieces after his death, thereby submitting herself to public exposure. Pull yourself together, Christine warns, while manifestly taking her own advice, "people are looking at you" (p. 167). And we recall that the party that led to Jurieu's murder was Robert's reward to Christine for having so successfully disguised the depth of her liaison with the new guest when Jurieu arrived. Those who live by disguises are destined to become what they only pretended.

At last, the façade of insouciance becomes the building; these people have reconstructed their hearts. As the General says in conclusion, "La Chesnaye does not lack class . . ." (p. 168). Finely, *Rules of the Game* dramatizes both the achievements and the costs of so complete a triumph over wildness and spontaneity.[30]

Hence the film must constantly show us what "class" attempts to resist. Theater in *Rules of the Game* is continually invaded by cinema —that is, the real world. The entire work consists in a battle between the two that ends with victory for the dramatic mode, both conceived as content (the La Chesnaye world) and as form.

Two principal scenes rupture the theatricalism: the hunt (literal wildness outside the chateau) and the ball, which was designed by La Chesnaye as a further manifestation of stylishness but which degenerates into a sexual hunt that brings wildness into the chateau. Even before the two forms of hunting are equated, we were prepared for the parallel. Soon after we had been introduced to the La Chesnayes, Renoir showed us Octave chasing Lisette around a hallway. Later, at the chateau, we saw Marceau pursuing the woman belowstairs. Between these two scenes comes the hunt for rabbits and after them, the hunt for human quarry in which, since men aren't as defenseless as animals, one of the hunters gets shot.[31] The hunt scene impresses us with the brutality latent in the rules but disguised by their elegance. By design, the scene contrasts sharply with everything we have thus far witnessed. Words are replaced by action, self-definition of the characters by an objective view of their behavior, and slow theatrical staging by a new frequency of cuts that inspires us with unwonted agitation. Whereas we had been lulled by the charm, charmed by the wit, and prone to take the La Chesnaye world at its own eloquent measure, the sight of beaters flushing rabbits out of the brush simultaneously calls forth our doubts.

Suddenly the play becomes a documentary—and a terrible one. Renoir trains his camera at the beaters who appear in overarmed, over-manned phalanx, distressing us by their relentless forward movement and by the cacophony of their sticks beating against the trees. The camera tracking backwards—as it had rarely done in the film— causes the rabbits to scurry toward us, as if seeking protection. A montage of guests loading their guns seems aimed at the audience as well. Next we have a lateral tracking shot that makes the beaters appear a hoard advancing on a single rabbit. There follows a series of cuts—unbearable in its speed, as well as in its content—of small animals serially murdered, ending with the graphic death throes of one of them, and then the victim clamped by the jaws of a dog and moved from dog to ground to beater to ground to gamekeeper as if it had never been more than a spineless piece of fur.

As far as possible, considering differences in content, Renoir repeats these techniques in constructing the ball sequence. As in the hunt, langorous talk gives way to violent action, while frightening images fill the screen. A high shot of piano keys moving by themselves starts things off on a semi-comic, semi-terrifying note. But the latter quickly dominates. Even though the performers have dressed themselves as skeletons and ghosts in costumes too makeshift to seem threatening, the audience in the film begins to scream. Renoir transfers their fear to the audience *for the film* with a series of quick cuts, each raked by lights, of people huddling in corners. One particularly bizarre image shows two spectators near a mirror that reflects the "ghosts" in a way which confuses us about spatial relations. The brouhaha increases, as we note a good deal of clandestine embracing; but the couples who are profiting from the simulation of death don't understand the portentous significance of their behavior. As their fear begins to melt under the heat of passions, ours increases because we realize that their heedlessness threatens. More and more, the sequence accomplishes this threat, as characters drop their masks of libertine elegance to reveal desperate and murderous frustration. Guns that were shot in sport during the hunt now go off in earnest. Yet when Schumacher fires after the fleeing Marceau, the General isn't sure whether this is all part of the program. Exasperatedly, Robert orders his major-domo to stop the performance, but this man also doesn't know where reality begins and performance ends.

In truth, the forms that appeared real to the La Chesnaye world kept them from recognizing the equal reality of the madness they were attempting to disguise. During the ball, this madness unmasks itself. By constructing the scene so as to parallel the hunt, Renoir makes clear that the game leads to murder. But the very elegance that constructed its rules allows La Chesnaye to pass the murder off as an accident. Style—which had been ruptured by truth's unmasking at the ball—reasserts itself, closing over the body of Jurieu. The film ends by taking us back to the tone and manner of its earliest scenes.

These had been staged in a markedly theatrical way. The combination of deep focus (permitting us to see as many planes simultaneously as in a stage set) few camera movements (except to follow the actors), and little cutting held our attention on the characters, whose elegance and wit we were permitted to savor. The hunt scene changed this, not only by focusing on the animals but by radically altering the form of the film. As Joel Finler reports, there are about 50 shots in less than four minutes during the hunt, whereas the rest of the film, running some two hours, contains only about 280.[32] This dramatic shift in pace is one sign of the film's brilliant use of cinematic techniques. Such contrasting examples of long and short duration that play on our pulses could not have been achieved onstage. *Rules* is a film because, unlike a play, it can first be a play and then cease to be one. *Rules* is a great film, in part, because this alteration precisely expresses the contrast between stylization and brute nature that is its theme.

Throughout, *Rules* communicates through means more resourcefully visual than are characteristic of Renoir's other films. For example, when we first meet Robert and Christine, they seem an extraordinarily amicable couple. Already dressed for the evening, she comes politely to fetch him from his room. As their conversation progresses, he returns the compliment by avowing perfect comprehension of her liaison with Jurieu, thereby putting her at grateful ease. But in one shot, when Robert asks her to admire a mechanical little negress that he has just added to his toy collection, Renoir cuts to an extreme close-up of the doll with Christine's sleeve and Robert's hand visible in the frame. Visually, this suggests a marriage that has borne no fruit and in which intimacy goes hand in hand with separation. In a later scene, when Robert is decorously throwing over his mistress, each is framed in reverse close-ups next to giant heads of Chinese statues that become the objective correlative of their own formalized repression of what they actually feel. At the end of the film, when the aristocrats have responded to Jurieu's death with awesome but heartless composure, they depart from the frame, leaving us to watch shadows flickering on the chateau walls. Renoir judges them by this image.

Like the shifts in tempo, these contrasts with the film's predominantly verbal language are powerful precisely because they are exceptional. By playing such cinematic techniques against the more pervasive theatricalism, Renoir makes us feel the force of what the plot, dialogue, and acting had made us understand.

Moreover (to repeat), these stylistic conflicts establish the film's aesthetic identity. As I have said, the theatrical medium provides no opportunity for internal technical contrast; a play cannot suddenly give up its essential language and turn into a wordless documentary.[33] By incorporating and opposing theatrical and anti-theatrical modes, *Rules of the Game* proves itself a film rather than a play. Yet this achievement is so unique, so grounded in a certain theme (the conflicting claims of civilized forms and brute reality), that it rather points us back to the aesthetic problem of literary film than ahead to a means of resolution.

As we have seen in the examples of Reed and Renoir, film begins with a rather close resemblance to literature. Despite the special resources of imagery and the possibilities of combining images with other images and with non-visual devices, film can choose plot, character and dialogue as its primary expressive means. This last choice threatens to make film a mere variant of theater. Even when non-verbal action is featured, as in the novelistic film, dialogue retains the key to meaning.

Nonetheless novelistic films are cinematic for granting a rough parity to images and words. A theatrical director like Renoir is in greater danger of aesthetic non-discreteness. Therefore, he needs to avoid independently communicative dialogue. As in *A Day in the Country*, he may use dialogue that restates the message of the images, or (as in *Grand Illusion*) he can seek to compose dialogue that communicates obliquely. Brilliantly, as in *Rules of the Game*, he can even play images against words, thereby achieving a synthesis not possible in the theater. More often, unfortunately, the relationship between dialogue and images in a theatrical film is contradictory rather than complementary. *Picnic on the Grass*, not *Rules of the Game*, is the prototypical theatrical film, with its contrived characters speaking rhetorical dialogue in a contradictorily natural setting. Instead of

65

counterpointing stylization and verisimilitude, it exploits the latter to lend a specious credibility to the former's mannerism.

The literary director who would make true films must want to give words and images, as it were, equal time. When Renoir's Octave (in *Rules of the Game*) says, "everyone has his own good reasons," he is suggesting something about the film's form as well as its content; for the film displays not only the pros and cons of stylization vs. spontaneity—it proves the equal centrality of both through its combination of obviously stylized and seemingly unmediated methods of execution. By contrast, *Picnic* springs from no such even-handedness: nature is all good; civilization, ludicrous. As a result, the film's theatrical elements are parodied, and thereby deprived of that minimum of credibility which would make them fit their naturalistic context. Unless a filmmaker has equal respect for words and images he will allow the former to claim the limelight and show himself a playwright in celluloid robes.

In conclusion, then, we must return to one of our first observations: a film can't be good unless it is good as a film. But, good as the films of Reed and Renoir (which is to say the majority of good films), their goodness is more equivalent to their intelligent representations of life than to formal distinctiveness. Even in the case of a film like *The Third Man*, which is more visually striking than any of the others so far discussed, our esteem should be based not so much on Reed's cinematic illustration as on the complex view of life in the Greene script Reed is illustrating. Renoir accurately represents himself when, in all his interviews, he says that he doesn't care for cinematic technique and is mostly interested in avoiding dramatic clichés and formulaic acting. Most important about the best films of such directors are items like thematic complexity, multi-dimensioned characters, credibly open endings, etc. Clearly, none of these things would be admirable were they not admirably expressed, but in each case the expression is not so distinct from expression in literature that we are more struck by the uniqueness of the form than by the fineness of the content. In the deepest sense—even when they are not actually adapted from pre-existing literary works—most good films are adaptations; they adapt a script for visualization on film.[34] What we have now to begin to see is that this isn't the only method for making a good film; indeed, that it is the least cinematic method for attaining cinematic excellence.

The glory of cinema is also its fundamental challenge: unalterably a mixed medium, it insists that the filmmaker make choices in the priorities he assigns to various components. No filmmaker can entirely eliminate the dramatic element in film (dialogue) nor the musical (rhythm), but he can grant them varying emphases. In this sense, film is less like prose than like poetry, which combines words with music (prosody) in combinations that vary from work to work.[35] That is to say, cinema moves toward fulfillment of its own formal possibilities, thereby distinguishing itself from essentially verbal modes like fiction and drama, insofar as it emulates the combination of verbalization and non-verbal elements characteristic of poetry.

This proposition needs, at first, some explaining and, more importantly, ample demonstration. But before either is undertaken, an obvious objection must be met. Most readers will probably grant that novels and plays—being essentially verbal constructs—are essentially discursive. But any reader can point to exceptions. A play like Wilde's *Importance of Being Earnest*, for example, mocks the very notion that drama speaks to us in order to illuminate life. We can also point to contemporary "anti-novelists" who seem to create fictions that exist only to work out their internal structural geometry. But such exceptions prove the basic rule, both by their rarity and because, as one sees in many of the "anti-novelists," life leaks in, bringing discourse with it.

On the other side of the issue, one might argue that although poetry is partly valuable for its music (an element that neither speaks about nor, except in a metaphoric sense, imitates life), most great poetry is also discursive or imitative. "Concrete poetry" alone proves that poetry impoverishes itself when it attempts to be pure form.

Nonetheless, after one has conceded that *some* novels and plays aspire toward purely formal excellence and *most* poems have content as well as form, it remains evident that fiction and drama are more resistant to the formalizing of content than poetry is. If nothing else, Gertrude Stein has shown that if you beat the sense out of words the music into which you convert them can seem bodiless and boring. On the other hand, Rimbaud and Verlaine present convincing demonstrations that a high degree of satisfaction may be obtained in verse by offering music and a roughly associational pattern of reference.

Film validates a similar choice. Since, by definition, images are non-discursive (or, at least, not necessarily or precisely discursive), it is possible to make a film that says nothing (as many non-narrative, "avant-garde" filmmakers have). In film, even more than in poetry, the medium itself invites one to more or less dispense with content, whereas in fiction and drama, the medium itself resists such an invitation.

But narrative films, "feature films," aren't purely imagistic. They tell stories, create characters, make observations. However, a film needn't emphasize story, character, theme; or rather, a film can turn such items of content into items of structure. For example, themes may be referred to by analogy to musical motif rather than in the literary sense of organizing purposes. What this contention means in practice we can now see by turning to the films of René Clair and Alfred Hitchcock.

HITCHCOCK

ALTHOUGH Alfred Hitchcock is the most primitive of major directors, he belongs in their company. Those who emphasize his primitivism also dismiss his achievement, but his achievement is fundamental to the art of cinema—more specifically, to the art of using cinematic means for audience manipulation.

It is not, however, fundamental to anything else; a truth that needs reestablishing because recent critics have misrepresented Hitchcock. Contrary to their view, he is not seriously interested in moral problems, as one can learn from *I Confess* (1953), a pertinent test case, since it treats explicitly those themes most reverently attributed to the Master: transfer of guilt, the need for absolution, *et cetera*. About a Canadian priest who receives a murderer in confession and thus cannot reveal the crime even when he is himself falsely accused, *I Confess* begins with a moral dilemma. But whereas a serious artist would use the thriller situation to intensify the moral dilemma, Hitchcock does the reverse.

This we can trace in his development of the villain: a refugee from a concentration camp, driven to robbery because his wife is dying from overwork and driven to murder by a reflex of fear. Such mitigating circumstances seem designed to reenforce the priest's sacramental vow of silence; but since Hitchcock is interested only in suspense (will the priest confess?) and melodrama (the priest is good and the murderer isn't), he gradually effaces all moral bonds between the protagonists by transforming the refugee into a sadist who torments his savior with periodic charges of betrayal. Eventually, the man is even made to kill his beloved wife, thus neutralizing the priest's obligations in the interest of a powerful conclusion for the plot.

Throughout his career, Hitchcock has posed moral problems only to evade them. In *Blackmail* (1929) and *Sabotage* (1936), for example, Hitchcock allows guilty heroines to go unpunished simply because their confessions are accidentally interrupted. In *Spellbound* (1945) and *Marnie* (1964) he depicts people falling in love with neurotics and has the queerer member of each couple draw explicit attention to the anomaly. Hitchcock was so titillated by the subject that he intended, in the later film, to have the hero rape the heroine

69

just as she was stealing cash from his safe, but he confessed to Truffaut that fear of censorship made him abstain. Obviously, no moralist could have conceived this scene, much less have avoided it for that reason.

Indeed, how could Hitchcock be a moralist when he does not reproduce the complexity of real experience? If he veers in the direction of realism, as in *The Wrong Man* (1957), he must first appear to his audience announcing that this true story is really stranger than fiction and must do so while standing in a V of light that magically leaves his own figure enshrouded—duplicating the cartoon printed throughout the credits of *The Lodger* (1926), his first typical shock fantasy.

Most of Hitchcock's ideas about the real world are indistinguishable from the commonest pieties—which, of course, helps to explain his unique popular appeal. To begin with, he is discomforted by intellectuals, as we see from *Spellbound*, for which Hitchcock solemnly employed a psychiatric adviser, although the film repeatedly intimates that psychiatrists are just as nutty as laymen. In that film the eminent doctor, who befriends Ingrid Bergman and Gregory Peck, tells us that he was so jealous of Peck's presumed victim that he once disrupted the man's lecture by kicking over chairs. Later, when he begins probing Peck's id for clues to solve the murder ("I'm going to be your father image . . . It's a shortcut, but we haven't got much time . . ."), he sagely pleads, as Peck balks at the nature of these revelations, "Try to recall the details. The more cockeyed the better for the scientific side of it." In *Rope* (1948), a gratuitous murder is attributed to Nietzsche, and the discovery of this link inspires a passionate denunciation, by James Stewart, of intellectuals who don't understand the unique worth of every human soul.

During World War II, Hitchcock became a super-flag-waver, dedicating *Foreign Correspondent* (1940) to those "recording angels" who first saw that Europe would erupt, and ending his irresponsible little thriller with the National Anthem. In 1957, he followed the vogue of *cinéma vérité* and even seemed to discover a theme in *The Wrong Man*'s detailed portrayal of the vagaries of law enforcement. But, at the film's conclusion, its hero indicts not society, which cruelly misjudged him, but the actual culprit, who presumably caused all the trouble by not turning himself in.

My previous remarks only suggest the lack of significant meaning that makes some critics dismiss Hitchcock as a mere prestidigitator or mechanic. But, in the narrow sense, he is an indifferent technician, and no magician who coaxes rabbits so rarely from his hat deserves the title. Everyone knows that setting is crucial to Hitchcock's effects, but no first-rate director, accustomed to big budgets, is so indifferent to authentic locations, so lavish in his use of filmed backdrops or stock shots (that is, bits cribbed from the studio library). Hitchcock boasts about his careful repositioning of fake clouds to signal the passage of time in successive scenes of *Rope*, but he does not remark that in any single shot the clouds remain firmly fixed, revealed to the most imperceptive as celestial cotton candy. Careless use of painted sets is a Hitchcock trademark. Recall, for instance, the last scene of *Vertigo* in which Kim Novak must actually jump from a tower, whereas she had previously only pretended. Considering the malarkey characteristic of the plot, there should at least be visual authenticity in the climax, but Hitchcock shoots the last sequence against a studio set, although the earlier scene had been photographed on location.

In first-rate entertainments like *The Lady Vanishes*, Hitchcock makes nationality functional to his plot. In more ambitious films, where accuracy is requisite to belief, he is oddly casual. Thus we get Montgomery Clift (in *I Confess*) as a French-Canadian priest adenoidally American in a house full of foreign accents or Gregory Peck (in *The Paradine Case*), Her Majesty's most gifted barrister with a down-east twang.

Film buffs rhapsodize about Hitchcock's trick photography, and one remembers marvels even from dreadful films—like the famous staircase shot in *Vertigo*. But frequently the tricks represent not skill but underhandedness. The shower murder in *Psycho*, for example, has the "mother" enter a dazzlingly lighted bathroom, but we can't make out "her" features because they are in the dark.

Often when Hitchcock does devise a clever trick, he uninventively repeats it. I refer not only to bits of business (cutting from a human voice to a train or boat whistle, as in *The 39 Steps* and *Foreign Correspondent*), or replanted clues (Marnie's neurosis: a fear of red; Gregory Peck's in *Spellbound*: a fear of parallel lines), or Hitchcock arcana: blonde heroines, mistaken identities, simultaneous pursuits by villains and cops. I would also point to repetition in incongruous contexts. Thus when Joan Fontaine's cruel employer in *Rebecca* squashes her cigarette into a jar of cold cream, we applaud so striking a way to make us hate her, but we are not meant to hate Jessie Royce Landis, the charming mother in *To Catch a Thief*, who squashes her cigarette into the yolk of an egg. In Hitchcock, an overhead shot is invariably used to suggest menace, and changes in locale are regularly signaled by shots of a façade, usually in tilt. Conventional editing techniques, like those dictating progressive movement in group scenes from long, to medium, to close shots occur more often in Hitchcock than accords with his reputation for unusual camerawork, and no other prominent director makes such lazy use of artificial dissolves.

Because Hitchcock commits so many errors and produces so many films that don't excite, he can't be credited with automatic expertise. The difficulty of achieving his special excellence is perhaps the best proof that it is an achievement.

Occasionally in all of his films and always in the best of them, Hitchcock is the master of evocation. Intellectual emptiness and spurious realism are preconditions for his effects. Since Hitchcock depicts a world in which anything can happen, and therefore everything is a threat, distinctions and priorities are forbidden.

Like Poe, the writer he most resembles, Hitchcock is obsessed by a small stock of situations which we can mistake for themes; but, as in Poe's case, these "themes" are only emotional stimuli born from the primitive stage of indiscriminate terror. Both men are sensationalists, but Hitchcock has the advantage of working in a medium that thrives on sensations which it can transmit with irresistible completeness. Sometimes Poe appears to be unveiling a metaphysical terror behind a physical threat, but since words can only point, and since Poe wielded one of the clumsiest pointers in English literature, he had to fall back on insinuation, validated by an aesthetic that argued for vagueness. Hitchcock's vocabulary is the very world from which he wants us to shrink, its items an inexhaustible stock of palpable terrors.

Yet Hitchcock never merely exhibits the sources of dread. As countless horror films and Hitchcock imitations prove, the naked ugliness is likely to excite only laughter. Not by accident do Hitchcock's excursions into direct brutality—*Psycho* and *The Birds*—contain his most elaborate contrivances, his most artful examples of aesthetic distance.

The secret of Hitchcock's terror lies not in the objects he employs but in the timing with which he presents them. He understands, as Poe understood, that emotion, which is imperious when it peaks, cannot be long sustained but may be extended through counterpoint. Like other romantics harassed by the essentially cognitive nature of language, Poe always yearned to transform himself into a musician —which, with a tin ear, he eventually became. For Hitchcock, no such transformation is required, since inherent resemblances between music and film have only to be exploited. Because a film is made from individual shots, the length of which is determined by editing, the filmmaker can control the speed of his revelation to a degree imperfectly approximated by the stage, with its cumbersome machinery, and unavailable to the writer (even the poet) who remains in thrall to the reader's attention span and rhythmic exactness. Therefore, by choosing precisely what we may see and hear at any given moment, by altering the amount of information and by varying the tempo at which it is conveyed, Hitchcock can play upon each spectator's emotions in much the same way that a piece of music plays upon his hand and feet.

Admiring interviewers seeking to pluck out the secret of Hitchcock's meaning forget that the secret is the absence of meaning, the absolute indentification of meaning with effect. Thus Hitchcock asserted to Ian Cameron and V.F. Perkins (in *Movie*, January 1963), "I'm more interested in the technique of story telling by means of film rather than in what the film contains." And when his interlocutors touched upon a question that Hitchcock was normally happy to emphasize—box office receipts of, in this case, *Psycho*—the director pressed on with his shrewd self-analysis: "[The money] was a secondary consideration. *Psycho* is probably one of the most cinematic films I've made and there you get a clear example of the use of film to cause an audience to respond emotionally."

INTERVIEWERS: It was primarily an emotional response you were after from your audience?

HITCHCOCK: Entirely. That's the whole device. After all, the showing of a violent murder at the beginning was intended purely to instill into the minds of the audience a certain degree of fear of what is to come. Actually in the film, as it goes on, there's less and less violence because it had been transferred to the minds of the audience.

The key to *Psycho* is less Sigmund Freud than Richard Strauss. That is why most of Hitchcock's best films are devoid of meaning, peopled by mere containers of stress, and set against backgrounds chosen simply because their innocuousness counterpoints terror. Primitive in insight, Hitchcock is a sophisticated man revelling in pure form, whose films are ends in themselves and so can please both the plebes who want thrills and the cognoscenti thrilled by such an arrogant display of craftsmanship. That is why, like music, Hitchcock films are often most striking at the beginning and the end (introduction and coda), and why he sustains interest only when there are enough crescendos to provide rhythm, paralyzing reason and achieving kinesthesia.

The 39 Steps, Hitchcock's first masterpiece (1935), exhibits his technique in its simplest form. Consider the first sequence showing Robert Donat entering a vaudeville pub where he enjoys the performance until it is interrupted by a shot. We divine no reason for Donat's presence and the pub itself seems utterly insignificant, yet Hitchcock's editing creates a rhythm of anticipation that makes the gunshot doubly effective. First he pans across the music hall sign as it is being illuminated (other directors simply start their films; Hitchcock emphatically begins them). Then, in a tilt shot that declares some approaching mishap, we see a man's back as he nears the box office. Increasing our curiosity, Hitchcock shoots his entrance at floor level, raising the camera only when Donat sits, but still not affording a frontal view. Immediately, the band strikes up, distracting our attention in a way that is obtrusive and therefore frustrating. He now cuts to a full view of the stage taken from the back of the theater, and from this to a close-up of the stage itself on which the mind reader is being introduced. Pans across the audience, in which Donat is casually revealed, and cuts between it and the stage, pile up new information and raise new questions (who is Donat? why is he here? what is his relationship to the mind reader? *et cetera*) with a speed that nearly defies formulation. The cutting and panning tempo now accelerates (that is, we get shorter and shorter bits of film alternately devoted to stage and audience), a movement augmented by the sudden exchange of questions and answers. Donat asks about the distance from Winnipeg to Montreal (whatever for? we wonder), someone challenges the mind reader's response, a fight breaks out in the hall, and Hitchcock further increases the editing speed. Suddenly we get a close-up of the gun; after a moment sufficient to inspire our surprise, it goes off. Then the frame fills with a mass of bodies seeking exit. Donat is pushed against a foreign woman; they talk, leave the hall, get a bus. Fade-out.

By showing the audience that the unexpected can occur, this scene builds up anticipation that will keep us tense even at moments that are relatively placid. This pattern of tension and relaxation, not the silly spy story, is what *The 39 Steps* is "about." The film's next brilliant sequence moves from the primitive fear of the unexpected to the somewhat more sophisticated fear of false appearances. Having witnessed the death of his mysterious guest, after she had told him about the 39 steps and the archdeceiver with the missing finger,

74

Donat seeks refuge from the police, at a farmhouse near the residence of a man he believes will epitomize "the right side." At first, the farmer rejects Donat's plea for shelter, but he relents at the hero's offer to pay. When he thinks Donat has begun making love to his wife, however, he determines to take vengeance. This he does by informing the police of the fugitive's whereabouts, but not before the wife has informed Donat that a police van has arrived.

Beginning with a close-up of the wife's face after Donat flees, the sequence then dissolves into the sweating face of a policeman in the same position: protection is literally replaced by jeopardy. Immediately, Hitchcock cuts to long shots of the pursuit across the moor, intercut with close-ups of solitary policemen silhouetted against the sky—an alteration suggesting that Donat will come through. Still, the police outnumber him and he has no place to hide. Excited by pulsating music and Hitchcock's use of fast motion photography, we are desperate for Donat to gain admission when he finally arrives at the house of the "key man." Donat being let in by the maid is immediately replaced by the policemen being turned away by her saucy lies. Relieved at the ease of this getaway, we settle down as Donat enters a highly civilized drawing room, presided over by suave Godfrey Tearle. The houseguests turn out to include a sheriff, but this reminder of pursuit is clevely evaded, as Tearle draws our hero to the window, through which we spy the police running in the opposite direction. The guests exit, Hitchcock moves in for a closer shot, and we are now back in a confined haven, very much like that of the farm. The relaxed Donat tells about his adventures, while the camera keeps Tearle in sharp focus and Donat in soft. At the end of his recital, Tearle holds up, for the camera's inspection, a hand missing one finger.

This *coup de théâtre* is effective because of Hitchcock's editing. The coincident use of close-ups and relatively slow pacing at the farmhouse and the mansion make them both valleys of rest below Donat's hill of effort. Moreover, Hitchcock controls the image size so as to emphasize the contrasting coziness of the farm and house scenes with the wide-open threat of the moor. For these reasons and others (like the splendid performances of Donat and Tearle, and of Peggy Ashcroft as the farmer's wife), the climax of the sequence is made tremendously powerful. Characteristically, the pace slackens immediately thereafter, as Tearle regretfully discusses his need to kill Donat, which creates an even greater shock when he does so. That is, he seems to have done so—until the next scene. The film's suspenseful rhythm is subsequently reinforced when Donat is joined in his ordeal by a woman, thus doubling the audience's apprehension, while also providing an opportunity for a different kind of suspense as the strangers are handcuffed to each other: will his bravery overcome her reluctance?

To this combination of exciting rhythm and speedy plotting, Hitchcock adds in his next major film a new kind of comedy rooted in national caricature, Hitchcock's only viable, because swift, means of creating people. Based on the famous story of a girl who can find no trace of her hotel companion on returning to their room, *The Lady Vanishes* (1938) features the shock of losing confidence in one's perception. Throughout the film, as Margaret Lockwood searches for Dame May Whitty (an incongruously mild-mannered spy of whose presence all signs have been erased), she encounters little help from her compatriots, who all have selfish reasons for denying that they saw the woman. Thus, for the British audience for which the film was made, national self-confidence is affronted in a way that parallels the affront to the heroine.

Pursued by the villains, Lockwood and Michael Redgrave turn to their British trainmates who, since it is teatime, must be massed in the dining car. This the villains have uncoupled and surrounded, but the occupants won't, at first, believe that they are in danger ("They won't do anything," one announces. "We're British subjects"); and when an emissary sent to entice them from the train reveals he went to Oxford, the poor dupes almost follow him. Only after a shot rings out do they acknowledge their error, rally round the protagonists, and simultaneously thrill the audience with affirmation of Miss Whitty's existence and of British grit.

Like *The 39 Steps, The Lady Vanishes* offers a nonstop display of Hitchcock's speedy, evocative construction. But this film is even more brilliant in its reliance on visual details to create desired effects. Shortly after the first scene, for example, as they prepare to board the train, Margaret Lockwood is hit on the head by a falling window box intended for Dame May. Immediately, Hitchcock cuts to a subjective camera shot of blurred vision, further representing Lockwood's vertigo by superimposing a train wheel. The speedy progress of surrounding experience is then established by close-up shots of tracks as they merge and separate before the onrushing train. Then, from an objective shot of the compartment with Miss Lockwood waking up, Hitchcock again cuts to a subjective shot, as the heroine's "eyes" pick up Dame May, a smiling man, a veiled woman peering at her, and, at her side, a mother and daughter. A bit later she returns to the compartment and prepares for sleep. Quickly cutting to the famous shot of the train as it crosses a graceful but narrow and enormously high viaduct, Hitchcock visually implies the dangerous vulnerability of the heroine's position, which she does not yet understand. So Miss Lockwood closes her eyes once more, after panning across the compartment where the man is playing with the little girl, Dame May is humming, and all seems safe.

This shot fades, we again see the train laterally, and again move to tracks merging and separating in their measurement of time. Abruptly there is a frontal shot of the train as it effectively runs us over, a whistle shrilly blares, and Miss Lockwood wakes up, glancing about the compartment in a direction opposite to the one used before and coming to rest on an empty seat. This skillful use of visualized time and parallel subjective shots creates for the audience the heroine's terrifying sense of having lost her grip on reality and thus involves us emotionally despite the blatant preposterousness of the plot.

While sacrificing the tightness of these early films—each photographed in a studio—*North by Northwest* (1959) contains the boldest display of Hitchcock's mastery of emotional rhythm. Critics faulting this extravaganza as self-parody misjudge the seriousness of its models. *The 39 Steps* and, more obviously, *The Lady Vanishes* are exercises in the terror of confinement; *North by Northwest* is Hitchcock's bravura answer to the question: how can you scare people in technicolor and a Vista-Vision screen? For this reason, the plot of the film is rooted in topography: the true star of *North by Northwest* is the United States map.

Therefore, Hitchcock's signatory appearance in this film is the most functional of his career. Materializing in the crowd of people as the credits are ending, Hitchcock reaches a bus that slams its door in his face just as we read "Directed by . . ." Like his creator, the hero of the film is a man with less than expected control over his environment.

At first, Cary Grant seems fully in charge, weaving through the crowd while dictating orders to his secretary that will simultaneously placate his girl friend and his mother, and climaxing his display of cool by commandeering a taxi—emblem of power throughout the New York scenes. Whizzing into the Plaza where he is greeted as a steady client, Grant seems on top of his world, which he is—until some thugs mistake him for someone else. From then on he becomes someone else—a man senselessly hounded through areas of differing dimensions.

North by Northwest is simultaneously humorous and frightening—not alternately one or the other like *The Lady Vanishes* and *The 39 Steps*—because it lets the viewer in on the joke of its sheer contrivance. We get the bravura idea near the beginning of the film through a scene with Grant drunkenly careening down a narrow road in a car, since we all know that this is a standard movie conclusion. This scene is, moreover, a model of shifting tempi to enhance a mood and of the centrality of landscape, for the horror of Grant's experience is equivalent to the narrowness of the road and the proximity of the sea at its side, a vision that comically sobers him enough to renew his self-control. Subsequently, he is trapped with his pursuers in an elevator from which he is literally saved by humor: the laughter his mother excites, providing cover for his escape. Menace in tight quarters reaches its climax in the film when Grant visits the United Nations, citadel of civilized safety, only to see a man stabbed in the back.

Henceforth, menace moves outdoors (with the single exception of the auction room scene, borrowed from *The 39 Steps*, needed to further the romance, borrowed from *Notorious*). Of the two set-pieces of outdoor menace, the crop-dusting sequence is the more adroit, making full use of the possibilities offered Hitchcock by his medium.

Sent to a rural bus stop, Grant finds himself on a wide open road, which Hitchcock emphasizes with aerial shots. Lack of music and the long-held emptiness of the setting also create a feeling that something tremendous is coming in a film so normally galvanic. Brilliantly, Hitchcock builds suspense by exaggerating the eventlessness of the scene. For some time, Grant merely peers up and down the road; the rare car that crosses moves on without stopping. When a truck comes through, Grant is rewarded only by a mouthful of dust. Soon, however, another car appears from a side road, depositing a man. Now we get a long shot of two figures at opposite sides of an immense vista. Something must surely be up! After a moment of hesitation, Grant crosses the road, an action Hitchcock shoots subjectively, thus heightening our expectation, because subjective shots invariably provide dramatic emphasis. Then exquisitely laconic dialogue assures us that this man cannot be the threat we have feared. A bus now draws up and the man mounts its steps, but not before remarking, "Funny about that plane. Crop-dusting where there ain't no crops."

Having thrown us off so long and so completely, Hitchcock now explodes the violence, hurling Grant across the wide expanse, in which there is no cover, before the swooping, gunfiring plane. Suddenly, Grant notices a cornpatch and makes a run for it; the camera closes in on his triumphant face. But he (we) had forgotten: the plane is equipped with poison gas. How can Grant get away? Running into the road, he stops a truck, but almost at the cost of his life. The marauding airplane, however, can't brake as easily as the truck into which it crashes, as we crash into laughter at the delicious coincidence. Artistically, Hitchcock ends the sequence with a wide-screen intersected by a forward motion of perpendiculars (people moving toward the debris) through which Grant moves backwards in the opposite direction. But this too dissolves in laughter, when we dissolve into the hayseed's truck, which Grant expropriated for his getaway, parked on a posh Chicago street, to the obvious consternation of the traffic cops.

North by Northwest is a prime example of contentless virtuosity. It is also notable for showing, with peculiar clarity, the function of Hitchcock's cynicism. Matching his display that no object is innocent is his belief that no person is. The ubiquity of guilt and of corruption in Hitchcock's world, however, contrary to the view of solemn critics, are rarely moral observations but usually emotional cues. Since no one is very good in the typical Hitchcock movie, we needn't take sides and can root for naked skill. This, in turn, concentrates our feelings on action, which is what the director wants. "Audiences are strange," he has asserted. "I know their reactions so well I don't have to go to the theater anymore; the emotional anxieties are pretty well standard. And they do not necessarily relate to right and wrong." As evidence of this proposition, Hitchcock repeatedly cites the scene from *Psycho* where Tony Perkins is trying to submerge a car containing the woman he has just killed. Hitchcock maintains that spectators root for it to sink, and they do: because the victim has been revealed as a thief and fornicator and because the action is irresistible in its appeal (the car almost sinks, stops, causes Perkins a moment of panic, and then goes to the bottom, bringing him and us relief).

In *North by Northwest* the release of the spectator from moral considerations is patterned every bit as carefully as the release of Cary Grant from his sources of control. First, we have the flaming-haired bridge-playing mother whom her son can bribe. Then we have venality on the train: when Grant escapes by stealing a porter's clothes we applaud his cleverness, until the camera cuts to the "victim" in underwear counting his cash. Even later when anxiety seems the only response, Hitchcock provides a tiny moral shock: when Cary Grant escapes from a hospital room by invading that of another patient, she screams until putting on her glasses, at which point she begs him to remain.

Morality is more seriously neutralized in the film through Hitchcock's characterization of the ostensible "good guys," who not only risk Grant's life but do so with outrageous callousness. Upon being informed that Grant must play decoy in the fight against foreign agents, a nice-old-lady C.I.A. officer sighs, "Good-bye, Mr. [Grant] wherever you are," and Leo G. Carroll, our head man, hatches the plot while photographed against the Capitol. The crucial contribution made by such cynicism can be quickly perceived by comparing *North by Northwest* to *Foreign Correspondent*, a film nearly identical in plot that is washed out by patriotic sentimentality.

Hitchcock's cynicism makes an advantage of his moral indifference by freeing him and his audience to admire pure aggression, including the aggression of film form. But his fear that nothing is what it seems (of which the skepticism about moral distinctions is only one consequence) sometimes approaches the status of serious belief, and then we see, most dramatically, the special underpinnings of his work.

Shadow of a Doubt (1943), often described by Hitchcock as his favorite film, culminates notions that can be traced back to *The Lodger* (1926). That silent movie is one of Hitchcock's many teasing thrillers (like *Stage Fright* and *Vertigo*) in which the audience is crudely misled about a character's guilt, in this case a man who is suspected of being Jack the Ripper. Surrounding the silly puzzle are scenes of real interest that establish the moral inferiority to the presumed criminal of more respectable members of his society. The opening sequence, which is astonishingly fluent for the period, emphasizes the public's prurient interest in crime, and the closing sequence, although a bit florid, makes the public seem reprehensible in its vengefulness (a characteristic emphasized, here as elsewhere, by the scapegoat's innocence).

Unlike the hero of *The Lodger*, Uncle Charlie, in *Shadow of a Doubt*, is guilty of crimes attributed to him; but he is given idealistic, if cracked, motives in Hitchcock's evident desire to create an approximate—and highly ironic—moral parity between Uncle Charlie and the innocent niece who is his alter ego. Although she had longed for him to relieve the dullness of her middle-class life, she instantly determines to banish him after discovering his crime. This discomforts us not only because her professed love should at least make her consider protecting him, but because her motives for wishing him gone are hardly edifying: she fears that his presence will compromise her father's job at the bank and will disillusion her doting mother. Throughout the film, Hitchcock pokes holes into the façade of respectability that he was initially careful to erect. When Uncle Charlie visits his brother-in-law at the bank, for example, and makes a joke about embezzlement, the brother-in-law cautions against such humor in such a place. Shortly after, when Charlie is introduced to a rich widow (his preferred class of victim), she reacts rather more libidinously than accords with her mourning. One of the family's best friends plots murders for his pastime, and the father enthusiastically joins in. Innocent small-town life involves a yearning for forbidden thrills, a point Charlie makes explicit in a cafe scene before the climax. When he is killed by his niece in self-defense, the thematic substructure of their relationship is perfectly externalized in action. In her attempt to preserve cherished insulation from a more mordant perspective on life, she turns lethal.

Shadow of a Doubt is erratically written (its collaborators running from Sally Benson to Thornton Wilder), but it almost succeeds in making a serious comment. Thus we get the first important example in Hitchcock of visual symbolism: in identical shots that introduce the protagonists in identical poses after setting has established the dramatic difference between their worlds. But Hitchcock ruins this subtle equation, not only through blatant details in the script (uncle and niece share first names and telepathic powers), but by his final submission to conventions of melodrama. Since these necessitate someone to root for, Hitchcock must ultimately dissolve the equation whose irony sustains the film. In totally amoral movies like *North by Northwest* rooting for the hero implies no disruptive judgment; in *Shadow of a Doubt* it is profoundly illogical.

Nevertheless, *Shadow of a Doubt* helps us measure the extent to which Hitchcock's art is based on his assumption that normality is merely a thin veneer covering a lust for thrills. Like the niece, we tolerate thrills just until they threaten permanently to taint our self-image, so Hitchcock obligingly neutralizes the threat with last-minute melodrama. But his concern for us is specious, only a reflection of his concern for the box office. ("... I have too much conscience," he once said, "to make a film that would please only me and the critics.") Only our money commands his respect and nothing so validates his contempt for the rest of us as our willingness to pay for manipulation. Hitchcock's sensitivity to audience tolerance alone restrains his contempt; when that tolerance loosens, he makes *Psycho* and *The Birds*.

In the best of his films, however, contempt for respectable pretension is reflected, more fully than in *Shadow of a Doubt*, in the plot as well as in Hitchcock's formal aggression. Thus *Strangers on a Train* (1951) almost succeeds in joining Hitchcock's mastery of emotional rhythm to the other qualities that we associate with narrative art.

Made in 1951 after four straight flops, from a novel Hitchcock discovered for himself, *Strangers on a Train* is a happy instance of an impulse suddenly finding its proper form. Throughout his work, Hitchcock had used, strictly for emotive purposes, the device of one character's being accused of another's crime. Patricia Highsmith's novel, while itself a pretentious, even brazen affair, has the virtue of making this device accord perfectly with Hitchcock's most fundamental attitude: that everyone is latently a killer. In this film, the victim of false accusation is, in a sense, morally guilty. What is only hinted at in the niece of Uncle Charlie is explicitly and carefully developed in Guy Haines.

In the film, as in the novel, Haines is a rather unformed young man who learns of his homicidal impulses by meeting Bruno Anthony accidentally on a train. Bruno, who hates his father, offers to murder Guy's wife (a woman of little virtue) so that Guy can remarry, if Guy will react in kind. Normal restraints make Guy refuse Bruno's offer, but we see that it has definite appeal. Seeing this too, Bruno follows the wife to an amusement park and strangles her. Then, when Guy balks at fulfilling his part of the "bargain," Bruno strikes back.

Hitchcock's interest in this plot is suggested by the few changes he makes in its initial details. First, he turns Guy from an aspiring architect into a famous athlete and thus from a genuine talent blocked by an unsuitable spouse into a tennis bum coveting a patrician Senator's daughter (transformed from the novel's interior decorator to clarify the shadiness of Haines's motives). Then he shifts the setting to Washington, from which he draws ironic contrasts between civilization and the baser impulses, as in the wonderful shot of a dark-suited Bruno standing before an august white pillar of the Jefferson Memorial.

Further evidence of the story's appeal are the visual analogies to which it inspired Hitchcock. Appropriately, the film begins by equating its protagonists, since the first shots are of taxis drawing up to a railroad station and depositing two sets of feet that don't possess bodies until they bump against each other in the dining car. Then, throughout the reverse shots of Bruno and Guy in conversation,

Bruno's face is barred with shadows cast by some venetian blinds while Guy's appears in white light. This contrast is exploited later in the film, after Bruno has murdered Guy's wife, when he is waiting across the street from his beneficiary's apartment. Bruno stands behind a metal gate, suggesting the expected consequence of crime, but he is composed and regularly photographed, whereas the agitated Guy soon appears in tilt. Heeding Bruno's call, Guy crosses, but, during the ensuing conversation about Bruno's father, Guy addresses him while standing clear of the gate. When some police unexpectedly arrive, Guy is forced to seek shelter, and we now see him at Bruno's side, slashed by the same shadows as his alter ego.

Similarly, respectable society is tainted by prurience and hypocrisy, like the Senator's guests who are charmed by Bruno's discussion of murder but fearful of the scandal caused by his excessive zeal. In the final chase scene, when the police expropriate a cab, its old lady occupant is delighted to be involved in a crime, and news of the murder has the effect of boosting the box office at the amusement park. On the other hand, Bruno, although a psychopathic murderer, is a figure of tremendous charm and even some semiserious moral ambiguity. Soon after entering the amusement park, he is accosted by a little boy who shoots a toy gun at him, to which he responds by bursting the child's balloon. But after the crime we see him guiding a blind man through traffic.

Before the end, however, Hitchcock has cut things down again to the dimensions of a thriller. In the novel, Guy actually kills Bruno's father, subsequently filling more than half the book with his anguish. In the film, Guy refuses to follow Bruno this far, preferring instead to incur the vengeful wrath that produces Hitchcock's most brilliant coda, in which Guy has to win a tennis match and reach the amusement park before Bruno has the chance to plant a clue that will convince the police of his guilt. No sequence in Hitchcock makes such brilliant use of the screen's fundamental method of producing suspense: parallel editing of simultaneous action. Moreover, the conclusion of the film, with Guy and Bruno struggling on a merry-go-round gone berserk, is both emotionally stunning and precisely suggestive of their entire relationship. For sheer invention, unfailing pertinence of every frame, and occasional suggestions of deeper purpose, *Strangers on a Train* is Hitchcock's masterpiece.

But, it will be said, the masterpiece of a low ambition. Such derogation is implied even in the applause of *Cahiers du Cinéma* critics and their numerous followers who have tried to elevate Hitchcock into the ranks of directors like Bergman, Antonioni and Truffaut. Although recent film criticism is typified by mindless emphasis on visual effects (thus Nicholas Ray can be thought an important director and *Lola Montes* an important film), most critics are made nervous by effects without theme or psychological insight. As a result, visual signs are read as if they were literary symbols, and directors like Hitchcock, whose meanings are his effects, become no less elusive for cinephiles than for traditionalists.

Yet no other director is so badly represented by translation into the assertions and propositions that criticism, being a tendentious, pattern-making activity, can scarcely avoid. A Hitchcock film can only be appreciated while it is seen, and is therefore perfect for the so-called "new sensibility." A critic like Susan Sontag, however, wouldn't be caught dead discussing Hitchcock because he is so relentlessly lowbrow and frivolous about meaning, whereas the new sensibility is only frivolous about craft.

As a craftsman, Hitchcock ranks with the best. He has taught essential lessons to directors with greater aspirations because he has realized one of the potentials of film form. From the first, cinema theoreticians recognized the unparalleled power of film, its ability to make the audience both a crowd and a collection of separate individuals (riveted to the screen in darkness that conceals the depth of their enslavement). Propaganda, it was thought, must inevitably result, and no one would be completely impervious to the appeal of screened messages. The history of film, however, has shown the form equally resistant to ideas and ideology. For the essence of cinema is action, gesture, surface: natural inciters not of reflection but of perception and feeling. What Hitchcock has supremely understood is that the line between perception and feeling can be manipulated by the director, can be sustained or broken, quickened or retarded so that the spectator feels only what the filmmaker intends. Moreover, he has understood that no other medium can simulate action with most of life's reality but none of its limitations. As a result, Hitchcock has produced a new experience, a new kind of art. It is low but powerful; it does not exploit the full range of his medium, but it takes to the limit one of the things that film can do more fully than any other art. In Robert Warshow's phrase, film is the "immediate experience." No director knows that better than Hitchcock.

(1970)

84

FEDERICO FELLINI:
JUXTAPOSITION

MOST OF the masters of the cinema make films in a certain way regardless of the material they adapt (Vigo, Truffaut, Bresson) or design material to suit a method of filmmaking (Antonioni). With Fellini, who began his career as a writer, the material he invents is determinant. He has few characteristic techniques of shooting or editing, no special use of the soundtrack; not even, as the similarly script-centered Bergman does, a singular way of directing and photographing actors. As we shall see when discussing his later films, spectacle, the most fully cinematic element in his work, is also the most demeaning to his art. One reaches less deeply into the latter by speaking of a "Fellini style" than of a "Fellini world or viewpoint."

Because the Fellini world is recognizably distinct—with its empty piazzas and deserted beaches, its grotesque faces hovering in the fetid air of parties gone flat—one reads much about his "symbolism," just as one reads about his "philosophy"[1] because, since Fellini is an *auteur* who writes as well as directs avowedly autobiographical films, distinctive interests shine through the apparent variety of subjects.[2] However, Fellini is no more a thinker about life, with an integrated philosophy and a special symbolic language, than, on the evidence of his style, is he a thinker about cinematic form. In the most impressive phase of his career (from *Variety Lights* [1950] through 8½ [1962]), he is, above all, an observer. Insofar as he has a style, it isn't narrowly technical but rather a general method of constructing films through juxtaposition; that is, through setting details of reconstructed reality side by side to point up a common denominator or, more often, to expose the ironic relationship between unlike things.

Both historically (owing to an association with Rossellini early in his career) and stylistically, Fellini's best films belong within the tradition of neo-realism, which he correctly defines as "the opposite of manufactured effects, of the laws of dramaturgy, spectacle, and even of cinematography. . . ."[3] Like his neo-realist forebears, Fellini tries to present the world naturally, without arranging things in order to create plots or entertainments.

What distinguishes him from his fellow neo-realists is an insistence on the primary force of human imagination. Fellini's characters aren't solely motivated by externals—the theft of a bicycle, social indifference, divorce—as De Sica's are. Nor, like Olmi, does he invert neorealism only in studying the human accommodation to such external circumstances. Rather, he denies the pure externality of events, choosing instead to show that reality and imagination interpenetrate. If not their inventor, Fellini is nonetheless master of cinematic devices that simultaneously portray the surface of life accurately and show that individuals see it through a haze.

This haze is romantic, the constant fall-out from explosions of hope. Fellini's characters never face a fact without dressing it up. If they are in an empty piazza during the small hours of night, they actively deny the implication that all human activities must pause. They are constantly going to parties, although the parties end in hangovers and a sharper sense of solitude. They are always on parade, decked out and boisterous, although, in effect, they are stepping in place on a treadmill. Continually awaiting an answer to their deepest needs, they are always disappointed; what we see of them ceases, but they never reach a destination.

Essential stasis is crucial to Fellini's world. Conventional dramaturgy exalts the will. Characters want something; they reach out for it; they get it or they don't. Sometimes they fail because of circumstances; sometimes, because of another character. Their fate is established in a conflict that peaks in a climax, after which there is a denouement. Such strategies, Fellini either rejects or transforms. Like other directors who wish to wean cinema from its addiction to popular fiction and melodrama, he tries to inject the bracing truth that life isn't very dramatic.

As we have seen, an anti-dramatic impulse can be felt even in directors who are literary. Hence Carol Reed may not give up plot but he tries to blur his endings, and Jean Renoir, who employs all the artifices of theater, strives to roughen their effect. Among the neorealists, episodic structure and open endings are fundamental strategies. Yet the scenarios of Zavattini don't avoid narrative causality and suspense, and although Olmi's characters seem to wander in and out of unconnected experiences, they eventually reach a turning point, so that in retrospect their wanderings appear to conform to a dramatic pattern. At his most characteristic, Fellini eliminates such remnants of conventional dramaturgy. Scenes are related in his films not by causality or in order to create a crisis but as illustrations of a state of being. At his best, Fellini shows us people in several versions of hopefulness that, because it is unchanging and unassuagable, can achieve only the resolution of the spectator's understanding.

Fellini's world is epitomized by the protagonist and structure of *Nights of Cabiria*, a film about a whore as sexual victim rather than profiteer because, night after night, she will not abandon the romantic readiness that makes her vulnerable. The point of the film is that Cabiria ends as she began, smiling despite her pain, out of an unshakable will to go on living.

This constancy, rather than any outer achievement or inner alteration, is Fellini's typical subject; and he wants us to find it both deplorable and marvelous. Not alone for defying dramaturgical artifice or for showing that perception shapes experience does Fellini deserve to be credited with having deepened cinematic realism; his films are especially realistic in precluding unequivocal judgment. Life, Fellini implies, is not dramatic but repetitious, not external but mediated by imagination, and neither to be admired nor despised.

Not wanting us to be partisan, Fellini must simultaneously put us outside his characters to show their errors and inside them so that we do not dismiss them as fools. This double exposure, a subjective view laid over the objective, is the Fellinian touch that first signals the presence of a personal and incisive refinement of realism.

Often cited as his masterpiece, *I vitelloni* (1953) clearly exemplifies Fellini's methods. A bit of regional slang, roughly translated as "the overgrown calves," the title designates five superannuated juveniles whose antics comprise a model of provincial stagnation. All the *vitelloni* recognize that they should leave Pesaro, but each prefers to gaze carelessly on its arid slopes, dreaming of green fields. They talk of girls and of honeymoons in Africa, but only one of them marries; and Fausto has to be beaten into fulfilling a role too lightly assumed. The others do not even come this close to maturity. Leopoldo dreams of becoming a playwright and pointlessly flirts with the next-door maid. Alberto upbraids his sister for trysting with a married man and thus worrying their mother. Yet he lives off the object of his sermons. Riccardo wants to be a singer, but not even fervently enough to earn him a large place in the film. Moraldo simply watches his friends.

What do the friends do? Little that is either impressive in itself or rendered so by dramatic arrangement. Most of the scenes concern Fausto's shotgun wedding to Sandra, the job he takes reluctantly and then flirts away, his wife's defection and their subsequent reunion. This slight plot, ending without Fausto's reform, is constantly interrupted for vignettes about the other characters, so that suspense is never allowed to build. We watch the *vitelloni* razzing a whore whom they accidentally meet in a piazza, playing pool and making feeble jokes about the waiter, going to a carnival or to the theater, and, when nothing else offers, gazing out on a wintry sea while wondering how much it would cost to get any of them to take a swim.

Such details, the random construction, authentic locales and natural performances—shot by an unobtrusive camera—make *I vitelloni* a convincing paradigm of life in a small town. Despite its brevity, the film has room for a host of minor characters, some of whom appear for less than a minute but manage to give the sense of an entire world. Parents, employees, friends flit through each other's lives and engage in activities no less important than what we see, as if to imply that Fellini could follow these too if he would.

Instead he concentrates on the *vitelloni* as viewed retrospectively by an unidentified former member of the group. This voice-over, in addition to offering the standard expedients of commentary (temporal elision, background information, etc.), helps to shape our response into the Fellinian "double perspective." Like the film's other non-natural device—Nino Rota's score—the commentary tells us to feel differently from the characters, teases us into seeing them more tenderly than they see themselves, protects them from the derision earned by their behavior.

Thus, when Sandra faints after being crowned Miss Siren at the film's opening kursaal scene, Fellini shoots the crowd of well-wishers from her angle, making us feel that she is being undone by the crowd and the excitement. However, a later glance from her brother (Moraldo) to Fausto, as he expresses bewilderment and the dawn of chagrin, establishes the true cause of her collapse. We are ready to laugh at this discovery, but the music, with its haunting strings, keeps us from mocking. Only after the following scene, when, bludgeoned by his father into doing the "right thing," Fausto collides with the *vitelloni*, who are howling at his predicament, can our laughter find release. Next Fellini augments our amusement and, by default, our sympathy for the trapped bull by dissolving from the laughing calves into a gaggle of tearful biddies, hypocritically concealing their delight about the inflicted respectability. Behind the priest officiating at the rites of the middle class, Fellini then stations a choirboy unaffectedly picking his nose.

The double perspective on Fausto, balancing sympathy and disdain, is reflected in Moraldo, who begins by romanticizing his friend and ends by repudiating him. Only in Moraldo's growing alienation from Fausto does *I vitelloni* have a progressive action; typical of Fellini, this action is perceptual disenchantment. At first, Moraldo is Fausto's admirer. He can't bring himself to condemn his unemployed friend for fearing marriage; when the match takes place, all he can see are Fausto's charm and Sandra's happiness. Moraldo doesn't witness Fausto's subsequent antics: his loitering on the job, his attempt to pick up another woman while at the movies with Sandra, his flirtation with the boss's wife, but had he done so, he might have concluded, as we do, that Fausto is a harmless boy. Who else would invite his wife to applaud the feat of lowering shutters on the shop when he works, or celebrate his sexuality by shadow-boxing after getting a kiss from the lady and doing deep-knee bends after making a pass at Giulia? Only when this last action causes him to be fired is Fausto's immaturity revealed as something worse. Convinced of his own alibi (that he was fired for resisting Giulia's advances) and childishly vindictive about this childish invention, Fausto proposes that Moraldo help him to recapture lost wages by stealing some of Michele's merchandise. Although reluctant, Moraldo agrees.

Now Fellini makes the audience and Moraldo join in seeing Fausto objectively. During the early stages of the attempt to sell the angel, sprightly music and the liveliness of Franco Fabrizi (Fausto) contrive to make it seem a lark. But as the sequence lengthens, the music turns heavy, and Fellini slows down the rhythm so that Fausto becomes tiresome. Then, after the prank has failed and Fausto has left the booty with his second accomplice (the village idiot, Giudizio), we are made to realize that the angel isn't only salable gilt. Placing it on a mound outside his hovel, Giudizio expresses worship, while the graceful tracking of Fellini's camera and Rota's music work to make the statue seem as beautiful to us as to the idiot and thus a severe indictment of Fausto's venality and lack of imagination.

Fausto later delivers the death-blow to Moraldo's esteem by trysting with a chorus girl while his friend awaits him in the street and, on his return, by boasting that the girl asked him to join her act. His new contempt for provincial *machismo* helps Moraldo accomplish the *vitelloni* dream of departure. Yet he cannot tell the young railroad boy who sees him off that he wasn't happy in his hometown and he has no idea of his destination.

His departure is neither happy nor sad because what he leaves is ambiguous. Fellini makes this ambiguity clear in the single departure from natural cinematography that substitutes a climactic image for a dramatic conclusion. As Moraldo's train pulls out and he looks back at what he is leaving, Fellini cuts to a series of shots—all shaking as if seen from the train whose movements are heard on the soundtrack—of the *vitelloni* asleep. Visualizing what is in Moraldo's mind, these shots suggest both the stagnancy of the others' lives and their enviable comfort to someone departing for the unknown. Incorrigibly somnolent, the *vitelloni* are also stable in their sleep.

Sleep is their life; they wake to dream. The film's rhythm, like that of all Fellini's major films, is an oscillation between humdrum reality and clamorous delusions. Appropriately, *Vitelloni* begins with a celebration, but the first shot is of a waiter expecting rain. Immediately after the narrator has introduced the protagonists, rain does fall, dousing their festivities. Alberto drinks a last glass while the wind blows and is indefatigably clowning during the downpour. Meanwhile, Leopoldo ducks under an awning not so much in search of shelter as hoping to be introduced to the starlet lured here by a lust for notice so like his own. Succeeding scenes repeat this view of people avidly pursuing respite from a place where, as Leopoldo says, "winter never passes" and "everything's all over by midnight."⁴ Particularly important are those scenes that show Leopoldo falling for the spell of the theater and Alberto following a party to its inevitable hangover because each is the model for all the other scenes in Fellini that place a character in an environment altered by his mode of perception.

When Leopoldo arranges a meeting with an actor he idolizes, by cutting between the bug-eyed fan and the tawdry vaudeville, Fellini shows what Leopoldo isn't noticing. Natali first appears in a neutral long shot, but when the camera cuts closer we see that he is a made-up has-been, engaged in a farago of nationalist sentimentality, poesy and burlesque. Backstage, Natali has a torn curtain covering a nook to serve as dressing-room; offers notoriously strong Italian cigarettes, while pretending that he smokes these cheapies because he must protect his throat; and confesses that his film career wound up on the floor of the cutting-room—but Leopoldo misses all such clues. He is equally unperturbed when the actor accompanies him to a restaurant so that eating can accompany the reading of Leopoldo's play. Nor does he blanch when Natali mistakenly appropriates a speech belonging to the heroine or when he invites Leopoldo out into a night so turbulent that they can scarcely hear each other's voices. Only when bidden into the shadows by the eerily lighted face of a grimacing queen does Leopoldo realize what we have suspected and take flight. Natali's demonic laughter follows him, drowning out our impulse to laugh at Leopoldo's folly. The fool drunk on excitement was laughable; the wind-buffeted victim of humiliation is not.

Alberto's disillusionment comes after a more literal inebriation than Leopoldo's. Throwing himself into the frenzy of the carnival, which, suggestively, he goes to in drag, Alberto is doomed to suffer the worst of mornings after. The music speeds up. A floor-mounted camera turns the dancers into a sea of twitching feet. Then a tilt shot from Alberto's perspective shows the ceiling as a whirling mass of streamers and confetti, until, as everything goes into double-time, there is a dissolve. We are now on a nearly empty dance floor, where a trumpeter plays flat and Alberto dances to the bitter end with the detached *papier-mâché* head of a carnival float.

In the bleak morning light, Alberto comes out to a piazza empty of all save a few early risers and the ball's debris. The wind, which blows so chill a reminder of reality during Leopoldo's walk with the actor, blows here as well. When Alberto arrives at home, he is just in time to say goodbye to his sister. Coming after the hilarity of the ball, piling up in a dizzy whirl very like what we were made to feel at the end of the previous scene, these events cause sympathy for Alberto. But the man himself is too drunk even to comprehend the grief that begins to break through his revelry. When he runs up to comfort his mother, and, out of commiseration, promises to find a job, drunkenness takes over. To her excited "have you found something?" he can only curl up in a chair and fall asleep.

Although Leopoldo and Alberto are not so prominent as Fausto in *I vitelloni*, they come to us through methods more typical of Fellini. Unlike Fausto, on whom Moraldo provides a judgmental perspective, Alberto and Leopoldo must be understood only through the details of their behavior. This explains the otherwise gratuitous scene, interrupting the search for Sandra, in which the *vitelloni* razz a road crew and are then beaten up by the irate laborers when their car breaks down. Besides keeping us from getting too worried about Sandra's defection, this scene underlines the insult to honest work implicit in the *vitelloni* hijinks.

Such a detail communicates directly and wordlessly whereas the voice-over and Moraldo are devices of a novelistic sort. Fellini's other great early film, *The White Sheik* (1952), is more wholly cinematic than *I vitelloni*. In details of background as well as through the major action, it also presents Fellini's most wide-ranging treatment of delusion.

This film concerns what ought to be a classic instance of people oriented toward reality: a provincial couple come to Rome for a honeymoon. Instead, Wanda Cavalli is obsessed with meeting her hero, the white sheik of the fumetti (live-action comic strips), and Ivan wants to live out his dream of public honor under the auspices of an influential uncle who can arrange an audience with the pope. As soon as they arrive, Wanda runs off to find her sheik, leaving Ivan to save face by stratagems while he tries to bring her back in time for their great appointment.

At bottom, *The White Sheik* uses the chase film formula. With each minute bringing him closer to loss of the papal audience and humiliation before his relatives, Ivan is very much in the position of Holly Martins searching for Harry Lime, or of Prospero and Michel racing each other to find the lottery ticket, of a Hitchcock hero beleaguered by crooks and cops, and of Ricci looking for his bicycle. This common denominator highlights the uniqueness of Fellini's interests. Unlike the other directors, Fellini doesn't develop a suspenseful plot, much less identify us with a questing hero. There are two chases in his film; both commence before we can take sides; and Fellini intercuts them only so as to point up their similarity. He does not indulge in thrills nor is he using the chase thematically. Rather, in the manner of De Sica, he wants us to focus on the society in which the chase occurs. Unlike De Sica, however, he doesn't show society as the antagonist; its relation to the Cavallis is synecdochical. Wanda and Ivan epitomize a world.

Artfully, this is never stated; it is to be inferred from countless details of characterization and event, of setting and music, even from small movements of the camera. This last technique actually gives us the film's theme.

When the couple finally arrives at St. Peter's, the uncle commands them to a trot in which they parade to the Vatican. Fellini then cuts to a close-up of the couple protesting their mutual fidelity. But since we know that Ivan had, in his grief at being abandoned, formerly assuaged himself with a whore, we wonder about Wanda's innocence. Nothing happened between her and the sheik. Of what might she be accused? Brunella Bovo's moon-struck stare in a direction opposite to her husband as she recites the line, "you're my White Sheik,"[5] answers our question. Faithful in fact, Wanda is incorrigibly faithless in imagination, implacable in not seeing things as they really are. Ivan notices this and registers his concern in a subsequent close-up. Fellini now cuts back to a long downward shot of the group, redoubling its efforts to reach St. Peter's, and from this tilts up to a nearby statue of the pope, dressed in a costume that unmistakably resembles that of the white sheik. Ivan is no less wedded to his spectacular icon than Wanda is. Married in the flesh, they remain separated by their dreams.

But this summary makes the film sound solemn, whereas *The White Sheik* is funny. The final parade is only the last example of a world comically in pursuit of constant spectacle. Descending the train that brings them to Rome, Wanda is nearly run down by a troupe of boy scouts, just as, later, while searching for her, Ivan runs athwart a parade of plumed, trumpet-blowing *bersagliere*. Although he is frantic with worry about his wife and indignant at having had his hat knocked off, Ivan is too Italian not to join his compatriots in applause, even after the parade has passed. Still later, when his failure to find Wanda has propelled him to the police station but his fear of losing face prevents a full confession, Ivan seems so crazy to the inspector that an ambulance is called; but he is able to escape because, for no purpose that we can see, the police are conducting maneuvers in the courtyard and he slips out by temporarily entering their ranks.

Here Fellini adds a detail that exemplifies the rich social expressiveness of everything in the film. As Ivan is running through the police station in search of the courtyard, his path crosses that of a functionary whose arms are loaded with paper. The man asks Ivan's help in unloading them, and when Ivan obliges, great clouds of dust emerge as the documents hit the floor of a corridor paved with an endless monument to Italian bureaucracy. The image is momentary, but it makes an important point about love of display in a country where nothing is too trivial for a writ.

Everywhere in this crowded canvas, Fellini sketches the social background. Some strokes are details of behavior, like Ivan absent-mindedly smelling and tapping a drawer in his hotel dresser, demonstrating by this gesture both his finickiness and a life-long acquaintance only with hotels that are provincial or tacky. Others are more inferred from a pattern of acts. Chief among these is the Don Juanism of the Italian male, regardless of class, profession or looks—the lady's and his own. When Wanda visits the *fumetti* office, the male assistant to the female editor primps as he ogles the visitor, although Wanda doesn't respond, and then turns his attentions, though she scarcely deserves them, to his ugly boss; the fat desk clerk flirts with a beautiful guest; even the bald old man who gives Wanda a lift back from her adventure with the sheik expects that she will repay him carnally. When she doesn't, he explodes in rage. The white sheik embodies a communal fantasy; he is no special case.

One of the film's wittiest transitions points this up. Fellini cuts from Wanda and the sheik in a boat to Ivan and his family applauding from their opera box. Juxtaposition makes it seem that the group is watching the couple, who were indeed performing. And since the family is attending "Don Giovanni," into which Fellini cuts when the libretto is most like the preceding dialogue, we infer that in Italy, at least, all the world's a stage.

The boat scene is hilarious because Alberto Sordi speaks so convincingly about having lost his lover through a magic potion administered by his wife and because Brunella Bovo responds to this nonsense in the idiom of pulp fiction as if her heart were breaking. But reality is always ready to break in: the sheik is first attacked by the unforeseen swinging of the mast and then by his opulently maternal wife, who reveals the child within the caftan. Now clad in a cheap modern suit, the sheik ultimately rides off on a motorcycle driven by his wife, while he clutches her from behind and attempts to cajole a little kiss. Ivan is equally plaintive when he is led off to consolation by the whore in the piazza.

That scene, like the *vitelloni* and the workers, is introduced as a seemingly anecdotal digression.[6] When the two whores enter the piazza, they appear to have wandered into the film from nowhere, yet they duplicate characteristics already familiar to us. As she turns the corner, the smaller whore is talking about a romantic movie she has just seen, and when she encounters Ivan she responds as if he too were enacting a drama. Soon the other whore takes him away, but the small one barely notices because the new appearance of a fire-thrower excites her everpresent desire for spectacle. Watching the fire-thrower in the empty piazza, the little whore becomes the representative of all the other characters in the film. Significantly, she is Cabiria, who will later get a film to herself and become Fellini's definitive representation of all life's irrepressible dreamers.

While we watch Cabiria exulting in the flames, the beauty of Fellini's pictorial composition and the eerie background music draw us into her wonderment. We are similarly seduced by Wanda's infatuation with the *fumetti*. When Wanda finds herself in the courtyard at the precise moment that the actors are coming down a staircase, Fellini makes us see their descent through her eyes. All in glittering costumes, the troupe appears to the strains of Nino Rota's loveliest march tune; just when the female star (Felga) reaches the center of the frame, a joke is whispered in her ear so that she can laugh delightfully, arching her back in natural grace as the march reaches a crescendo. The effect is magical. Pointedly, Fellini then dissipates the magic. Looking at her with mean suspicion, the actors pass on either side of Wanda, and are then hauled off in army trucks, presided over by an obese workman eating an oversized sandwich and followed by a mob of yowling kids that irritates the star "bedouin" into a vulgar lip-fart. A cut back to Wanda shows that she hasn't become disenchanted.

Nor is she disenchanted by her first view of the white sheik, on whom she stumbles while trying to return from the beach where the *fumetti* troupe had taken her. Surrounded by lush vegetation, the sound of crickets, and bird calls—with romantic music on the track—Wanda is suddenly arrested by a whistling whose source can't be seen. Then Fellini cuts back to show above her head the sheik swinging from stately palm trees at an impossible, fabulous height. As John Simon has said, this image "manages to be at once glamorously exalted and thoroughly ridiculous."[7] The former, because of the miraculous height, the graceful swinging, Sordi's look of utter imperiousness; ridiculous, because of the excessive costume, the spread legs and crotch that every forward swing inflicts up on the lens.

However, other characters beside Wanda regard Fernando Rivoli as delightful. When Fernando takes her to a local cafe, toasts her in soda pop and performs a marvelously outrageous tango to music from the radio of a passing car, Fellini inserts cuts not only of Wanda's worship but of onlooking women, the waiter, a policeman, and even of the car-owner, who applies suntan lotion in time to the music while he gazes lovingly at the dancers (thereby suggesting the narcissism that underlies romantic folly).

Equally susceptible—and this is the film's best joke—are the dream merchants themselves, who take their still photographs on a real beach, employ a troop of drummers to supply suitable background music, and treat their director as if he were shooting a movie. Throughout *The White Sheik*, as when one of the "bedouins" hurls a rush as if it were a spear, or "Felga" on her lunch break is turned by the drums into a dancing houri, Fellini shows that the actors have fallen for their own make-believe. To dramatize its ubiquitous appeal, he shows two hard-bitten fishermen dazedly watching the performance and has the car-owner from the cafe scene get so carried away by the oriental fantasy that he wanders into the shooting area and ruins the stills.

What hinders the *fumetti* director is what makes *The White Sheik*.

Fellini communicates his incisive joke about Italian society by setting examples side by side so that the spectator can add them up. Relying on accretion of detail rather than on analysis or statement, he shows that he understands the difference between film and fiction or theater. Fellini enriches his representation by juxtaposing not only items of reality but reality's items and man's subjective response. Subjectivity is the medium through which objective facts come to us. Because of the speed with which it can make transitions and because of the copiousness with which it can impart information (visual, auditory, linguistic, musical, etc.), cinema is particularly able to represent the combination of mind and matter. Fellini's films comprise a veritable textbook demonstration of this fact. By juxtaposing parts of the real world and by superimposing subjectivity on the result, Fellini proves that presenting the world's surface can also go beneath it. Without upsetting the illusion of reality, Fellini is able to reflect those mental transactions without which we would not even know the world.

Such procedures create the masterly portrait of provincialiam in *I vitelloni* and of the Italian character in *The White Sheik*, but they aren't confined to these masterpieces. Fellini's other films employ the same means. For clarity's sake, we can designate two major strategies: the "Leopoldo method," in which neutral and biased views of the same subject are juxtaposed, as in Leopoldo's meeting with Natali, and the "Alberto method," in which an accelerating rhythm of hopefulness peaks in despair. Since I am concerned not only with individual artists and films but with techniques that exemplify the art of filmmaking, we can perhaps scan Fellini's other early works in order to concentrate on examples from each that establish his way of using cinematic resources.

The first scene of *Variety Lights* illustrates the "Leopoldo method," as does virtually every representation of theater in Fellini up through *Roma* (1972). As always, Fellini creates a negative reaction in his audience to what an audience in the film is enthralled by.

After an establishing shot of the theater, Fellini cuts inside to the back of the auditorium and from this to a close-up of some chorines finishing their act and making way for Checco. While the latter sings his number, Fellini moves about the hall, breaking the audience down into types of response. Although a few young blades feign uninvolvement, most of the poorly-dressed, obviously unsophisticated viewers are rapt. Some can't even smile; others hold up clapping children; one shot from the back of the hall shows a little girl in the aisle aping

Checco's movements. For a long time we see the glowing Liliana only as a member of the crowd, which makes her its effective representative when she later assumes dramatic prominence.

To create a different response in us, Fellini now strips back the veils of showmanship. An off-angle shot turns the chorines into dumpy grotesques. Then the camera peers down into a hitherto unseen part of the orchestra pit where a stringy 60-year-old drummer, seedy looking and with a cigarette dangling from his mouth, rises before every downbeat, on which he hits his chair with a thud. At the curtain call, a series of intense close-ups, lighted from below, makes death masks of the performers' faces.

Without dialogue or narration, Fellini shows that the theater is glamorous only from far away. And though he has chosen an inept company to make this point, he extends it, at the end of the film, by treating a Ziegfeldian review. This sequence shatters the illusion in advance. Backstage, an ancient blonde, bedecked in features, scowling and picking her teeth, assumes a classic glamor pose only to find herself squirted under the arms by a stagehand wielding a gigantic atomizer. "Beast," she hisses, as the elevator ascends. Then the curtains part, Fellini cuts to a front long shot, and—lo!—the hag becomes a goddess.

More inventive and suggestive is the equally funny encounter between Cabiria and the movie star in Fellini's later film. Here the acting makes more of a contribution than in *Variety Lights* because Cabiria herself, though invincibly a Leopoldo, tries to pretend the contrary.

When the actor and his girl friend come out of a nightclub, a fast track-in to Cabiria informs us that she has recognized an idol, and throughout the ensuing argument she behaves like the viewer of a film. When the star orders her into his automobile, she pretends not to know what he wants, but soon she agrees to being treated as befits her profession. However, she tries to maintain a certain dignity, as we see from her hilarious attempt to sit upright while the car careens through Rome.

When Nazzari takes *her* to a nightclub, we are made to see the gap between her joy and the contemptuous treatment she is accorded. Upon their arrival, Nazzari bounds out of the car, leaving Cabiria to negotiate the embarrassment of an unescorted entrance. Inside, the headwaiter orders her to deposit her umbrella, but the hatcheck girl won't even deign to look up. Cabiria slams the umbrella down on the girl's newspaper, but this small triumph in self-assertion is followed by her daunting inability to part the thick velvet drapes between the vestibule and the dance floor.

Cuts about the club show it as tawdry and boring. In one, we see an octogenarian lady dancing with a handsome young man; in another, waiters loiter, urging the dancers on with professionally offhand enthusiasm. Intercut with these are shots of Giulietta Masina (as Cabiria), her face frozen into a worldly scowl but with eyebrows held rigid above swooning pupils. Despite her attempt to appear blasé, Cabiria can't keep herself from applauding when the m.c. announces Nazzari's presence; and when the actor asks her to dance, she breaks into a delirious solo, to his obvious bemusement.

The vulgar decor of the house to which the actor takes her highlights the error of Cabiria's appreciation. Then, to suggest her coming fate, Fellini mounts a camera at the bottom of a long staircase so that Masina's figure is reduced and the climb exaggerated. We arrive at the actor's bedroom before she does so that we can see its sham splendor (including mirrored closets that open to music) and thus laugh at Cabiria for loving what we found absurd. A close-up of Nazzari affectedly listening to Beethoven finishes him off for the audience, but Cabiria doesn't seem to note that he is a poseur.

For a few moments, Nazzari begins to warm up to her, but soon his girl friend reappears. Suggestively, Cabiria has to finish the episode hiding in his bathroom, forced to peer through a keyhole at the beautiful lovers—reduced once more to the voyeuristic status of a moviegoer. Hours later, the actor ushers her out, while a camera tracking from her perspective makes a longingly lyrical sweep of the mistress sleeping off love. Cabiria collides with a glass door and is finally seen hobbling down a road, flanked by pretentious plaster statues, while trying to shake a stone from her shoe.

Cabiria also includes an example of the "Alberto method," which occurs, as is common in Fellini, at a religious festival. After a fast series of cuts that show the event's carnival atmosphere—with balloon sellers, busloads of tourists, and Cabiria's friends having their pictures taken—Fellini places his camera within the crowd of pilgrims stampeding the church. Their fervor is conveyed as well by accelerating music and by subjective tracking shots of crutches and other cast-off disabilities hanging from the rafters. Cabiria's increasing involvement appears through intercutting between her and the crowd. Eventually she kneels at the altar and kisses the madonna, her soul ready to receive grace. Bringing this to a pitch of intensity, Fellini then cuts to a sick pimp as he is urged to drop his crutches and move forward for the miraculous cure. The pimp does so, instantly falls, and the scene ends with a cut to his head lying on the pavement. From this, we dissolve swiftly to a group of cyclists zooming past Cabiria's picnicking friends, who show blithe detachment from the previous upswelling of hope.

With equal frequency, Fellini's characters are caught up and then dashed to earth during secular festivities. Again, *Variety Lights* offers the model for later variations. The relevant sequence starts when a rich theater-goer invites the vaudeville company to his house so as to get his hands on Liliana. Late and bleakly cold when they emerge from the theater, they are forced to make a long walk toward their destination because Anselmo didn't order a carriage. Fellini stages this parade at a slow tempo with long-held shots, frequently at diminishing down-angles, and few cuts.

A dissolve through the flames of Anselmo's fireplace radically alters the mood, and the tempo is accelerated by a montage of the group happily preparing supper. The next shot, one of the funniest in Fellini's career, consists of a circular track around the table during which each of the troupe is shown eating in characteristic fashion, while all we hear on the track is the amplified sound of chewing.

On a swell of laughter inspired by this shot, Fellini floats us to the next scene—a nearly frenzied weaving of the camera through the characters' excited dancing. Both for us and them, pleasure is mounting, until Liliana and Anselmo pass before Checco in a close shot that shows them as posteriors twitching in front of his glowering face. Immediately, he announces that they must all leave, but Anselmo offers them lodgings. We then get a montage of sleepers, and after that the final confrontation between Checco and Anselmo when the latter sneaks into Liliana's room. The sequence concludes with a parade back to the theater in the same bleak coldness of the opening.

Scenes like the above create rhythms that made the audience feel the anticipation-disappointment cycle as viscerally as if it were a musical motif. Neither fiction, with the inescapable abstractness of printed language, nor theater, with its cumbersome machinery and fixed perspectives, could achieve the same effect so vividly, if at all. Fellini's speedy and evocative juxtapositions remind us that life is not only events but responses. Yet, on the evidence of his weaker films, such responses can't be too complex. His great subject is the reaction to surfaces. Any deeper probing of character is beyond him. Thus, when he attempts to depict internal change, he falls back on literature and theater (i.e., language and dramaturgy), betraying both cinema and credibility.

The model for this problem is *La Strada* (1954), a film largely devoted to the subject of spiritual conversion. Zampano, who is too bestial to requite Gelsomina, must lose her in order to understand that she was worth loving. But Fellini is unable to dramatize Zampano's emotional change. Indeed, the film does not even focus on him but rather on Gelsomina, who should be catalyst rather than protagonist. The result is a misplaced dramatic center that produces redundancy to no good end.

As we have seen, since his subject is human incorrigibility, repetition is crucial to Fellini's films. However, in *La Strada*, repeated demonstrations of Gelsomina's goodness say nothing about mankind but merely solicit our admiration for this wholly fabulous creature. Half-fool, half-saint, Gelsomina is the only one of his protagonists whom Fellini asks us to adore; but, in so doing, he forfeits a typically ambivalent, hence creditable, portraiture. Not accidentally, Gelsomina doesn't hold together; daft in certain scenes, she becomes normally intelligent in others. For the latter, she even achieves rhetoric, most deplorably in the famous scene with that other figure of dubious mental status—"the fool"—who gets her to remain loyal to Zampano by arguing from the example of a pebble that everything has its function in God's universe and that hers is to love a brutal master.

Without such a speech, which is both rhetorical and corny, we wouldn't know what the film meant, in contrast to Fellini's other films that mean what their data add up to. Equally unusual and imposed is the creaking plot. By coincidence, "the fool's" car breaks down on the highway, thereby exposing him to the rage of Zampano, so that the latter may kill him, thereby provoking the guilt-ridden descent of Gelsomina into madness that causes Zampano to abandon her. Equally by coincidence, years later, Zampano happens to hear a woman singing the tune associated with Gelsomina so that he can learn in conversation what happened to the waif, thereby provoking the delayed grief that leads to his epiphany. That the latter occurs after so long a hiatus is plausible because a man like Zampano would take years to become acquainted with regret; but it relegates the subject of the film, since we don't see the process of his change.

Fellini shows slightly more of the interior action in *The Swindle* (1955), but, as in *La Strada*, he must employ dramatic contrivance.

As in the preceding film, the early, more documentary scenes are superb (scenes of the con-men at work and of the dreams that work on them). Then, without prior warning, Fellini introduces the hero's cast-off daughter to prepare for Augusto's final revulsion against his crimes. In the last scene a similar figure keeps him from repeating the buried-treasure ploy with which the film began. Susceptible because of his violated paternity and impressed by the girl's sweet-tempered acceptance of paralysis, Augusto seems deeply ashamed. Later, we learn that he only thought of rejecting his ill-gotten gains, so his cohorts beat him for what they regard as a trick to keep them from their shares. This introduces a note of plausible ambiguity (is Augusto shamming or did his past fatally delay the birth of a moral sense?), but since the final moments show the girl's determinant effect upon him, the sentimental contrivance is only mitigated, not erased.

La Strada and *The Swindle* prove that Fellini can't plot.[8] As is once again demonstrated in *Juliet of the Spirits* (1965), whenever he chooses to chart a process of development, he falters. Either he omits the subject, as in *La Strada*, or, in the cases of *The Swindle* and *Juliet*, it comes too late and coincidentally to seem the effect of character rather than authorial manipulation. Juliet could just as easily have had a liberating vision during the film; the lateness of her epiphany, even more than Augusto's, comes simply from the need to sustain a certain length of film.

Juliet attempts to show how the repressed wife of a philanderer frees herself from equally tempting opportunities to be vengeful or libertine and instead deals honestly with her predicament. In place of insight into her liberation or her prior bondage however, Fellini chooses surrealist phantasmagoria to make neurosis photogenic and pop-Freudianism to make analysis pat. Offspring of a beautiful mother and a moralistic father, Juliet grew up feeling it neither possible nor proper to be sexy. After consulting a series of gurus and being haunted by ghosts, she outbraves her mother in a last fantasy and then goes off to face life. Fannie Hurst meets Jean Cocteau.

Banal in conception, *Juliet* is vulgar in execution. Already in *Nights of Cabiria*, there had been disturbing signs that Fellini, the satirist of fake theatricalism, was himself attracted by the genre's least creditable form. After the phony Festival comes the hypnotist, who, though he harms Cabiria, is authentic in his power. In *8½* Fellini asked us to believe in a mind reader and even associated the art of his alter ego with such trickery. Now Fellini asks us to accept spooks.

As drama, *Juliet* has no more substance than a specter. After some two hours of playing-time, Juliet frees herself, during a vision, from puritanical masochism. But people have been urging her to just this action throughout the film. One might argue that they represented hedonism in too sinister or uncontrolled a form, yet this argument is circular since their excesses were gratuitously invented by Fellini. "Gratuitously" unless Bhisma, Don José, Susy, the psychiatrist *et al.* are meant to represent real snares set for the troubled soul by the world's self-styled healers; and in our interview, when confronted by the charge that these figures are instead expressions of purposeless sensationalism, Fellini fell back on the defense of verisimilitude.[9] Yet the gurus aren't even minimally credible; when one seems so,— like Bhisma, whose grotesqueries are a mystic's act—he is accidentally appropriate to the film's style. Otherwise, we have the private detective, whose activities are as bizarrely staged as the kinky Susy's, or Juliet's mundane relatives, who seem to have been outfitted at a freak-show. This film has no place for reality; even Juliet's trees are swathed in gauze. Yet Fellini's stagey effects, garish colors, and factitious bustle appear in the service of a plot arguing against excess and for moderation.

In Fellini's good films a character takes as true and beautiful what the camera reveals as fake and tawdry. Now we find Fellini playing the dupe. Juliet walks out on the tableaux; Fellini lingers over them. Not her character but his showmanship concocts a world that is part circus, part *Playboy* eroticism:[10] the very gaudiness he once made art out of satirizing. Most terribly, Fellini becomes boring (since even marvels pall without development), whereas formerly his characters were bored, thereby giving him his chance to move and enlighten us.

In *8½* Fellini made fun of critics who condemned him as an artist with nothing left to say. However, each of his subsequent films supports his critics. *Juliet* is an avowed imitation (albeit travestied) of *8½*; *Satyricon*, a literary adaptation by one who had always invented his own material; *The Clowns*, a documentary exploiting the appeal of the circus; and *Roma*, a piece of arrant self-cannibalizing. One scene in *Roma* shows that Fellini is now given to inferior imitation of familiar effects. Despite having earlier created many incisive criticisms of the church, Fellini now expresses anti-clericalism through an ecclesiastical fashion show that simply attributes to the church implausible vulgarities. Long after whatever might have worked in this sequence as critical hyperbole, Fellini is still training his camera on

Danilo Donati's eye-catching costumes. By coming to laugh and stay-ing to goggle, he contradicts his premise.

Contradiction replaces ambivalence in Fellini's disastrous second decade. *Satyricon*, the last of his fiction films, is contradictory to the point of chaos. Talking to Alberto Moravia, Fellini said that the work was designed to have the "enigmatic transparency, the indecipherable clarity of dreams."[11] Instead, Fellini produced almost the opposite: a film whose general meaning is clear while individual details (some-times literally) are fogbound. Through much of *Satyricon*, we are looking through mists or, as in the early walk through a red-light dis-trict, are tracking so swiftly through so crowded a background that we can hardly see. Elsewhere, we can see but not comprehend. Even more than in *Juliet*, Fellini is turning people into mute images; not— as he used to—examining the love of spectacle but rather indulging it.

And to what end? Half his published remarks about *Satyricon* indi-cate a realistic intention, as when he attributes a surfeit of deformed characters to the likely absence of medicine in ancient Rome;[12] half the time, he is comparing the film to "science fiction."[13] Now his choices are true to Petronius (according to his co-scenarist that is why he dubbed the actors in a "jumble of dialects"[14]); now he is denying any allegiance to his original.[15] He proclaims his abandonment of narrative at the same time that, like all feature film directors, he de-pends on narrative expectations to hold our attention. When all else fails, he consigns himself opportunistically to the "very young people. ... They understand."[16]

Understanding is less of a problem, however, than Fellini contends. His theme is as blatant as its presentation is wayward. Petronius's Rome was sick: a world between two dispensations, afflicted by po-litical upheaval, sexual perversion and religiosity. Hence we get wars and assassinations, nymphomania, impotence and homosexuality, bizarre cults and, ultimately, cannibalism. Although many of these items come from Petronius, Fellini betrays the satirist's urbanity and, by so doing, also the complex objectivity of his earlier films. Instead, we get an ugly battening on ugliness, the exploitation of what only insight could redeem. This Fellini specifically foreswears, and his film—coldly voyeuristic and monotonously sensational—amply bears out his contention that we can never penetrate an alien way of life.

Only *auteurist* critics, who confuse signature with quality, could miss the self-betrayal that accompanies the self-reference in *Satyricon*. After we peel back the surface of Donati's physical production and discount the travestied borrowings from various ancient texts, all of Fellini that remains is the celebrated eye for odd or striking faces. In *Variety Lights* two minor characters (an impresario and his assistant) are played by an actor who looks like a rodent and one who resembles a bloodhound; in *The White Sheik*, when Ivan searches for Wanda at the asylum, Fellini wheels in front of him a cigar-smoking catatonic in a crib: these are piquant touches to extend laughter created by more meaningful material. In Fellini's latest films, such touches are the material.

As his compatriot, Antonioni, has said, "the greatest danger for those working in the cinema is the extraordinary possibility it offers for lying"; by which he means revelling, as Fellini now does, in colorful objects that deflect attention from human significance.[17] However, during the middle of his career, Fellini found ways to make objects reflect what he was trying to say. Without ignoring reality, as he does in the later films, Fellini arranges and stylizes data so as to go beyond the accurate imitation of his early phase into something more propositional and even symbolic.

Nights of Cabiria was both a culmination and a dead end. Whether or not he was conscious of having taken a wrong turn into *La Strada* and *The Swindle*, in *Cabiria* Fellini avoided interior psychology and came up with his definitive portrayal of incorrigible hopefulness. In one person he encapsulated qualities that in his two best early films he had shown as permeating groups. The result is more moving because of the new concentration but, for the same reason, poorer in implication.

La Dolce Vita (1959) represents an obvious attempt to extend Fellini's range. As in *The White Sheik* and *I vitelloni*, local mores are accurately reproduced, but they have become vehicle rather than subject. Fellini has repeatedly insisted that *La Dolce Vita* isn't about Rome; rather, its Roman tableaux are meant as paradigms for an epoch. Each episode contributes to the general theme, but Fellini isn't yet as fragmentary as he was to become in *Satyricon* and after. Recalling *I vitelloni*, to which this film is something of a sequel, Fellini includes an observer character who invites audience empathy.

From the beginning of *La Dolce Vita*, Marcello, a gossip columnist, serves as guide and reactor. In the film's second scene he appears slightly defensive about his job. By the end, he is bitterly adjusted to it. In part, the film shows how disillusionment with a series of alternative lifestyles leads him to become the self-lacerating malcontent of the final scene.

First, he tries to woo the rich and bored Maddelena, but her avowed interest in love is too undiscriminating to offer stability. Then there is Sylvia, the natural, healthy animal—or so he thinks. After the fall of the movie star come others whose solutions tantalize by being intercut rather than self-contained encounters. Thus, Marcello meets Steiner, the atheist humanist, who seems to represent intellect and culture; but after other encounters—with a father who is provincial but would embrace sophistication if he could, and with some decadent aristocrats—Marcello discovers that Steiner has killed himself, thereby finally invalidating tradition as an alternative to "the sweet life." Marcello then goes to pieces, rejects the mistress who had tried to draw him into domesticity, and sinks to the lowest stratum of his world. Becoming a p.r. man who sells the talent we had been told was worthy of books, Marcello, by the end of the film, is too enervated to heed a final call to innocence.

Incremental and sympathetic, Marcello precludes the *Satyricon's* cold spectacle and, because he doesn't change, the false dramaturgy of *Juliet* and *The Swindle*. But his story occurs at the periphery, with even a whole sequence lacking relevance to his condition (the false miracle). Although he gives the film some dramatic shape, he is too sparsely characterized to warrant much attention. Far more striking than Marcello is what he experiences because for the first time in his films Fellini makes juxtaposition discursive. The events, images, transitions, etc. of *La Dolce Vita* objectify a certain analysis of the modern world. That the analysis is a commonplace of modernism only highlights the particular brilliance of many of Fellini's devices, which breathe new life into this survey of ersatz gods.

As in the justly famous opening, ideas are translated into images. A helicopter comes gradually toward us with a life-size statue dangling from a cable. While it passes over ancient Roman aqueducts, it casts a shadow. When it eventually reaches modern Rome, a worker waves, kids run to catch up with it, and sunbathing women attempt to answer the request by passengers in a second helicopter for their phone numbers. But the motor's din blots out communication and the helicopter flies off. When St. Peter's is reached, Fellini gives us a full frontal view of the Christ effigy carried by the first vehicle and then sharply cuts to the trembling face of a buddha that turns out to be the mask of a nightclub performer.

Without a word of explanation, this scene establishes the film's principal themes: the contaminating force of publicity, the desanctification of religion, the uncommunicating contiguity of past and present. Yet the characters in the film don't appear to be startled by what the audience must find bizarre. That simple disjunction places us in ironic relationship to them. Moreover, we see that they are disjunctively related to each other, either because of a physical distance suggestive of distances in age and class or because their voices are drowned out by a modern artifact. By varying this slightly at the end, Fellini will be able to create a fittingly discursive climax for this discursive film. *La Dolce Vita* concludes when an affluent but haggard Marcello is prevented from responding to an innocent country girl whom he had compared to an "Umbrian angel" and who thus recalls the opening Christ; but this time they can't hear each other because of the sound of waves. Nature ultimately becomes a context as alienating as civilization.

This point is preshadowed in the film's best sequence, in which a sylvan goddess, as her name implies, descends to earth—via airplane—and is met by a covey of worshippers—with cameras—who, like acolytes in a fertility cult, beg her to bare her bosom and offer her the fruits of the harvest—in this case, a pizza.[18] Throughout the Sylvia scenes, irony is created from juxtapositions within the action as well as within implied religious and classical parallels. So we get the interview during which Sylvia makes oracular responses, fed to her by her press agent and the priapic rite staged at a night club in the baths of Caracalla, featuring two movie stars as nymph and satyr and climaxing when the satyr hoists the nymph into an imitation of the propeller through which she descended to earth.

Yet Marcello, who had previously chased a vestmented Sylvia through St. Peter's, is convinced that salvation has come. Agreeing with every banality as if it were holy writ and all the while looking for some place to couple, Marcello drives the pneumatic goddess through Rome. Expertly mixing blasphemy and farce, Fellini satirizes the confusion between lust and primitivism. Convinced, as he later says, that Sylvia proves "we've all been wrong about everything,"[19] Marcello rushes into the Trevi Fountain where the nymph is temporarily playing Venus and begs for a resurrecting kiss. Obligingly, Sylvia drips water over his head, but after this mock baptism and before the embrace, the fountain is shut off for the night. Subsequently, in a Fellinian bleak dawn, the demystification is completed. The night with a goddess ends in a street brawl for the scandal sheets. A real lover knocks Marcello down.

Witty in conception, this sequence is also brilliantly made. Because we have seen Sylvia before Marcello does, we are slightly ahead in recognizing her absurdity. But the physical appeal of Anita Ekberg, the music, and the staging all contrive to build up in the spectator an excitement that dissolves almost as powerfully as Marcello's.

Later scenes, even when this well executed, are not as powerful because they do not so smoothly combine the characterization of Marcello with the exemplification of modernity. Thus, the Steiner party sequence is meant to dramatize another false religion (the cult of art) as well as a world understandably seductive to the hero. The first purpose dictates satire; the second, more sympathetic treatment. This mixture leaves us in doubt whether it is Marcello or Fellini who is so naïve as to take these pseudo-intellectuals for the genuine article. Similarly, although the aristocrats' party and the final orgy scene differ because the second shows a development in Marcello, because he is so slightly individuated, the orgy seems only to be repeating the general point about culture made by the party.

These scenes reveal a second problem. They can't be too titillating without belying their subject (sterility) or too boring without being artistically ruinous. Fellini's obvious solution—moderated shock—doesn't work. As Stanley Kauffmann has remarked apropos the strip-tease during the orgy, "if we could collect five dollars from every suburban New Year's Eve party at which there has been a striptease, we could finance Fellini's next picture";[20] and at the end of the aristo-crats' party, when Marcello discovers that the son of his sexual partner had been along on their expedition, we seem to be offered an equally inadequate proof of the decline of the West.

The realistic impulse that insures credibility works against the discursive intention to illustrate cultural decay. As examples pile up, the film starts to resemble the very scandal sheet style that is one of its major targets. Then we begin to suspect that Fellini likes what he is exposing.[21] In his equally repetitive illustrations of Italian character (*The White Sheik*) or provincialism, Fellini's obvious ambivalence seems warranted by his foolish but sympathetic characters. The same cannot be said for the denizens of "the sweet life."

8½ (1962) is far more successful because it locates its subject in the central character and juxtaposes scenes from his life toward an incremental purpose. Even more than *La Dolce Vita*, 8½ aspires to universality through what seem highly parochial circumstances. But Guido Anselmo, though a film director like Fellini, is a man suffering from problems that are more widespread and less tendentiously represented than anything in the earlier film.

Torn by the knowledge that he has not lived up to youth's ideal visions, Guido approaches age with a contradictory hunger for what is real. Burdened with unfulfilled responsibilities, he nonetheless expects nurture and gratification. Maturity should mean professional productivity and a stable marriage, but Guido is honest enough to admit his desire to escape both. Like most men, Guido is still half a child. Duty calls, but pleasure beckons. Everything is deadly serious, but he can't repress an urge to laugh.

Even if we should want to resist this image of middle age, the film won't let us. Minor characters and the settings are carefully designed to mirror Guido's situation. Recalling Fellini's other films that give us group rather than individual representation of their subjects, 8½ presents a spa full of geriatrics refusing to abandon pleasure. There is Guido's friend Mezzabotta, who is leaving his wife of many years for a girl young enough to be his daughter and introduced to the accompaniment on the soundtrack of "The Waltz of the Sugar Plum Fairy." But the fairy has teeth; our last views of Mezzabotta show him courting a heart attack while trying to keep up with Gloria's dancing and making a fool of himself while she flirts both with him and with Guido. Other characters share the problem of aging: the actress who though shamed by needing to exploit waning sex appeal, desperately tries to vamp Guido into padding her role; Conocchia, the production director, who vengefully reminds his boss of their shared diminution in power; Cesarino, the middle-aged production secretary, who resists age's deprivations by bringing along two "nieces." All these are seen against a backdrop of old people drinking mineral water as if from a fountain of youth or partying at the rest home's night club and descending into its baths with the same grim determination to live forever.

These characters suggest that Fellini might find something very similar did he choose to probe their psyches as he does Guido's. Therefore, the memories, dreams, and daydreams of this film director feature what unites him to ordinary people rather than the specific nature of his creative temperament.

Guido is portrayed at a moment of stasis and he doesn't change. But in his case, more than in the similar cases of former heroes, Fellini illustrates the consciousness that is blocked. Guido's problem, like that of any man temporarily paralyzed, is the vulnerability of his present to his past, of his intentions to his daydreams, and of his ego-drive to nightmares of annihilation or salvation fantasies bubbling up from the Id. His state of mind is a mélange of images that Fellini brilliantly enacts.

After the title on a black ground, the film begins without credits by tracking into a tunnel crammed with cars. The sounds of breathing and a beating heart, which are all we hear, establish that this is a dream. Guido, whom we do not identify, since he is seen from behind, tries desperately to wipe the windshield, which is beclouded by rising smoke. As he looks about him, we see, among other things, his mistress (as yet, unknown to us) being fondled by a stranger and the companions of his traffic jam peering at him with hostile curiosity. Eventually, Guido succeeds in kicking himself out of the car and in soaring free. But he turns out to be a balloon ballasted by a rope in the hands of one of his associates and thus is vulnerable to forced descent; this happens, waking him up.

Impossible to stage and more powerful to see than read about, this sequence uses sound, camera movements, and imagery to turn the audience's first feeling—which is simple puzzlement—into vicarious anxiety. Yet, it is not—like similar sequences in the later Fellini—merely spectacular. Rather, it precisely objectifies Guido's condition. That his blockage merges professional and sexual fright is reflected by the image of a fancy automobile immobilized in a tunnel. The woman being fondled by another man, even though we do not identify her as Carla, establishes Guido's fear of losing potency. The breath that fogs the window, like the heartbeat, informs us of the physical symptoms accompanying the nightmare and provides the later transition to Guido's waking at the spa. Guido's many attempts to escape responsibility in the film are prefigured by the dream soaring, just as the coldly inquiring spectators suggest the colleagues, journalists, and hangers-on who harass Guido in real life. The forced return to earth under such auspices also indicates the stress of Guido's real situation.

Guido's second dream is equally telling. In a cemetery, dressed in the cape of a schoolboy, Guido talks regretfully to his father about their estrangement, but he is interrupted by his producer. With time enough only to help his father back into the grave, Guido is told by the older man that his mother will smooth the path of life. Soon the mother appears, kisses Guido passionately, and, in a cut, turns out to be Luisa, his wife.

Very quickly, this scene establishes what Guido suffers from: his sense of not having had paternal guidance, his desire to please his father, the connection between this drive and his Catholic upbringing (since he wears the same cloak we will see in a later parochial school scene), the producer as a father-surrogate and the wife as a substitute mother. This last fact is the most disturbing to Guido, for the maternal component in his wife inevitably mixes censure into her satisfaction of his sexual desires. Subsequent dreams show why Guido has a mistress and can't be at ease with his wife.

Such scenes reveal a new alertness in Fellini to the uses of visual analogy. Not only do we understand his meaning because of what the characters do but because of how they look and through visual connections among their backgrounds. The memories and dreams clustering about the conflict between Guido's lust and his religious training exemplify this visual technique.

Shortly after the cemetery dream, Guido is going to meet his producer in the hotel lobby. His descent in an elevator is staged to recall the opening dream sequence. As it passes each floor, the elevator makes a sound like that of Guido's heartbeat, and the other inhabitants of the car (a cardinal and some assistants) peer at Guido like the people in the tunnel. This scene also points forward to the Saraghina memory because the elevator's grillwork resembles the carving of the confessional.

In turn, the Saraghina memory refers to the earlier "Asa Nisi Masa" memory scene, in which Guido recalls being bathed and tended by a nurse and then being put to bed where he and other children chanted words that were supposed to unlock a treasure. Now stalled as he is attempting to unlock treasure in his profession, Guido thinks back to that earlier time when gratification came without effort. But, as he also recalls, the Church frowned on sensuality. After delighting in Saraghina's rhumba, he was forced to do penitence and was censured by his mother. Saraghina is linked visually to the nurse, just as Luisa was linked to the mother. Guido's mistress, with whom he tries to find the unjudging gratification that Luisa cannot give him, also inspires guilt feelings, like Saraghina. So he tries to create fantasies that will preclude guilt, makes use of his directorial skill to stage a tryst with Carla in which she is told to enter the room as if by accident. This the woman dutifully performs, opening wide the sheet in which she was told to shroud herself, to let Guido feast on her treasure. The sheet recalls the opening of the "Asa Nisi Masa" scene in which Guido is removed from his bath and swathed in sheets by the nursemaid. By such analogies does Fellini clarify the causes of Guido's sexual behavior.

Dreams can never be realized, not even when one is a film director and can stage them. Luisa's superiority to Carla leaves Guido unsatisfied, so he begins to daydream, imagining that he can have both wife and mistress because both sing harmoniously when they chance to meet at a cafe. Later, he even imagines a harem living amicably with only the thought of pleasing him. Appropriately, the harem scene takes place in the same locale as the "Asa Nisi Masa" sequence and thus establishes the infantile source of masculine sex fantasy.

Many minor visual links serve the same purpose. For example, throughout the film Guido sees a beautiful woman whom he never gets to talk to. After the "Asa Nisi Masa" scene she makes a particular effect on him because he hears her talking to a lover and assuring him that she is all forgiving. Thus she embodies in adult form that total acceptance which Guido had thought only children were granted. Since at the end of the scene in which he is punished for watching Saraghina we see a madonna with this woman's face, we understand that the promise of such acceptance is one of the things that drew him to the church. However, the male half of the church, represented by the cardinal, harries him with threats of damnation and criticizes his films for godlessness. Religion, like sex, torments him by its ambiguity.

The overheard conversation that establishes the significance of the mysterious woman also shows how brilliantly Fellini designs his transitions in 8½. We arrive at the conversation after a significant ebb and flow of anxiety that begins with the frantic scene at the night club spa, during which Guido is beset by the actress, Carla, the disquieting view of Mezzabotta and Gloria, importuning guests, etc., all shot by a constantly tracking camera and accompanied by frenetic music. But when the mind reader comes up with the code-word to Guido's past, everything changes. The camera now tracks lazily through billowing sheets while a sweet soprano is heard singing. This, in turn, modulates through a slow dissolve to the lobby where Guido hears that his wife has called him, so he must order a response that will surely bring him in contact with her complaining. Here he happens upon the conversation in which the woman offers forgiveness, and we therefore understand his later impulse to ask Luisa to the spa; perhaps she too will appear in an accepting mood. But when she appears, Guido and the audience learn what both must realistically acknowledge—that a real wife, with real needs of her own, cannot fulfill a man's childish and narcissistic demands.

For most of its length, 8½ is Fellini's most expansive and precise film. Only a very fluent novel could so convincingly illustrate the intersections among dreams, wishes and experience, and no novel could do this as vividly or swiftly as Fellini's 160-minute film. Culminating a career devoted to showing the force of dreaming on actual behavior, 8½ displays Fellini's richest assemblage of techniques for bringing such yearnings to the surface, where they may be felt as well as seen. At the same time, like the more realistic films of his first period, 8½ teems with life, observed accurately and with great humor. But the seeds of his later rank overgrowth are also planted in this film, bursting occasionally into an opportunistic love of pure spectacle that turns human beings into delicacies for the visually jaded.

This bad habit first shows itself in the scene that introduces us to the spa. Both in moving to this from Guido's room and in its presentation, the scene in which Guido joins a crowd of patients is illogically and irrelevantly showy. Since we already hear its background music while Guido is staring at himself in the mirror of the previous scene, we, first of all, don't quite know if the new image presents a real locale. This confusion is exacerbated, as in *Juliet*, because Fellini allows Piero Gherardi to costume the patients in a style too flamboyant even for the moneyed class. Equally disorienting is the camerawork, which moves unrealistically from shots that are subjective (as when some people wave at the camera or when a nun turns coyly away) to others that are plainly authorial-omniscient. One long track passing through the orchestra so that we can see the conductor, in the context of the frequent subjective shots, forces us to the absurd conclusion that Guido is in danger of knocking into the players. Later, a shot of Guido looking about him is followed by a distant down-angle of the entire scene that shatters any illusion that we are seeing what he sees. Yet this doesn't stop Fellini from treating the most important elements as subjective; for example, the vision in which Claudia Cardinale replaces a waitress or the entrance of Mezzabotta. Wanting to exploit the scene's opportunities for satire, but wishing to retain the intense identification between audience and Guido that characterized the film to this point, Fellini indulges in capricious technique. For the same reason, he confuses us about the scene's status with the music bridge from Wagner's *Die Valkyrie* because he likes the ironic effect of matching that virile tune to the march of geriatrics.

Other scenes are equally confusing because of Fellini's love of shocking details. The shopping area near the spa where Guido meets Luisa, for example, incredibly mixes a Ford dealership and a fakir in a glass case. But the most subversive of these scenes is one which gave 8½ its advertising motif and caused American distributors to purchase rights even though the film had not yet been finished.[22] Because this harem sequence includes every woman in the cast, it dramatizes the comic imperiousness of the male sex-drive. Moreover this important observation is inferred from one of Fellini's most delightful pieces of staging. But he doesn't know when to stop. Illogically, for a wish-fulfillment fantasy, Guido imagines not only the harem but a revolt. This may perhaps be accepted as an additional thrill, since he puts down the temporary resistance; but what are we to make of his speech to the assembled ladies about the definition of happiness ("to be able to speak the truth without hurting anyone")?[23] At the cost of logic, Fellini is not only indulging in effect (the revolt permits the crowd-pleasing moment in which Guido controls the women with his whip); he is violating the dream status of the scene so as to permit Guido to articulate the film's theme. This sins against the clear distinctions among levels of reality that is one of the most delightful signs of Fellini's artistry in this film, as well as against its cinematic freedom from rhetoric.

Interestingly enough, the harem scene was one of two seriously transformed in the movement from script to film. In the original screenplay, it was shorter and more logical: the women rebelled because of mutual jealousy not resentment at Guido's dominance, and, after putting the revolt down, Guido was shown being upbraided by Luisa and involuntarily remembering their wedding. Consequently, the next real-life scene in which Luisa stalks out of the rehearsal for Guido's film is more expected and consistent than it is in the finished version of 8½. Fellini sacrificed this consistency and violated logic because he was carried away by the chance to elaborate an effect.[24]

In such previews of his later penchant for meaningless spectacle as well as through its more admirable features, 8½ stands as Fellini's definitive work. This much is evident in the film's other drastically altered sequence. Originally, 8½ was to end with Guido and Luisa departing from the spa and talking about the possibility of divorce. During their conversation, in which the husband preaches resignation to an imperfect arrangement against loneliness, Guido has a vision of all the characters in the film joining the couple while they sit in the dining car of a train that takes them back to Rome. But when he tries to formulate the import of this vision, it fades, and, signalling his frustration, the film dissolves into a blackness that will cover his future life. Notoriously, Fellini had not decided between this and the present ending shortly before the film was to be premiered. This hesitation, together with the supposed evasiveness of what he did choose, has earned the last scene widespread denigration.

After keeping dream and reality sharply delimited (which is why the scenes I've criticized are harmful), Fellini deliberately mixes the two, moving into a realm of pure vision in the final images. Prior to the end, Guido nearly breaks down under harassment by hostile reporters, importunate fans, and colleagues who badger him about the film he no longer wishes to make. Since all either announce or imply his death as an artist, actual death comes to seem like a relief. A production assistant places a gun in his pocket. Then, in a moment of carefully dubious status, Guido shoots himself.

Fellini now cuts to the same location empty of the preceding crush of people except for Daumier, the critic who had throughout 8½ served as Guido's antithesis and who had himself been hanged in a dream moment during the earlier rehearsal scene. Congratulating Guido for having decided to give up the film, Daumier asserts that artists must stop creating when they have nothing to say. Yet an interior voice, asserting Guido's joy in life, gradually grows louder until it drowns out the critic. This voice bids Guido to express himself in continued presentations even though he has no theses to promulgate and can't even resolve his own personal confusion. Now all the characters we had seen in 8½ march down the steps of Guido's abandoned movie set, filling the screen with life, and then parade under his direction until night falls. Light gradually diminishes, the accompanying orchestra also walks off-screen, and we are left only with the figure of Guido as a little boy, playing the flute while spotlighted. He too goes, and darkness takes over.

This *tour de force* of staging sums up the nature of Fellini's cinematic art. Affirming that "he nothing affirmeth," Fellini says that the meaning of Guido's representative life can no more be reduced to intellectual assertion than can any other true image of living. Like 8½ itself, any film that Guido might have made could deal honestly with its subject only by juxtaposing carefully staged images and then shutting the lights. Film, 8½ implies, is only honest when it is non-dramatic and anti-rhetorical: that is to say, when it seems neither to have interfered with the flow of life nor to have reduced it to statements. Hence Fellini presents an ending which is no conclusion but rather a literal parade of the human elements that have comprised Guido's life.

Luisa's willingness to join the parade, bitterly deplored by critics who believe that the film should make some judgment about Guido's infidelity, is plainly no more real than anything else in the sequence. What we are witnessing is the enactment of a vision which holds that art resembles a chemical rather than an intellectual solution, with life's components remaining in suspension. Fellini wants to say that saying can't be judgmental because judgment involves exclusion and images of life are true in the degree that they are copious. Fellini doesn't ask that Guido be forgiven for this amorality in the face of art as well as life. He merely asks us to recognize that inclusiveness offers the only satisfaction of the heart's desire. Guido has been seeking freedom not only from the limitations of duty and monogamy but from the neatness of form that would falsify the inchoate grandeur of content. The last scene announces that neither Guido nor Fellini will ever escape such stresses, except through the art of film whose power of inclusion is greater than any yet devised.

Were 8½ not so rich in images of life, its assertion of inclusiveness as the supreme definition of art would seem arrogant. But in this film, as in all of Fellini's successes, art is achieved through accretion of detail because almost every detail is full of observation, rich in feeling for the bedeviled dreamer who is man. But, in his later films, when observation gives way to fabrication and people flatten to the dimensions of objects, Fellini begins to make only galleries of stills that are contradictorily and purposelessly moving. Then he offers negative proof that cinema must be impelled by observed life or the craft loses its justification. In its unresisting enchantment before the human parade, the last scene of 8½ epitomizes Fellini, the film artist; the ending of Satyricon, in which the characters dissolve back into the fresco from which they came, epitomizes Fellini the decorator, the fabricator of dead though garish pictures. As Fellini himself shows, pictures alone don't make a film.

PART TWO

SIGHTINGS

THE BLOW-UP:
SORTING THINGS OUT

For an esoteric director, Michelangelo Antonioni inspired surprising publicity when *Blow-Up* opened at New York's Coronet Theatre. Spoken in English, produced by a big American company, *Blow-Up* became "copy" for columnists who had formerly ignored the dour Italian and his arthouse masterpieces. Now much was heard of the absence of Monica Vitti (Antonioni's favorite leading lady) and of the artistic consequences of that fact. With each passing interview, new parts of London were added to the list of those actually painted by Antonioni in his search for expressive color. While to Rex Reed, who sketched the director in poison ink for the Sunday *Times*, Antonioni's zeal was mere arrogance; to MGM, it was integrity. When the director refused to make deletions required for a Production Code seal, the studio staunchly supported him. Yet when the flap subsided, MGM hid behind its subsidiary, Premier Productions, declining to acknowledge its sponsorship so as to avoid offending those Catholics who had wanted the film banned. In his review, Bosley Crowther voiced concern lest the publicity attract the wrong audience. But while saving *Blow-Up* from the prurient, Crowther invited another philistine response: the film was a mystery; he would not unveil its plot.

That Antonioni might have a plot to reveal was as novel an idea as that he might attract the masses. But soon the Coronet Theatre seemed as crowded as the Music Hall. To make matters more confusing, *Blow-Up* was admired by Crowther and Judith Crist, *Time* and the *Saturday Review*, but disliked by many reviewers for more intellectual journals. Several of the latter split off from the New York Film Critics just in time to give *Blow-Up* the annual prize bestowed by their more conventional colleagues on *A Man for All Seasons*, but the most influential members of the new group (Brendan Gill, Pauline Kael and John Simon) all disparaged the film.

Before long, Crowther's restrained synopsis turned into a joke. A few critics now denied that *Blow-Up* had a plot; others denied that it articulated a meaning. William Zinsser (in *Look*) provided an appropriate apex for the controversy by proclaiming *Blow-Up*—along with *The Homecoming* and Andrew Wyeth!—an example of art meant not to be understood but only experienced.

Were *Blow-Up* less significant and Antonioni less revolutionary, the imbroglio I have sketched would merely support Dwight Macdonald's warning about cults in collision. But because Antonioni has done more to define cinema than probably any director since Eisenstein, the criticism afforded *Blow-Up* tells a good deal about current consideration of the art.

Some critics, notably Stanley Kauffmann and Ian Cameron, have accurately described Antonioni's effort to disentangle cinema from theater, but they have not perceived the radical lengths to which he has gone. Every important director, from popular artists like Hitchcock to serious *auteurs* like Kurosawa and Bergman, has exploited cinema's unique ability both to imprison the spectator in the lens's grip and to free him through speed and scope of movement; but Antonioni stands alone in making the visual image his fundamental mode of expression. He does not tell a story; he presents gestures and tableaux. He does not explore characters; he moves figures through a landscape. Yet, although his films are filled with things to look at, he does not shoot scenery.

To begin with: plot. Antonioni's plots are really antiplots, since his characters are chronically unable to engage in productive action. Thus, in *L'Avventura*, Claudia and Sandro cannot truly search for his lost fiancée because they cannot truly care whether she is found. In *La Notte*, the unhappily married protagonists accomplish nothing in their long, eventful day, while the lovers' appointment in *Eclipse* is never, so far as we can tell, kept. Giuliana, of *Red Desert*, performs the one significant act in Antonioni, but that is only a spiritual adjustment to the modern world. Plot suspense is utterly avoided; our desire for knowledge focuses on character.

But not on character as unique personage, with determinant past and significant future. Antonioni's people are simply what we see, which is why they are always defined by dead-end jobs. Sandro, once an architect, is now an appraiser; while Giovanni, in *La Notte*, is a writer who doubts the possibility of another book. The sensitive heroine of *Eclipse* is doomed to the soulless and the secondhand: her lover works for the stock exchange, while she translates for a living. Even Giuliana has a depleting job, that of full-time neurotic. Unlike characters in other works that are similarly focused, Antonioni's do not develop. Their stories show them assuming a role—Claudia becoming Sandro's lover—or understanding the roles they have always played—Sandro facing his emptiness.

Since Antonioni's characters do not really engage in action and do not radically change, their inward fixity calls for a new kind of film movement. Whereas most directors move your eye across the surface of the action, Antonioni tries to move your eye into its depths. For most directors, a close-up represents, as it were, the locus of event and dialogue. In Antonioni, events occur behind faces, which express themselves not in dialogue but in gesture: a flick of the eye, a grimace. Antonioni's close-ups must be "read." Furthermore, whereas most directors bombard the spectator with images or hurl him through space, Antonioni holds his eye in front of the carefully composed scenes.

This last characteristic is the heart of Antonioni's method. A director who emphasizes action will photograph the background as an agent; as, for example, Hitchcock photographs the windshield wipers of Janet Leigh's car in *Psycho*: normal servants turned by the plot into menacing blades. A director who explores character will arrange the background into an "objective correlative"; as, for example, Fellini does in 8½. Antonioni handles decor in neither way. In his films, the background does not enhance or reflect the foreground but rather interacts with and interprets it.

In his first important film, *L'Avventura*, the two main female characters are established by the simplest visual means: Anna, who has dark hair and scowls a great deal, represents withdrawal from society to which blond, always smiling Claudia is innocently attracted. In the film's second scene, Anna leaves Claudia inspecting a Roman square while she deliberately stages a test of her love for Sandro. As we watch Anna's face disgustedly receiving Sandro's caress, we see the nullity of their relationship and, since we shall later see the faces of Sandro and Claudia turning in the same erotic dance, we preview the essential anonymity of relationships in this world.

That Claudia is destined to replace her, Anna realizes when, with a smirk, she forces Claudia to wear her blouse in the subsequent yachting scene. This image must come back to our minds when, at Taormina, Claudia playfully dons a black wig, accepting a life in which identities may so easily be changed. In the film's last scene, when Claudia is herself replaced by a common whore, she has no moral force left from which to condemn the fickle Sandro. Now totally sophisticated, she can only join him in a gesture of resignation at their common incapacity for commitment.

The plot, or aborted action, of *L'Avventura* advances by means of visual analogies and small appearances; Antonioni can spend seconds shooting Claudia as she sits exhaustedly in the train station where she hopes to escape Sandro's tempting importunities. Above her head, in this actionless scene, are some pictures of madonnas. The moment's meaning is a contrast between the despair registered on Claudia's face and the serenity in the pictures. This is how Antonioni's decor interacts with and interprets the characters.

It also helps to establish the significance of their behavior through visual symbols and allusions, like the modernist devices of *The Waste Land* or *The Magic Mountain*, that realize Antonioni's modernist themes: lovelessness, paralysis of will, loss of faith. Fundamentally, *L'Avventura* contains an implied parallel with the *Odyssey*, which mostly took place in the same Sicilian locale, and which provides the Western mind with its definitive image of adventure and search. The point of the comparison, of course, is that the modern quest, indifferent to its object, must turn inward. Thus Antonioni fills the background with symbols of former validity to point up their debasement in the modern world. I will cite only a few examples. Patrizia, the yacht's owner, works a jigsaw puzzle of a classic scene while the playboy Raimondo fondles her breast in a gesture that is "unreproved, if undesired." On the island, while searching for Anna, the modern Romans find an ancient amphora, and after some humorously uncomprehending guesses about its possible function, Raimondo carelessly lets it fall. The *carabinieri* to whom Sandro goes at Messina are housed in a baroque palace before whose splendid marble walls they have set up ugly wooden slabs to form an office.

Throughout the island sequence, Antonioni is careful to train his cameras on the rocks so that the humans are always seen entering large barren areas, as if they come too late and too punily to dominate the alien landscape. For their humanity has been wrecked by a cultural debacle in which, as in much modern literature, a debilitated pursuit of pleasure competes with activities that had traditionally nurtured the soul. This theme, which gives the meager events their large significance, permeates the film. On the church tower at Noto, for example, when Sandro asks Claudia to marry him, she refuses a proposal so lightly made by ringing the bells which actualize attunement. The Sicilian men milling about Claudia with sidewise lust are visually counterpointed by the choirboys marching in orderly sexlessness from the cathedral. The Sicilian journey progresses through a culture in ruins (symbolized by the succession of church towers progressively abandoned and incomplete—one without a bell), coming to rest at Taormina, haunt of the rich, before a shattered building of which all that remains is a ruined tower and a fragment of façade.

Because *L'Avventura* shows an unformed girl realizing her latent sophistication, it comes closer than any of Antonioni's films to presenting a character in transition. Although we know little about Claudia (except that she was born poor), we can sympathize with her decline. Thus *L'Avventura*, Antonioniesque though it be, is moving in a conventional way. The later films are more representational in their enactment of cultural malaise, their characters are more fully symbolic, and their effect is more sensory and intellectual.

In *L'Avventura*, although hints exist only to demonstrate the deterioration that is modern worldliness, we learn something not only of Claudia's but of Sandro's past. Once a creator of buildings, Sandro now merely measures their cost. When he vindictively spills ink on the young boy's sketch of the cathedral at Noto, the personal and public meanings of Sandro's behavior merge; he is both a success reacting against lost innocence and modern man reacting against lost faith. In *La Notte*, we do not know why Giovanni can no longer write; the personal drama now merely illustrates the public meaning of a day that begins with the death of an intellectual and ends at an industrialist's party. Similarly, we do not know why Giovanni and Lydia have fallen out of love. Their unhappiness is not explained; it is merely displayed.

To establish Lydia's feelings, for example, Antonioni shoots the famous walking scene in which Lydia's state of mind is revealed through her reactions to a postman eating a sandwich, some fighting youths, a man firing off rockets, etc. Stopped clocks and flaking walls suggest the era's sickness; later, at the party, Antonioni achieves one of his best visual symbols of deterioration by showing the industrialist's cat staring fixedly at a Roman portrait bust. "Maybe he's waiting for him to wake up," the millionaire's wife announces. "Try and figure cats out." When Giovanni takes Lydia to a night club, they witness the erotic dance of two splendid Negroes; but the act turns out to be acrobatic, concluding when the female manages to get her legs around a glass of water. Milan's sterility is highlighted at the party which becomes vital only when a rainstorm strikes.

With a few exceptions (the explicit last scene or some excessive business at the party), *La Notte* dramatizes its insights subtly. But the film is impure. As if frightened by its increased abstractness, Antonioni relies too heavily on dialogue to clarify his points; and, as we might expect from an artist who thinks with his eyes, the dialogue is banal.

Eclipse is more abstract than *La Notte*, heightening its emphasis on meaningful gesture and replacing dialogue, as often as possible,

with expressive natural sound. Vittoria, the heroine, is even less explained than Giovanni and Lydia. We never learn why she has
broken off her first affair or why she takes up with Piero. Although she
has a job, it is minimally emblematic, whereas the jobs of Sandro and
Giovanni represent obvious problems. Vittoria is created almost exclusively through what she does. She constantly fusses with flowers
or disports herself with the primitive and the natural. These meanings come together when Vittoria is fascinated by one of the men who
is wiped out by the stock market slide. Whereas the other investors
sweat and fan themselves furiously, rush around, or, like Vittoria's
mother, blasphemously turn religion to the service of Mammon, this
man exits calmly. Vittoria follows him to a cafe, where he orders a
drink and writes intently on a piece of paper. When he leaves, drop-
ping the paper behind him, she retrieves it. It is covered with flowers.
She is delighted. This is the moment before she begins her affair
with Piero.

Living in a sterile modern world, Vittoria seeks escape on an airplane ride above the clouds, as well as through love. When down to
earth in Piero's arms, however, she learns that people nowadays
care only for things. The liveliest, noisiest scenes in *Eclipse* take place
at the stock exchange (significantly, built in the ruins of a Roman
temple), where men sweatingly pursue goods that truly excite them.
But, try as they may to stir it, the air cannot cool their agitated bodies.
Only above the clouds, or in one small moment when the Exchange
halts out of respect for a deceased broker, does the air quicken; during that unique respite from noise in the ruined temple, a large overhead fan, like a propeller, whirs freely.

Setting aside *Red Desert* for the moment, this brief survey of Antonioni's films should suggest the atmosphere of *Blow-Up*. Yet faced
with a murder witnessed by a photographer, Bosley Crowther inevitably recalled the Hitchcock of *Rear Window*, and this utterly
misleading comparison has been perpetuated by many critics. In
fact, the antiplot of *Blow-Up* is *vero Antonioni*.[1]

Like *L'Avventura*, *Blow-Up* concerns the search for something
that is never found. As in *La Notte*, the peripatetic hero fails to accomplish anything. Like the other protagonists, the photographer is
the embodiment of a role, although here he is so fully defined by his
function that he is not even named. As in Antonioni's other films, the
climax is reached when the protagonist comes to face his own impotence. There is even a concluding disappearance that recalls the
absence of Vittoria and Piero from the last minutes of *Eclipse*: as the

124

camera slowly draws away from the photographer, he slowly diminishes in size, an effect made more significant when Antonioni literally causes him to vanish before "the end."

The events in *Blow-Up* dramatize the same theme one finds in Antonioni's other films. The photographer, a creature of work and pleasure but of no inner force or loyalty, is unable to involve himself in life. He watches it, manipulates it; but, like all of Antonioni's male characters, he has no sense of life's purpose. Thus, when faced with a challenge, he cannot decisively act. Unable to transcend himself, except through ultimate confrontation with his soul, he represents modern paralysis.

Most reviewers have denied that this or any other theme is apparent in *Blow-Up*, while those few who believed that Antonioni was up to something were either uncertain or wrong, I think, about what it was. Since Antonioni demands closer attention than even professional film watchers are likely to be familiar with, and since reviewers usually have the sketchiest knowledge of a serious director's canon, the errors are not surprising. But what are we to make of the critical misconceptions perpetrated by John Simon?

Simon is, in my opinion, the best American film critic now writing. Expectedly, he was the one critic who saw the need to summarize *Blow-Up*'s events; yet in his exhaustive résumé, he missed the crucial moments. As a result, he determined that Antonioni's theme was Pirandellian, despite the total absence of any metaphysical concern in the director's other work. Together with the common emphasis on Hitchcock, this Pirandellian analogy has done a great deal to obfuscate Antonioni's meaning.

Because the body vanishes, and because the photographer ultimately hears a tennis ball that doesn't exist, some people have thought that Antonioni means us to question the existence of the corpse. Incidental details such as the photographer's initial appearance as a bum who surprisingly enters a Rolls Royce have been cited in support of this interpretation. Yet the point of the first scene is that the photographer *isn't* a bum, that he took part in the doss-house life merely to exploit it for his picture book. The body exists; what is significant is that the photographer didn't realize he'd seen it.

When the narrator enters the park, we see him performing his first spontaneous gesture. Emerging from the antique shop, he notices it and, for no apparent reason, enters. Perhaps he is attracted by the lush greenness, the melodically rustling leaves. Chancing on the love ballet, however, the photographer responds automatically, according to a settled routine. Love, as his agent, Ron, later tells him, would make a "truer" conclusion to his picture book. But when the girl tries to get his film and a young man (apparently the murderer) peers through the restaurant window at his lunch with Ron, the photographer begins to suspect that he has witnessed something less than innocent. After the girl leaves his studio, he blows up the photographs; and it is here, I think, that Simon and every other critic I have read misinterpret the action.

What happens is this: While the photographer is studying the shots, he spies something suspicious in the still of some shrubbery behind a fence. What he does not see but what the audience does, as Antonioni's lens pans across the row of blow-ups, is the still showing a body. The audience, but not the photographer, knows that a body exists. (When Vanessa Redgrave ran away from the photographer during the park scene, she stopped to look down at the tree, from behind which a head was unmistakably visible.) But the photographer chooses to blow up only the still showing the murderer and his gun. Exulting in what he thinks is a meaningful action, he rushes to the phone to call his agent. "Somebody was trying to kill somebody else," he says, "I saved his life."

That the photographer jumps to this erroneous conclusion despite contrary evidence is logical in view of subtle but clear hints we got earlier of a latent dissatisfaction with his normal mode of behavior. His studio is dominated by photographs of a sky diver and a skin diver, his living room by a shot of camels (recalling a similar photograph in *Eclipse*), and he clearly would like to get away. Vittoria made her frail gesture in a plane; the photographer buys a propeller. Lydia had gone on a solitary walk; the photographer, so far as he knows, takes a stroll in the park. As he tells his agent, "I've gone off London this week. Doesn't do anything for me. I'm fed up with those bloody bitches. Wish I had tons of money, then I'd be free."

Freedom and mastery are cheaply purchased when the photographer allows himself to believe he has saved a man's life. Had he done so, his action would have symbolized a separation from the aimless mod world. What he witnessed, as he believes, was the attempt by a young swinger to murder a gray-haired, older man in a garden. Catching the snake hidden in the bushes, the photographer had preserved the intended victim. The fact of the matter is different.

While on the phone with Ron, he hears a noise at the door. Apparently suspecting the murderer, he opens it surreptitiously; in tumble two teeny-boppers. Although he had previously expressed contempt for these "bloody bitches," he now becomes involved with them. Meanwhile Ron rings off. When the girls, who have come for some exploitation of their own, begin to undress before a clothes-rack, the photographer seizes the opportunity. An orgy ensues, and here Antonioni works his most audacious trick.[2]

While the photographer is romping with the girls (avidly attended by any normal spectator), for perhaps five seconds, in the upper right hand corner of the frame, above the purple paper, we see a man dressed like the murderer, watching them. Antonioni then cuts to the girls as they are pulling on the photographer's clothes, and the photographer, who is sitting up, now notices the shot he had previously overlooked. Much to their chagrin, he ejects the teeny-boppers, blows up the fatal still, and learns that he had saved nothing.

However, instead of calling the police, asking for help, or in any way dealing with what he now realizes, he returns to the park to prove that the murder took place (although in calling his agent, he had acted far more precipitately with no more evidence). Back at the park, he sees the body; but behind him he hears a click, as of a gun or camera, and he runs away. Again, he does not go for the police. Instead, he returns to his studio and looks longingly at the propeller, an old part without a plane, lying on a white floor—useless. He then goes to his friend's apartment, where he is shocked to find the wife fixing her attention upon him while having intercourse with her husband.

Reentering his studio, he discovers that the blowups have been stolen, presumably by the man who entered during the orgy sequence. After a brief, apparently fruitless conversation with his friend's wife, he takes off in his car. While driving, he thinks he sees the murderer's accomplice; but his attempt to chase her degenerates into his meaningless involvement with an absurd experience at a rock 'n roll club. Once again, he has recourse to his agent; but he finds Ron in a marijuana trance, which he soon joins. In the last scene, returning to the park, he discovers that the murderer has made off with the body. He has accomplished nothing.

For he is part of his world. Hiding behind a tree, like the murderer, he shot with a camera what the latter shot with a gun; and he did not save the older man. He is blond, and so is the murderer. For all his aloof contempt, he is as frivolous as the mod clowns who frame his experience. In the last scene, when he hears their "tennis ball," he effectively actualizes the charade existence that they share in common. His final gesture of resignation—like Sandro's tears, Giovanni's loveless copulation, or Piero's and Vittoria's failure to meet—shows clearly that the photographer cannot change.

The actions I have sketched are nearly pantomimed; their larger implications are also established through visual means. As with the *carabinieri's office* in *L'Avventura*, the first shot in *La Notte* (showing a graceful old building standing in front of Pirelli's glass box), the forbidding sleekness of E.U.R. in *Eclipse*, Antonioni fills the background in *Blow-Up* with examples of tradition being razed to make way for a grey, anonymous wasteland. As the photographer drives through London, the camera pans along the colorful walls of the old city only to be abruptly lost in blank space surrounding a new housing project—all grays and browns. When he visits the antique shop, scouting real estate for his agent, he advises purchase since the neighborhood seems to have attracted homosexuals—those great contemporary buyers of the past. The old caretaker, however, refuses to sell him anything, but the young mod owner is only too anxious to turn the shop into cash for a trip to Nepal, where she hopes to escape from the antiques. "Nepal is all antiques," the photographer dryly observes.

The modern world, however, seems bent on destroying its traditions. On the wall of the photographer's apartment, an old Roman tablet is overwhelmed by the hallucinatory violence of the modern painting at its side. More important, traditional human pursuits are being drained of their force. Politics is now playacting; a pacifist parade marches by with signs bearing inscriptions like "No," or "On. On. On." or "Go away." Pleasure is narcotizing, whether at the "pot" party or in the rock 'n roll club. Love is unabsorbing, as the photographer learns from his friend's marriage. Art has lost its validity. Murder is ignored.

These last implications are forcefully portrayed in the film's main scenes of human interaction. The first of these scenes shows the photographer visiting his friend Bill, who is a painter. When the hero enters his flat, the painter is standing affectedly before a large canvas. Attempting to engage the photographer's interest, he explains his condition:

> They don't mean anything when I do them, just a mess. Afterward, I find something to hang onto [pointing]—like that leg. Then it all sorts itself out; it's like finding a clue in a detective story.

Although we are likely to find Bill rather pretentious, particularly in view of the obviously derivative nature of his painting, the photographer seems unusually impressed. When the painter's wife enters, he tells her that he has wanted to buy one of the canvases. When we see her massaging his neck with obvious interest on her part but mere friendly comfort on his, we know what this oasis of art and domesticity might mean to a man so cynical and frenetic. Later, in his puzzlement concerning the murder, when he turns to them for help, he discovers that the oasis is dry.

In the second important scene, the murderer's accomplice meets the photographer at his studio because he blew his car horn when he reached his street so as to inform the pursuers of his whereabouts. When he tries to calm her, she replies:

"My private life is already in a mess. It would be a disaster—"
P: "So what? Nothing like a little disaster for sorting things out."

Through turning sparse, functional dialogue into a system of verbal echoes, Antonioni achieves the economy of tight verse. Yet he does not sacrifice naturalness. The painter, in an observation appropriate to the scene, had suggested that visual experience is comprehensible only through recollection, during which process it performs the function of a clue that helps to "sort things out." The photographer, in a casual remark to the girl, asserts that the sorting out process is facilitated by disaster. This verbal cross-reference points to the meaning behind the action.

The most subtle use of dialogue occurs in a sequence which has been either ignored or misinterpreted as a sign that Antonioni's theme is failure of communication. When the painter's wife enters the photographer's studio, she comes upon a distraught man; he has lost his evidence and his faith in his friends. Although laconically, they do communicate:

P: "Do you ever think of leaving [your husband]?"
W: "No, I don't think so."
P: [Turning away with annoyance] "I saw a man killed this morning."
W: "Where? Was he shot?"
P: "Sort of a park."
W: "Are you sure?"
P: "He's still there."
W: "Who was he?"
P: "Someone."
W: "How did it happen?"
P: "I don't know. I didn't see."

W: [Bewildered] "You didn't see?"

P: [Wry grimace] "No."

W: "Shouldn't you call the police?"

P: [Pointing to the one still the murderer didn't take] "That's the body."

W: "Looks like one of Bill's paintings. [Turning to him, helplessly] Will you help me? I don't know what to do. [He doesn't react. She looks at the shot.] What it is? Hmmmm. I wonder why they shot him."

P: "I didn't ask."

W: [Looks up at him, smiles sadly, and, after some hesitation, leaves.]

I record this dialogue to show how clearly and economically Antonioni establishes his meaning.[3] When the painter's wife comes to his apartment, she hears the photographer's confession of failure and declares her own. Bill's art is no alternative to the destruction symbolized by the murder; his art is another version of it. They can no more deal with their marriage than the photographer can deal with the crime. She can only slink away in compassion for their mutual impotence, leaving him to futile pursuit, marijuana, and his depressing moment of truth.

In *Blow-Up*, as in *Eclipse* and *L'Avventura*'s island sequence, Antonioni achieves his meanings through the use of sound effects as well as speech. When the photographer shoots his model in a parody of intercourse, and when he poses the mannequins, music, as he says, is "noise" to inspire their artificial vitality. When Vanessa Redgrave comes to his apartment, fresh from the murder, he tries to teach her the lesson that music maintains one's "cool." While giving her some "pot," to which she sensuously yields herself, he shows her that really to enjoy it and the taped jazz he is playing, she must hold herself back—draw slowly and keep time against the beat. Before he begins to inspect the blowups, he turns the jazz on. But the music quickly fades when he becomes involved; as he looks deeply into the frames, we hear on the sound track a rustling of leaves.

The incredible greenness of a park that was the ironic setting for murder suggests another of Antonioni's means. When the photographer discovers the body's loss, he looks up at the tree, whose leaves now rattle angrily, and sees the leaves as black against a white sky. Like the sound analogies and the verbal cross-references, the color in *Blow-Up* aids comprehension.

The film is composed mainly in four hues: black, white, green and purple. The hero's studio is black and white, as are most of his clothes and those of Vanessa Redgrave. So too are photographs. In fact, the meaning of the event in the park was "as clear as black and white" before he photographed it, which is what makes for significance in his initial failure of perception as well as in his underlying failure to understand the implication of his way of life. The green park was penetrated by evil. Suitably, the door of the photographer's dark room, in which he brings to light the dark deed, is also green. Not, however, until he copulates with the teeny-boppers in a sea of purple does he realize that he did not prevent the crime. Appropriately, the door to the room in which he blows up the fatal still is also purple. One of the teeny-boppers wears purple tights; the other, green.

Colorful though it is, *Blow-Up* seems to be moving toward color-lessness, black and white—almost as if Antonioni were trying to make us face the skull beneath the painted flesh. But that is not what most reviewers have done. That they should, if my reading is correct, have missed the film's meaning so completely is a phenomenon almost as significant as the film itself. What, after all, does their error tell us?

The familiar things are aspects of a fixed condition. As I have said, few reviewers know the director's work; fewer still have sophisticated ideas about film art. Their collective sophistication, if not their intelligence, is modest; when they simulate brilliance, it is only through the perfervid prose we associate with *Time* magazine. I doubt that many serious readers would choose books on the advice of the same sources to which, *faute de mieux*, they are forced to turn for evaluation of films. This much, I think, is sadly inarguable, but not limited to consideration of avant-garde film-making in general or Antonioni in particular.

The confusion about Antonioni comes from the unusual demands he makes. Most films are to be looked at; Antonioni's are to be inspected. Decades of film as a commercial form of escapism have atrophied our perception; like all great artists, Antonioni insists that we see anew. Unfortunately, most reviewers can't see. Although many disguised their ineptitude by reporting little of what goes on in *Blow-Up*, distressing errors of fact tend to characterize the more venturesome accounts. Thus one reviewer (Richard Corliss, *National Review*) has the photographer buying an oar, while another (Joseph Morgenstern, *Newsweek*) has the orgy spread out on sky-blue paper. John Simon suggests that the photographer makes eyes at Sarah Miles, whereas the reverse is true. As a result of error he can give no accurate reading of the subplot. John Coleman (*New Statesman*) loftily deems *Blow-Up* a "very superficial film . . . about people reckoned as leading superficial lives"; but since he asserts that the photographer saw the body and the gun *after* the orgy sequence, Coleman is in no position to call anyone superficial.

Such errors of fact are less important in themselves than as manifestations of a cavalier attitude toward Antonioni's difficult style. More than their mistakes, the arrogance of reviewers is what rankles. Confronted with a famously complex director whose films are widely acknowledged to be important, the journeyman critic, both here and in England, treats *Blow-Up* as if it were indeed a mechanical piece of Hitchcock. Despite museum cults, the emergence of cinema's right to be considered a form of art is notoriously recent. A parallel growth in movie reviewing is long overdue.

Among critics, the sources of confusion are more profound. Misunderstanding *Blow-Up* is not only failure to scrutinize with sufficient care a highly wrought method of expression; it is the consequence of some false, but currently powerful, ideas about the nature of art. Although these ideas are more blatantly damaging with an art form so ill-defined as cinema, they have their origin in wider cultural presuppositions.

The first of them, to use Norman Podhoretz's phrase, is the demand that art "bring the news." Widespread dissatisfaction with contemporary fiction, lack of interest in poetry, and the inflation of nonfictional forms like the book review all indicate the dominance of this aesthetic program. Thus Norman Mailer's lucubrations attain significance because he styles himself a social prophet, confessional poetry becomes the accepted fashion in verse, and non-fiction, a form defined by what it isn't, now begins to absorb whatever it lacks.

From the neonaturalist perspective, *Blow-Up* is offensive because it manipulates the materials of contemporary London to express not the city but Antonioni's version of modern life. If one can bear the hip language—not unrelated to the ideas—he can see this attitude clearly expressed in Richard Goldstein's article in the *Village Voice*, entitled "The Screw-Up." Condemning a lack of "understanding that can only be called Parental," Goldstein insists that Antonioni misrepresents the swinging Samarkand and derides the film for the expressiveness that—*autres temps, autres moeurs*—would have guaranteed its status as a work of art. Whatever can be said for such documentary emphasis, it easily degenerates into mindless fixation on the up-to-date. That people old enough to know better don't avoid the trap can be seen in Pauline Kael's review, where, amidst a veritable fusillade, she criticizes Antonioni for not catching "the humor and fervor and

astonishing speed in youth's rejection of older values." Godard, *sí!*
Antonioni, *no!*

The other new aesthetic barbarism has quickly filtered down to its
rightful level, having been recently promoted by the arts editor of
Look. Given a more respectable formulation by Susan Sontag, Richard Gilman and other less conspicuous gurus, the conception of art
as "sensuous form" might seem a useful antidote to excess verisimilitude, but it comes to much the same thing. Like those who wish art
to be a form of sociology, the advocates of a "new sensibility" reveal
a fatal affinity for what's "in." Thus Miss Sontag finds that formal
heights are scaled by happenings, pornography and science fiction,
while critics like Gilman opt for novels (promoted by magazines like
the *New Yorker*) in which insouciance becomes art by imitating the
era's bafflement. (Collusion between the documentary and nonin-
terpretive definitions of art was nicely indicated by the appearance
of Robert Garis's review—which argues that the film is good because
it is "exciting to watch"—in *Commentary.*)

One error encourages the sentimental social pieties of some reviewers; the other authorizes their imperception. Thus reviews of
Blow-Up express outraged social optimism or a kind of aesthetic
trance induced by globules of "surface beauty." The skillful creation
of symbols for insight—art, in short—becomes an achievement of
negligible appeal.

A third aesthetic error (born, in part, out of reaction against the
other two), despite a devotion to artistic seriousness, runs the risk
of blocking new modes. John Simon is rightly opposed to art without
discursive implications or rational validity. In *Hudson Review* pieces
concerning Albee, Pinter, and thinkers like McLuhan and N.O.
Brown, Simon shows himself a powerful demolition machine for a
culture besieged on all sides. But in his splendid assaults, he sometimes finds himself forced backward into old-fashioned demands for
situational realism, psychologically valid motivation, and human-
istically oriented themes. These requirements should be suspended
with considerably less alacrity than most critics now show, but they
must be abandoned for those rare cases, like Borges, Beckett or Antonioni, in which authentic art is being produced in a new way.
Significantly, Simon is receptive to such art when reviewing books—
a further indication that people automatically relax their aesthetics
when discussing films.

A similarly based lack of sympathy is detectable in the otherwise
laudatory pieces on Antonioni's earlier films that Dwight Macdonald

wrote for *Esquire*. Although Macdonald, along with Stanley Kauff-mann, was one of Antonioni's few discerning American champions, he became displeased by the Italian's progressive refusal to motivate his characters. Even Kauffmann was made nervous by the abstractionism of *Eclipse*, although he rejoiced, wrongly as I think, in the colored abstractionism of *Red Desert*.

Still, despite a few hints of retrograde commitment, Simon, Kauffmann and Macdonald are the most sensitive of Antonioni's American critics and the most useful, intelligent film critics of recent times. The fumbling responses of their colleagues remind us that the always thinly staffed legion of competence is now threatened with depopulation or, as was seen when Wilfred Sheed replaced Dwight Macdonald at *Esquire* and Pauline Kael took over Stanley Kauffmann's post at *The New Republic*, with specious new recruits.

As a novelist and book or theater critic, Wilfred Sheed has behind him an estimable body of work. As a film critic, he has nothing—either in experience or rumination—a fact that he candidly admitted in his first *Esquire* piece. Despite his avowed respect for Antonioni's other films, his review of *Blow-Up* expresses nearly ruthless contempt. Much of the piece is not about the film at all, concentrating its attention instead (complete with feeble jokes about old musicals that Sheed *does* know), on Rex Reed's interview with Antonioni in the *Times*. The rest of his review repeats Judith Crist's complaint that Antonioni let a good story get away, Richard Goldstein's complaint that Antonioni didn't really capture London, and the blank raving about "surface beauty" that characterizes most other reviews. Finding the symbolism "non-organic" and the ideas banal, Sheed disdains to argue either point.

Such offenses against criticism are compounded in Miss Kael's review by offenses against taste, logic and the reader's patience. In a piece so staggeringly verbose that one cannot, as in Sheed's case, attribute the lack of argument to lack of space, Miss Kael serves up that combination of personal exhibitionism, obsession with fashion, and irrelevant inside dope that has become her special ragout. She reviews not the film but the audience.[4]

> Will *Blow-Up* be taken seriously in 1968 only by the same sort of cultural diehards who are still sending out five-page single-spaced letters on their interpretation of Marienbad? (No two are alike, no one interesting.) It has some of the Marienbad appeal: a friend phones for your opinion and when you tell him you didn't care for it, he says, "You'd better see it again, I was at a swinging party the other night

134

and it's all anybody ever talked about!" (Was there ever a good movie that everybody was talking about?) It probably won't blow over because it also has the *Morgan!-Georgy Girl* appeal; people identify with so strongly, they get *upset* if you don't like it—as if you were rejecting not just the movie but *them*. And in a way they're right, because if you don't accept the peculiarly slugged consciousness of *Blow-Up*, you *are* rejecting something in them. Antonioni's new mixture of suspense with vagueness and confusion seems to have the kind of numbing fascination for them that they associate with art and intellectuality, and they are responding to it as *their* film—and hence as a masterpiece.

Two bad reviews by two irresponsible critics prove little; but when we search for alternatives, the point gets made. There are frequently fewer interesting plays or books in a given season than interesting films. Yet I think the *Blow-Up* controversy suggests how ill-equipped American criticism is to discuss them. With the exceptions of John Simon and Stanley Kauffmann, who recently returned to *The New Republic*, there are at the moment, no aesthetically sophisticated and informed guides available for the growing audience that seeks enlightenment about films. Of the journalistic film reviewers, there is scarcely one to be taken seriously. The mass magazines used to employ men like Agee or Macdonald, but such critics have been ill-replaced. Smaller film quarterlies (when they last long enough to be useful) are made up either by film buffs capable, like the *Cahiers du Cinéma*, of ontological analysis of Jerry Lewis, or they bear the same relationship to live film criticism that a philological journal bears to the vital discussion of books.

Artists like Antonioni will continue to progress, unperturbed by widespread ignorance. (Moreover, they will prosper; *Variety* says *Blow-Up* is "k.o.") But scores of interested viewers will be left behind.

(1968–1969)

135

BONNIE AND CLYDE

A BUNCH OF decayed cabbage leaves smeared with catsup, *Bonnie and Clyde* has been judged an artistic bouquet; not by middlebrow critics like Bosley Crowther but by reviewers whose very names stand for the setting and guiding of taste. Admittedly, the film is well-acted, slickly paced, and brilliantly edited. Yet after granting its technical polish, one is left with its meaning, which is heavily obvious when not confused; its tone and characterization, which are both implausible and inconsistent; and its violence, which is stomach-turning. One who measures its cynical falsity will realize how worrisome is its success.

To begin with, *Bonnie and Clyde* is presumed to be making serious comments about crime. So far as I can see, the comments are these: crime is joyless, it is sick, it is less concerned with money than fame. As an example of the first point, we have the scene at a motel in which Clyde's brother hoots and hollers, "Whooee, we'll have ourselves a time."—Long pause—"What we gonna do?"—followed by Clyde's account of how he avoided prison work by cutting off two toes, concluded with a broad smile and an "Ain't life grand!" To establish the bankrobber's sickness, we have at least four instances of Clyde's impotence that presumably explain his reliance on more lethal weapons. By way of asserting that the criminals seek publicity rather than gain, we have the Barrows stealing a newspaper from a rural mailbox before they count the proceeds from their latest bank. It is difficult to understand how insights so dramatized can be taken seriously; but Joseph Morgenstern, who on first viewing thought *Bonnie and Clyde* "a squalid shoot-'em-up for the moron trade," acknowledged great purposiveness and subtlety when *Newsweek* permitted him a public reversal the following week.

Viewers might well find themselves confused, for the film shuttles back and forth between radically different tones. Through most of the gang's activities, fast pacing and banjo music contrive to turn mayhem into zaniness and the bloody Barrows into charming hicks; but, in addition to being primitive, these scenes violate characterization and plausibility. Take, for example, Clyde's first bank robbery. As Bonnie drives him to the site of the crime, he seems as nervous as a raw recruit, yet we know that he has already served time for what he here contemplates with dread. (One might argue that this shows Clyde to be a frightened punk, but usually, as in the woods or the café before this job, he is made to seem authoritative, even sensitive.) When Bonnie finally shames him into action, he discovers that the bank is out of business. Considerately, the management has left a teller behind to inform him of the fact; but, of course, without the teller, there would be no comedy. Even more absurd is their second job, during which the get-away man, C.W. Moss, nearly ruins everything by backing into a parking place—guided less by his own stupidity than by the scriptwriters' desire for laughs. Eventually Moss pulls out, but his delay permits the bank's employees to chase him. Here the film turns suddenly gory, a fact that has occasioned its admirers' most sophistical argument.

Pauline Kael asserts that the comedy purposefully turns into violence in order to implicate the viewer, who will be harrowed when he realizes that crime isn't, after all, fun: "the whole point of *Bonnie and Clyde* is to rub our noses in it, to make us pay our dues for laughing." What Miss Kael neglects to admit is that we laugh only because the director and writers have forced us—by wrenching their materials to fit a comic mold. Penelope Gilliatt recognizes that "the movie is full of scenes of giggling and show-off, but the mood belongs to the characters, not the film." One would be interested to see how she might go about arguing this distinction.

When sexually motivating the protagonists' crimes—that is to say, when introducing psychology to tone matters up—the film becomes not only implausible but dishonest. Scenarists David Newman and Robert Benton have recently confessed that Clyde was originally to have been homosexual rather than impotent, "but we [made the change] because homosexuality took over the whole movie and colored all responses." Translated less ingenuously, this comes out: whereas homosexuality repels the average spectator, impotence is likely to make him sympathetic. After all, Clyde is a hero.

Similarly motivated are the many hints that Bonnie and Clyde were heroes because America was undergoing a Depression. This note is first struck when Clyde invites a dispossessed farmer to shoot the sign placed before his house by the bank. Throughout the film, its director and set designer take great trouble duplicating the thirties in order to surround the Barrows with an ambience of social decay so palpable that mere presence might suggest causality. Thus we are disposed to believe Clyde when he promises Bonnie's mother that they will stop stealing as soon as times improve, and we can sympathize when the couple is forced to steal food because the bank they had previously attempted had already failed. But apart from the offensive facility with which it yokes public circumstance and private crime, occasionally the film argues against its own implication. Before they are killed, for example, when Bonnie asks Clyde what he would do with his life to live over, after an intense moment of concentration, he replies that he would pull his jobs in other states.

Bonnie and Clyde runs off in many directions at once (even Pauline Kael, who runs off in quite a few herself, calls it at one point, "the first film demonstration that the put-on can be used for the purposes of art"). Yet though all of its admirers are aware that the film might be called wayward, they either de-emphasize or ignore its banal confusion. But since *Bonnie and Clyde* is so confused, its violence shows all the more lurid against the vague thematic background. The interesting questions to raise about the film therefore are why so many reputable critics condone violence lacking expressive purpose and why customers are willing to pay for a movie both repulsive in its bloodshed and disorienting in its tonal shifts. What holds the film together for these groups who themselves form so unexpected a combination?

We can approach an answer by way of the movie's most discussed episode. When Bonnie returns to her mother, the director shoots the scene in soft focus, emphasizing not only the dusty atmosphere in which it transpires but the haze of nostalgia and family feeling through which its participants perceive themselves. Bonnie's family is delighted to welcome the returning prodigals; they have kept a scrapbook of the gang's exploits. Bonnie romps with the children; Clyde, the good son-in-law, enjoys the vittles. We might be witnessing the family picnic of all our dreams—until Bonnie's mother tells her daughter and Clyde to keep on running from the cops. This ironic reversal, however, is too pat and unsurprising to dissipate the foregoing effect of lyricism, especially since the picnic is preceded by another scene of lyricism so fruity that we are now thoroughly confused. In the earlier scene, Clyde pursues Bonnie as she flees the gang to make her way home. Catching up with her in a golden wheatfield, he wails plaintively, "Please don't never leave me without sayin' nuttin." Accompanied by soulful music, the loving couple embraces, while the camera draws back, leaving them a poor tangled speck in a giant sea of grain over which portentous clouds glide, casting shadows. Under the circumstances, this might seem a sick joke: casting the crooks—previously clowns or desperadoes—in the roles of Mr. Newly-wed and the young wife who wants to run home to mother. But like several other scenes, it creates unmistakable identification between the Barrows and the audience; and it is this identification which holds the spectator. Then, having persuaded the audience to identify with the Barrows, the film goes on to suggest that the crooks are superior to society. Here the serious critics seem to have found their delight.

It may seem tedious to recall the many ways in which the film slanders society, but I don't think one can understand its current popularity until this motif has been explored. Its presentation is relentless, beginning when the hungry but penniless Clyde attempts to steal groceries. While he inquires after peach pie, a piggish clerk flies down at him with a meat cleaver, thus nearly validating his subsequent chagrin: "He tried to kill me. I didn' wanna hurt him. You try to get somep'n to eat round here, they come at you with a meat cleaver." Throughout the film, the forces of property and law respond with excessive, even sadistic zeal. Not only do they require 1000 rounds of ammunition to finish the lovers off but when the gang tries to settle down in tidy domesticity, the cops intrude without even the chivalrous warning one has come to expect from earlier gangster movies ("All right, come out now; the house is surrounded!"). Ambushing the Barrows at a motel, the police unfairly arrive in an armored car at just the moment when Bonnie is showing Clyde how she has taken in an old dress; and when they kill Clyde's brother by surrounding him as he's down, the deputies shout like Comanche savages, in whose classic formation they have been staged. Yet though the besieged gang kills its share, the lawmen, unlike the criminals, never bleed.

If we turn our attention to the Barrows' only differentiated antagonists, the film's bias becomes unmistakable. The sheriff who finally kills the lovers sports a devilish mustache and, in the death scene, wears a black shirt, though everything about Bonnie and Clyde, including their car, is white. Critics have admired the film's insight into the crooks' pathetic desire for publicity. Sheriff Hamer is similarly motivated, but in his case the impulse is bad: he goes after Bonnie and Clyde out of vengeance, because they humiliated him by circulating the photo in which they forced him to pose as their captive.

Because the gang's antagonists are pigs and devils who wear black shirts and don't bleed, and because they have formed a society actually inferior to that of the criminals, in which brotherhood and love predominate, we can sympathize with the Barrows, even though they are hard to keep in rational focus. But because the criminals are sick, dumb, and ludicrous, we can bear to watch them die. Citing this latter characteristic, Pauline Kael argues that *Bonnie and Clyde* is less sentimental than standard Hollywood gangster films because they used to make the criminals innocent. But in drama, if not in life, innocence is relative. The movie clearly authorizes Bonnie's doggerel characterization of herself and Clyde as scapegoats whom society will not leave in peace.

At no time is the film's comedy more heavily thematic than when the gang kidnaps the couple, Eugene and Velma. By turns, we are treated to exposures of the couple's prurience, cowardice, and secret regard for crime. Though blatant, all this has some relevance. Why though, do we get the revelation that Velma has lied to Eugene about her age? For the same reason that the respectable Mr. Moss, who will betray Bonnie and Clyde, shouts at his son, "I'm glad that your ma ain't alive to see this thing," meaning not C.W.'s crime but his tattoo. And for the same reason that the one member of the gang who is disloyal, dishonest, and greedy is Blanche—the preacher's daughter.

Thereby forced into partisanship, a spectator can actually approve the blood as the red badge of Bonnie and Clyde's undeserved suffering. Critics, of course, have found something deeper in it. More or less overt in every favorable review is the notion that *Bonnie and Clyde* makes a valid comment not so much on their lives as on ours. We know better than the thirties that violence may substitute for love, that it is often perpetrated by moral morons, that America today incites violence by its disrespect for law and people. "All this should strike the viewer with icy familiarity," asserts Robert Hatch (an editor of *The Nation*) "in our day of motorcycle gangs and flower children, Nazi insignia, cheap beads, incense, drugs, apathy and motiveless violence." Whereas the audience probably identifies with Bonnie and Clyde as surrogate social victims, serious reviewers identify them as surrogate social problems. No wonder, despite the bloodshed, that everyone is happy.

But the movie's inventors give a less edifying account of their product's appeal: violence in the arts, they say, is "fun," "and if that idea causes you to blanch or cluck the tongue reprovingly . . . then you are not only soft . . . you are something worse: out of step." As Pauline Kael reports with equanimity, "in the spoofs of the last few years, everything is gross, ridiculous, insane; to make sense would be to risk being square."

Ironically, whereas Newman and Benton (creators of *Esquire's* "What's In and What's Out" and Dubious Achievement Awards) think violence fun and significance a drag, reviewers and moviegoers have, through their earnest pursuit of the movie's purpose, turned *Bonnie and Clyde* into the year's most successful and—the ads bray —"most talked-about film." This irony is the true key to the film's meaning, for as *Newsweek* reports, Newman and Benton "always seem to know what's going to pop up next in American culture."

Lurid example of a vulgar, wornout genre, *Bonnie and Clyde* nevertheless seems up-to-date. Not because of its technique, out of Godard and the vaudeville blackout; not because of its ideas, out of *Sanctuary* (the impotent gunman) or Erik Erikson (the identity crisis), but because of an attitude which persuades the viewer to swallow its violence: the attitude—it is precisely nothing more—that society and normality are frauds. Since this is close to having become a contemporary article of faith, it is no wonder that violence has become as entertaining in art as it seems to have become excusable in politics. Oppose the latter, and you are a soft-hearted liberal; oppose the former, and you are "something worse: out of step."

That Bosley Crowther is "out of step" should come as no surprise. When for once, however, he marched slowly in a good cause, he brought down upon his head anger so fierce that we can now see how precious a possession the film's attitude has become. Thus Penelope Gilliat, obviously thinking of Crowther, said that one would need "a head full of wooden shavings" to think that the movie glamorized crime, though if the word "glamorize" is correctly understood it is entirely to the point. Thus Pauline Kael, obviously thinking of Crowther, begins her piece in a manner uniquely wistful: "How do you make a good movie in this country without being jumped on?" (Miss Kael, it should be explained, thinks "*Bonnie and Clyde* . . . the most excitingly American movie since *The Manchurian Candidate!*") Thus Andrew Sarris felt called upon to begin his review in *The Village Voice* by informing readers that "*Bonnie and Clyde* has become the subject of a Crowther crusade that makes the 100-Years-War look like a border incident" (a remark whose inaptness would inspire hyperbole had Sarris not already pre-empted the heights). In fact, so enraged is Sarris that he charges poor Crowther with a crime of which Crowther was manifestly innocent: calling for censorship, "at a time when too many bigots see a golden opportunity to lash the Negro with fake rhetoric of law and order."

Sarris' absurd political analogy suggests the covertly political basis of most of the film's support, a phenomenon even more strikingly displayed by the irate letter-writers who bombarded the *Times* after Crowther's review appeared. But at the same time that the film's attitude suggests affinities with some current political notions, its supporters don't want it taken too seriously. One almost hears them tremble: if the establishment really sees what is going on in *Bonnie and Clyde* they may spoil the fun by taking it away from us! Thus, after coming to realize that its use of violence was relevant, Joseph Morgenstern spins about to assert that "when we talk about movies, even artistic movies, we are not talking about urban-renewal programs, nuclear nonproliferation treaties or rat-control bills." Yet Morgenstern then goes on to argue that the film's violence takes its significance from the fact that "most of humanity teeters on the edge of violence every day."

Does *Bonnie and Clyde* have political or social significance far beyond its significance as a work of art? To answer "yes" is not to contend that the film incites acts directly, for against such a contention Morgenstern would be right and Sarris would have reason to fear thought control. But art initiates action in more subtle ways: by reflecting contemporary attitudes and thus, through the power of reflection, confirming them. How much more potent is this process when performed by a piece of mass entertainment.

It would be foolish to equate the growing approval of violence, even among humane and liberal persons, with the specific advocacy of a bloodthirsty, cheap film. Those who riot against conditions in the Negro ghetto or the war in Vietnam can claim precisely the moral validation for their acts which the Barrow Gang so conspicuously lacks. But each form of behavior embodies a similar lapse of commitment to organized society, and in accepting one we may find ourselves accepting the other. Each expresses the underlying belief that society represents not law and order but only convention and force. When society is no longer felt to represent legitimacy, protest itself becomes the only legitimate response. But with standards of legitimacy confounded, the criminal may seem to resemble the rebel, the hippie to merge with the reformer. Surely *Bonnie and Clyde* did not produce society's current disrepute or our desperate reaching out for any alternative. Just as surely, by playing with the disrepute it exploits the desperation, helping us to celebrate what we once condemned.

If seeing the film as a reflection of larger social issues seems far-fetched, I commend the reader's attention to an important study of the German expressionist film after World War I: Siegfried Kracauer's *From Caligari to Hitler* (Princeton, 1947; reissued, 1966). Assuming that movies are an index to national mentality because they are collectively produced and massively consumed, Kracauer traces through the period's chief films the rise of Nazism. In short, he implies that popular entertainment acts as a national fever chart. In the thirties in Germany, the disease was authoritarianism; in the sixties in America, it is anarchy. Through the stream of anarchic art which flows high and low in our culture today, *Bonnie and Clyde* thrashes prominently, its protagonists folk heroes in a national epic struggle.

The day after I saw the film, at the school where I teach—a very good school with intelligent students from comfortable homes—I saw scrawled on a bathroom wall, "C.W. in '68." If this example of collegiate graffiti is portentous to even a small degree, then investigating the importance of *Bonnie and Clyde* can't be left to reviewers.

(1968)

143

PUPPETS: FROM Z TO
ZABRISKIE POINT

FOR the serious filmgoer, this is a bad time. If he can find anything not obviously trash (a skin flick, a youth valentine, the latest Godard-icy), it will likely prove a specious cliché tarted up with zooms and flash pans or edited on the chopping block. Z and *M*A*S*H*—the season's most prestigious hits—typify this genre.

Thrillingly packaged with fast intercutting and bouzouki music, Z also excites audiences because of its timely subject. However, although its villains are Greek generals responsible for the recent *coup*, they might as well be Western gunmen faced down by Gary Cooper (as Charles Brooks points out in the May *Commentary*). Trying to redeem an old melodramatic formula through allusion to politics, Z proves utterly devious. Its plot records an emotionally satisfying victory for the "good guys" and then tacks on an epilogue to remind us that *actually* the villains are still in power. Yet this, too, is undercut when the fade-out tells us what the letter Z means: revolutionary fervor cannot die. Unsurprisingly, this film is so popular that a dubbed version had to be rushed into production—for even the less literate want to share the contradictory pleasures of suffering the Greek tragedy at secondhand (thus bearing witness painlessly) and of assuring themselves that it will pass (while being helped to forget how little our government has done toward that end). Z is thrilling all right, but not for its suspense.

Pauline Kael maintains that *M*A*S*H* is thrilling because it "talks dirty." And so it does, about normally sacrosanct topics like Duty and God. It also talks dirty about War, by not talking about war at all even though it transpires in the midst of one. The mad scapegraces of *M*A*S*H* plot practical jokes and shack up with each other over the bleeding bodies of soldiers they are supposed to heal. Many critics, therefore, have taken the film as "black comedy," a demonstration that war is brutal and absurd. Instead, *M*A*S*H* is no more concerned about war than are its characters; the comic antics are authentic, whereas, in effect, the bleeding soldiers are props. One might as easily argue that *Some Like It Hot* was meant to expose the gangland murders and sexual ambiguities with which it comically surrounded Tony Curtis and Jack Lemmon (whose opposite numbers in *M*A*S*H* are Donald Sutherland and Elliott Gould). Each film asks us to laugh at aggression and opportunism. But whereas Hollywood's formulas haven't changed, the cultural climate has: today opportunism and aggression are deemed revolutionary, so long as they are openly displayed, because everyone is culpable, although less candid. Only if you take that as an article of faith can you find *M*A*S*H* anything more than a fitfully amusing piece of college humor, performed and directed with an insouciance appropriate to its modest budget.

Dismayed by the season's "best" films (Costa-Gavras' *Z* won an Academy Award for best foreign film; a process reversed when Robert Altman's *M*A*S*H* won the *Palme D'Or* at Cannes), I decided to devote this column to the work of more esteemed filmmakers—Federico Fellini, François Truffaut, Ingmar Bergman and Michelangelo Antonioni—each of whom recently opened a new film in New York. Four works misbegotten by masters create for the serious filmgoer not merely a "bad time" but something of a cinematic crisis.

In Fellini's case, the crisis seems largely personal, although several of his remarks might make one think otherwise. To an interviewer from the New York *Times*, he asserted that his *Satyricon* lacks meaning in the conventional sense of the term; when pressed for elaboration, he hid behind the film's appeal to youth, who presumably share his hatred of words. Such comments help us to understand why *Fellini Satyricon* is popular; one must look elsewhere to learn why it fails.

From the beginning, Fellini's work has revealed a complex attitude toward his favorite subjects: fantasy, spectacle and theater. His first film (*Variety Lights*), which he coauthored and codirected, tells of a provincial girl who takes up with a tacky vaudeville troupe. Because she unscrupulously exploits its leading comedian to further her career, she inspires a contempt that throws our sympathy to the vaudevillians, who would otherwise seem only ludicrous. The resulting balance between satire and sympathy characterizes Fellini at his best.

This balance underlies his greatest films: *The White Sheik*, a comedy about *fumetti* (live-action comic strips), and *I vitelloni*, about the fantasies of some small-town loafers. In each case, Fellini mocks the phony dreams that seduce his simpletons, while at the same time providing poignant evidence that their barren lives might make tinsel seem gold.

But between *I vitelloni* and his next feature a shift occurred. With

La Strada, Fellini begins to imagine the star-struck dupe as a divine innocent and the theatrical antagonist as a downright villain. This melodramatic perspective suits a parable like *La Strada*, but it wrecks *Il Bidone* and almost wrecks *The Nights of Cabiria*. In *La Dolce Vita*, Fellini sees in glamor nothing more than corruption. His new moralism, however, is oddly indistinguishable from prurience. Passing over the problematic 8½, we find Fellini's prurience gone wild, so that in *Juliet of the Spirits*, the theatricalism that was formerly his subject becomes a lurid method. From the empty circus of *Juliet*, it was but a short step to the freak show of *Fellini Satyricon*.

Or, as Fellini would have it, to the dream. In an interview with Alberto Moravia, he said that his film was designed to have "the enigmatic transparency, the indecipherable clarity of dreams." Instead, Fellini has produced almost the opposite: a film the general meaning of which is clear while the details (sometimes literally) are fog-bound.

Only the conception can be understood; to Fellini, ancient Rome equals orgies, cruelties and sacrilege: in short, *La Dolce Vita* pushed back two thousand years. But *Fellini Satyricon* lacks even the minimal verisimilitude of its prototype. As a result, we rarely know why any one of the characters goes anywhere or why he acts as he does when he arrives. All we comprehend is that his action is meant to be disreputable. Surely a zeal for thematic clarity lies behind Fellini's few additions to his source in Petronius. Thus a nymphomaniac tied to a cart and wheeled about in search of assuagement tells us that Roman hedonism is self-punishing, just as the scene in a hermaphrodite's cave shows us that Roman religion is futile.

When a sequence seems designed to make a somewhat different point, Fellini blurs the distinction. So he makes the Villa of the Suicides a placid, elegant place where a patrician kills himself, presumably to seek a better world (compare Steiner in *La Dolce Vita*); but he stages the suicide in a way that makes it scarcely less bloody than what it is meant to counterpoint. Similarly, when the hero Encolpius tries to have his virility restored in The Garden of Delights, Fellini employs the same species of painted harridans and deformed servants who populate less delectable spheres.

Nothing appears redundant to Fellini if it can inspire revulsion. The printed script shows that one of the few scenes he elaborated in production was the visit to the hermaphrodite, to which he added a Lourdes-worth of cripples. Perhaps we need to see an actor's hand chopped off in the early sequence of Vernacchio's play to learn how indifferent a Roman audience was to suffering. But why must a lamb's throat be cut before Encolpius marries Lichas, and why must its blood be carried in a bowl by a deformed dwarf, as if we didn't already get the point that it is kinky for one male to wed another?

Fellini is in a sweat to show us that Rome is terrible, although that doesn't keep him from exploiting its vices. How foreign this is to Petronius, who documents his fellow Romans with the neutral high spirits of intelligence—exactly as Fellini documented *his* Romans in earlier films. Now Fellini has become a sort of Savonarola, but at least that ancestor had a real world to inveigh against. Fellini, on the other hand, is heavily moralistic about a figment of his imagination. Although misunderstanding the implication, Fellini delivered the definitive critique of *Satyricon* when he reported that his historical researches were undertaken to help him forget the actual Rome and that the real inspiration for his dream of ancient malefaction was the cinema.

But whereas cinema usually permits a convincing re-creation of reality and externalization of motives, Fellini makes it difficult for one to believe what is going on. Why, for example, does a platform piled high with immobile people pass by an open window in the art gallery sequence? Why are Trimalchio's guests seen in phalanx formation in some gigantic pool? (Are they too poor to bathe at home? If so, how could so snobbish a host have invited them? Are they there for group sex? If so, why don't they turn toward each other?) Why do they hop up and down when Trimalchio enters? Why does the ghetto crumble after Ascyltus leaves with Giton? Why is a monstrous fish hauled on Lichas' barge? Why is Encolpius beaten to restore his potency? Why does anything happen in this film? Because Fellini wanted the effect.

Yet effects are consistently bungled. Through much of the film, as in the early montage of a red-light district, things go by so fast that we must be assiduous if we want to perceive them. When Lichas is decapitated, Fellini ruins the powerful image of his head sinking into the sea by preceding it with the fall of an obvious dummy. Encolpius begins the film by declaiming at such a pitch that we suspect him of being crazy. And what are we to think of Ascyltus, who delivers his first speech while crawling on all fours toward or away from the camera? The actors babble in different languages, and Fellini dubs them asynchronously. At one time, he attributed this seeming error

to his desire for Brechtian distance, but elsewhere he gave a less ingenuous reason for the effect: *Satyricon* was made with relatively little
money.

Heavy-handed in meaning, simultaneously garish and obscure in
detail, Fellini's dream is only self-referring. If it succeeds at all in
reaching the audience, credit must go to the designers, scene painters,
costumers and make-up men. Characteristic techniques appear—from
lavish parades to constant panning—but, of Fellini's talent, all that
remains is a casting director's instinct for faces. Formerly the faces
belonged to people. Now they are masks, grotesquely painted and
randomly hung in a carpentered space utterly devoid of human relevance.

In some ways, Truffaut's new film is no less vulnerable to criticism.
Like *Fellini Satyricon, Mississippi Mermaid* raids its creator's previous
work. Its theme and heroine wanly reflect prototypes in *Jules and Jim*;
a principal scene, in which the hero undresses his lover while she
pretends to sleep, comes from *The Soft Skin*; the final locale is borrowed from *Shoot the Piano Player*, and its snowfalls from *Fahren-
heit 451*; the very footage from the hero's dream in a hospital seems
to have been reproduced from the last film.

Also, like *Fellini Satyricon*, Truffaut's film violates its source. But
Fellini desecrated a classic; Truffaut doesn't desecrate enough,
doesn't subvert his trashy detective story as he formerly subverted
pulp novels to produce the tragicomic masterpiece, *Shoot the Piano
Player*, and that underrated morality play, *The Bride Wore Black*.

On its face, this new plot is no more preposterous than the others.
A rich French planter engages a mail-order bride and finds, to his delight, that she is lovelier than her photograph. Smitten with the girl,
he gives her access to his bank account, only to have her rob him and
flee. After discovering that she had also helped murder his original
fiancée, he hires a detective to track her down; but when he does so
himself, he is forced to admit that his hunt was inspired not by vengeance but by love. Because he loves her, he kills the detective who
now threatens their future. Nonetheless, the couple doesn't get on
well, and she tries to eliminate him with rat poison. When he reveals
that he knows of her intentions, love, formerly repressed but now
energized by guilt, wells up in her; and the two establish a relationship, mingling joy and pain, that, in Truffaut's view, typifies all
romance.

Truffaut is very deliberate about turning his thriller into a love story. Late in the film, his couple leaves a cinema where they had just seen the Nicholas Ray Western, *Johnny Guitar* (a *Cahiers du Cinéma* classic; *Mississippi Mermaid* is full of such private references, *comme il Truffaut*). "You're right," the girl says, "it's not a film about horses." "Yes," he replies, "it's a film about people and feelings." To which she responds, "They [the film's stars] were both wonderful."

Unfortunately, in addition to being physically unbelievable in their roles, Catherine Deneuve and Jean-Paul Belmondo are not wonderful, and so cannot transform Truffaut's cops-and-robbers story into a study of people and feelings. Belmondo can climb balconies, as he does in a long, irrelevant scene that is merely in the film to let him perform his specialty; but he cannot convey the depth of obsessive love. Miss Deneuve cannot convey anything, although she is beautiful and has lovely breasts (which Truffaut halts the film twice to display). We can imagine a man desiring her, but she is too boring to inspire such maniacal fidelity.

That Truffaut threw his film away on two vapid stars suggests a hypersensitivity to cinematic conventions, which produces on the one hand his serious parodies endowing old forms with life, and on the other his tendency to confuse life with movies. *Shoot the Piano Player*, for example, can use a Humphrey Bogart mannerism to expose its hero's willed isolation; *Mississippi Mermaid* treats movie mannerisms as inherently meaningful. Dedicated to Jean Renoir, it begins by illustrating the history of Belmondo's island home through a film from *La Marseillaise*, as if Renoir's film were indeed a document and not a fiction. Later, when Truffaut masks the sides of his screen during an important love scene between his principals, we are reminded—superfluously in so incredible a story—that, after all, we are only watching a film.

This effect is heightened by Truffaut's emphasis not on the intricacies of his characters—that is, on what makes fiction seem relevant to life—but on the hoary conventions and coincidences of its plot. Yet his film is obviously not designed as a thriller; at many points it does turn stereotypes into interesting people. After Belmondo kills the detective, for example, Deneuve, who had consistently dominated her husband by either offering or withholding sex, loses herself and insists that he take her without disrobing. Later, when he awakens from postcoital sleep, he is disturbed to find her in the kitchen, eating oranges. Or we have the lovely scene at Aix in which Belmondo explains the poignancy of having revealed his dream in a want ad. Consigned to real actors, this love story might have worked. Had the girl's dormant emotions been suggested earlier, we might have believed the release of love by guilt.

Unlike Fellini's, Truffaut's theme is a good one. Except for his principals, each of his characters is lifelike, which can be said for none of Fellini's. Consider, in the Truffaut film, the murdered girl's sister, a hard-nosed Frenchwoman with darting eyes. She pridefully refuses to let Belmondo pay the entire fee when both consult the detective. As Belmondo begins to sign his check, the camera cuts to her face while it trembles between frugality and suspicion. Finally she bursts out with her belief that this is no time for him to be gallant. The camera then draws back for a medium shot as both persons begin to write. Still distracted by conflicting emotions, she has difficulty getting her pen to work.

Matching such triumphs of staging are the editing of certain sequences. When Belmondo discovers that Deneuve has fled, he drives frantically in search of his banker. The camera frames his head and shoulders while his automobile negotiates a corniche, and we hear on the sound track the conversation he will later have at the bank. This departure from realism enlivens a scene that would have been routine if actually dramatized; it is psychologically right that Belmondo's anxiety elide the time between starting out and arriving at his destination; and asynchronous dramatization makes more comic the final dialogue: "How much did I have in the bank?" "28,000,000 francs." "How much did Madame withdraw?" "27,850,000. I will need *your* authorization to close the account."

Fellini's film turns a sour grimace of content into a lurid smile of execution, self-regarding and self-important. By comparison, Truffaut tells a nearly meaningful story with a set of inadequate dolls. But if his primitive puppets are hardly more intense than Fellini's baroque masks, they at least intimate some general truth.

General truths are Ingmar Bergman's stock-in-trade. Other directors surpass him in mastery of form or produce individual films that are richer in both thought and feeling, but no one else has created an *œuvre* unified by a comprehensive view of life. Occasionally portentous, sometimes naïvely solemn, Bergman's seriousness nevertheless demands our respect. Unlike Fellini, he could never be guilty of sensationalism, nor could he, like Truffaut, waste his artistry on trifles. (Who but Bergman can be grimly meaningful even in farce?) Although he has produced more bad films than any director of comparable stature, he has also produced more great ones (*The Naked*

Night, Persona, Shame, Winter Light), and more fine ones (*Smiles of a Summer Night, Wild Strawberries, The Magician*).

For these reasons, and because he seemed with *Persona* to have entered his greatest period, the failure of his latest film is dispiriting. Whenever I see a Bergman opus like *The Passion of Anna*, I am reminded of an old skit in which Nancy Walker played a beleaguered ballet dancer, among whose many torments was a boyfriend with a solution looking for a problem. Similarly, Bergman formulates answers and then casts about for characters capable of putting the right question. In the new film, we can locate the exact moment at which these characters fail.

The Passion of Anna begins with a ravishing shot of sheep crossing a meadow and then cuts to a terra-cotta roof being worked on by the hero, Andreas Winkelman (Max von Sydow). In voice-over, he introduces himself, while we discover him through action. Persuaded by the eloquent realism with which his chores are shot that this is a happy workman, we are slightly disturbed when the brilliant sunset he stops to watch ominously clouds over. But the sound of sheep bells and the sight of his heavy instep on a ladder rung renew our sense that we are watching a man in his element. Then a cement bucket falls. He picks it up. It falls again. He leaves it there. Although comically, the image of perfect attunement is shattered. Subsequently, it is shattered again by his fruitless contact with an old peddler Johan, and by Anna, who intrudes on his resumed labor. She asks to use his telephone and, although he mimes his shame, he listens in on her conversation. Tearfully, she begs the man she called to give her some of the money left by her late husband. Apparently the man refuses, and when the call is finished she breaks down. Recovering herself, she takes leave of Andreas, but we see how deep an impression she has made. Then, when we feel we have the hero and the plot in focus, a clapstick is struck, and we leave both to hear Max von Sydow discuss his role. "It is very difficult for an actor," he says, "to express a man who is expressionless."

When Bergman stops his story to interview his star, we immediately recall that uneasiness about art is a characteristic theme, which can be traced from his first original script (*Prison*, 1948), through the troubled apologia of *The Magician* (1958), to a magnificent climax in *Persona* (1966). But *Persona* dramatizes Bergman's self-doubt; in *The Passion of Anna* Bergman's doubt serves rather to explain his failure to dramatize. An actor should be able to express expressionlessness or, at least, to try, just as a writer (Bergman) should try to create, not assert, his characters. In *The Passion of Anna* Bergman has not devised enough scenes to fill in the outline of Andreas Winkelman, so he and Max von Sydow must sit around discussing him.

The film is full of expedients replacing drama: there are interviews with three other principal actors, much voice-over narration, and the kind of "key lines" that make one smile at Bergman's incorrigible rhetoric. Worse, all these are unnecessary, for the plot is inherently rich.

Andreas was driven to his island retreat by legal difficulties and a failed marriage. Anna's appearance makes him come out of himself when he finds a letter, written to her by her husband, which shows that she too married badly. But when he tries to return the letter, and thus becomes involved with her friends, he discovers her passionate denial of the truth. Anna's friends aren't well-married either, and Andreas drifts into a casual affair with the wife, Eva. Shortly afterwards, however, he takes up with Anna, although they too have problems.

A subplot triggers the conclusion. On the island, animals are being mysteriously tortured or killed, and Johan, although innocent, is punished for the crimes. When Johan tells Andreas the latter is his only friend, Andreas seems disgusted at his own moral pretensions and releases his disgust by attacking Anna. A brutal fight ensues. She acknowledges his charge of false romanticism, but they can never again come together. So the film ends with him, standing alone, decomposing through an optical effect, as narration tells us that he is her second victim.

Unfortunately, key connections in the plot are missing. We never learn why Andreas committed the crimes that sent him into hiding or what bearing they have on his character. We never understand why Eva comes to him for comfort or why (if?) their affair caused him to live with Anna. Some symbolic connection may be inferred between plot and subplot—the humans are sometimes compared to animals and both are presumably tortured by an unidentifiable force—but the distinctions are too great to make the inference seem valid. And if we accept it, what is the function of Johan's ordeal? It illustrates human cruelty, the waywardness of human justice, but what do those matters have to do with the film's featured wickedness: the ironic moral bullying of Anna's romanticism? Is Bergman saying nothing more than that the world in which Johan suffers can't support a view like Anna's? If so, he is both redundant (the film is full of such suffering) and excessive (Johan's experience is to painful to prove a point so obvious).

Because of these vague connections, the ending—although photographically powerful—seems pretentious. Surely we can't expect the couple to stay together after so roundly exposing each other, but why must they part in so operatic a fashion? And in what sense has Andreas been her victim? Bergman does not even show us enough of their life together to dramatize causality, if indeed there is any warrant for it.

He doesn't take the time because he is too busy alluding to other characteristic themes. In a brilliant dinner party sequence—awash in tones of gold and conviviality—Eva suddenly brings up the question of whether she believes in God, who appears here much as Hitchcock appears in one of *his* films—as a trademark. Later, her husband gives Andreas a lecture on the falsities of photography and on the viewer's responsibility for what he sees: matters that fascinate Bergman and relate to the actors' interviews but that have little to do with the plot. We are constantly reminded of Anna's duplicity through intercuts of her letter, a device that is artificially intrusive. Similarly, we discover the cause of Andreas' marital failure by an intercut sequence in which some woman—presumably his wife—accuses him, after intercourse, of having cancer of the soul. When Bergman cuts from this to Andreas, who says he's thinking of cancer, to which Anna replies, "I'm thinking of lies," the characters become puppets tangled up in Bergman's blatant strings.

Like *Fellini Satyricon* and *Mississippi Mermaid*, *The Passion of Anna* seems ultimately more a pastiche than an independent film. Bergman's work is self-referring—like Fellini's and Truffaut's—and therefore we expect a degree of repetition. But virtually everything in this film derives from an earlier—and better—appearance: the island setting and Anna's dream (both from *Shame*), some minor details, such as a moment when the couple watches a scene from Vietnam on TV (just as Elisabeth Vogler did in *Persona*), and even dialogue: Eva asks Andreas, "What is this deadly poison that daily corrodes the best in us, leaving only the shell?" just as twenty years earlier an unhappily married woman in *Prison* asked the man from whom she sought relief, "Did you ever think how life eats us away bit by bit?"

Such echoes wouldn't disturb us were the film more internally coherent, less of an omnium-gatherum. Still, much of what is gathered is first-rate. Chief among these is the superb color photography of Sven Nykvist, which makes *The Passion of Anna* a masterpiece in that regard. Moments in the film are immensely powerful: a dog appears suddenly in close-up dangling from a crude noose, its pathetic whimper an unanswerable indictment; after sleeping with Eva, Andreas moves aimlessly about his house, lies down in the middle distance, and howls like a wounded animal; exasperated by her romanticism, Andreas beats Anna so mercilessly that we almost echo her screams. Such moments, despite the story's fragmentation, create a reality more potent than Truffaut's or Fellini's. They coexist, however, with moments of rhetoric or abstraction with which they remain unintegrated. In *Persona*, Bergman created one of the cinema's few masterpieces in an abstract mode (the mode, *mutatis mutandis*, of writers like Kalka and Beckett). Then in *Shame* he made almost as great a film with realism (employing a modicum of abstraction only to extend his implications). *The Passion of Anna* lives uncomfortably between the two modes, borrowing promiscuously from Bergman's other films, and depending on Sven Nykvist's color to disguise the seams. As a result, it doesn't work; yet, if only because of the photography (this is Bergman's second film in color), it bears witness to the most astonishingly fruitful career in films. For that, one must be thankful.

By common consent, *Zabriskie Point* gives us scarcely anything to be thankful for. Of the four films featured here, only *Fellini Satyricon* is clearly inferior, but even it avoids some of the absurdities that earned Antonioni such contemptuous reviews. Why then do I give Antonioni pride of place? Because, despite manifold weaknesses, *Zabriskie Point* represents a radical attempt at revitalization. Whereas the other three directors, with varying results, imitate or parody themselves, Antonioni opts for transformation—a choice that is, at once, more promising for him and the medium.

In every sense, his latest film is a work-in-progress. This is literally true, not only because MGM excised a line of dialogue after it was greeted with derisory howls at the premiere, or because, in an attempt to boost sales, it added a rock-hymn to the ending, but because Antonioni himself seems to have been uncertain what form the film should take. Scripts were written, rewritten, discarded; the film was edited to excessive or deficient length and then reedited, uniquely for Antonioni, with outside help. He decided to release it, then hesitated, and had to be coaxed into going ahead by his producers. For a long while it looked as if the history of *Zabriskie Point* must eclipse the film.

But *Zabriskie Point* is a work-in-progress in a deeper sense. Heretofore, Antonioni's theme has been the running-down of modern culture. In contrast, *Zabriskie Point* contemplates the possibility of revival, and this shift in theme necessitated a shift in technique. Antonioni's previous films are almost documentary, showing his characters enacting dissolution, and asking that the viewer's eye fathom its meaning and cause. Now he employs a less realistic technique, more suitable to an optative vision. Unsurprisingly, he has not mastered the new mode, and *Zabriskie Point* succeeds only in suggesting what a satisfactory work in his new manner might look like.

Alone among the four directors, Antonioni's films have been wholly realistic. With the exception of *Red Desert*, none includes dreams, fantasies or suppositions. Significantly, the dream in *Red Desert* indicts dreaming. Showing Giuliana's false romanticizing of nature helps us to understand why she cannot adjust to the industrial world, for the dream's mood must be firmly outgrown for her to begin reintegration. In contrast, *Zabriskie Point* has two dream sequences; each is central and both are affirmed by the director.

Zabriskie Point is structured in three parts. In part one, we meet the hero and heroine amid a cartoon-like montage of American society. Part two dramatizes their encounter in the desert, culminating in their vision of a new society, and part three shows each character reentering the world—the hero at the cost of life, the heroine at the cost of hope. In her despair, she has a second dream, but this time it is of destruction.

Of the three parts, only the first and a bit of the last seem acceptable, but even they have been violently criticized. Part one has been accused of caricaturing national faults that are overly familiar. Yet that, I think, was intentional and appropriate. Given the movement from reality to dream, reality must be broadly sketched to make the shift in style not too jarring and to excite in the audience a distaste as unqualified as the hero's. Once that is allowed, we can see how economical and witty, if not subtle or probing, are the film's first moments.

Especially good is the opening *cinéma vérité* sequence of a student protest meeting. Antonioni deliberately edits image and sound so as to baffle our perception, much as Fellini does in the red-light-district scene from *Satyricon*. But, whereas Fellini's method titillates, Antonioni's describes: the point about such a meeting *is* its confusion—some of the students talk about burning the school down, while a girl sweetly asks if any of them wants coffee. Fed up with such chaos, Mark, the hero, walks out, announcing that he's willing to die for the cause, but not out of boredom. A friend tries to excuse him, explaining that meetings aren't his "trip," whereupon a hot-eyed radical retorts, "If he wants to be a revolutionary, he has to learn to work with other people."

This line wittily deflates the group. And there are many such incisive touches: a custodian sitting within a fortress of TV monitors, when all there is to see are people coming out of elevators; a gun salesman who advises the hero (pretending to want arms in anticipation of black riots), "Law says you can protect your house. If he dies in the yard, drag him inside"; a lavish office building, its mica-studded walls gleaming like Ali Baba's cave, where Rod Taylor, a real-estate executive, sits before an immense picture window outside of which an American flag flaps powerfully in the breeze. Antonioni picks off as many targets as time allows, even fleetingly, as when a short-haired lady executive in a gray-flannel suit responds with a smile of distaste to a TV commercial's celebration of kitchens ("just the perfect place to cook for the man of the house"). There is even a nice inside joke: among the many billboards and signs that Mark sees is one reading, "MGM Auto Sales."

Part three begins when Mark decides to return a private airplane he had stolen from the Los Angeles airport. When he lands, police surround him as if he were a prehistoric beast—which his plane resembles, with its weird colorings and stenciled slogans. The latter almost literally cause his death: before he lands, the control-tower men express indignation at "all those jokes." Shortly afterwards, the girl, Daria, learns on the radio of his death. Arriving at a posh desert house where she is to meet Taylor, she retaliates against all it represents by blowing it up in her mind—again and again—in a scene that is technically brilliant and emotionally powerful. Here is the film's one moment of characteristic complexity, as we watch everything go— books as well as TV set, food as well as refrigerator—and can scarcely sort out our responses, for the apocalypse is beautiful, although terrifying, and impotent in the midst of its force.

In such moments of serious caricature, *Zabriskie Point* is incisive. Unfortunately, like Bergman in *The Passion of Anna*, Antonioni hasn't created a coherent style for his film and cannot sustain the hard-edged caricature through the long middle section. Part two is stranded between notation and presentation.

Curiously, *Zabriskie Point* is the most conventionally plotted of

Antonioni's later films. Even more than *Blow-Up*, which is, on some level, a murder mystery, *Zabriskie Point* seeks narrative suspense. Yet (like *Fellini Satyricon*) it never clarifies its characters' motives, so that suspense becomes mystification. To the extent that motivation *is* established, dialogue accomplishes the task (in strict contrast to Antonioni's other films). The second curiosity about *Zabriskie Point*, by the most notoriously nonverbal of major directors (Antonioni's heroes embellish their plane with the motto "NO WORDS"), is its heavy reliance on rhetoric. And what rhetoric! Only through his fey "I wanna get off the ground," do we understand Mark's theft, just as we are meant to understand his return because he says, "I need to take risks." Sans dialogue, everything seems arbitrary. Why does Mark fall for Daria (Pauline Kael is right to quip, "His Cessna fell for her Buick")? Why does she go to Rod Taylor and what is the nature of their relationship? Why do the cops kill Mark—when he is clearly unarmed—with such brutal precipitance?

In addition, the central part, which is meant to show a possible antidote to the first, is totally unappealing. Chief culprit is the dialogue, but eloquence would grate in the mouths of Mark Frechette and Daria Halprin. In a famous short story, "The Real Thing," Henry James showed that if you want to re-create aristocrats, for models, you need servants; the artist reorders life, he doesn't simply use it. Antonioni forgot this basic truth for the one time in his career. Fearing that he did not understand the hippie or flower-child mentality, he laboriously searched for actual examples of the breeds. What he found, unfortunately, were a pretty-boy hippie with silent screen mannerisms and an overblown flower-child. That Antonioni should have not only hired such blanks but hung his film on their putative vitality shows how dangerously unsure he was from the outset.

But *Zabriskie Point* probably would not have been much better with other actors and a new script. Nothing could have helped once Antonioni made the mistake of trying to capture America. Following old instincts for social reality, he ignored the fact that vision doesn't work through what James called "density of specification," and so opened himself to the charge of simple-mindedness. In this respect, *Blow-Up* was right to take place in "London," whose abstraction is established by the masked troupe that opens the film, by the studious avoidance of topical reference, and by the stylization that turns a rock 'n roll audience into an impossibly catatonic mob. If Antonioni had not tried to render America, even in shorthand, but had created a stylized equivalent for it, his film would not raise expectations that its second and third parts—even if better acted and written—are unable to satisfy.

Zabriskie Point is a failure; still, just as one would have to be deaf to like it, one would have to be blind to despise it. Antonioni has an eye of genius, although he falters by trying to see into the future as well as the present. At the very least, however, since it contains the first of Antonioni's love affairs that doesn't perish of attrition, *Zabriskie Point* excites interest in the *director's* future. It is interesting that his next work may be a two-part film—in which he joins Fellini in a project that Bergman dropped—called *Love Duet.*

I began discussing these films as examples of a crisis. I want to end by saying what it is:

In an interview I had with Antonioni, he said that lying was so easy in films; and when I asked him what "lying" meant, he added:

> To give an interpretation that we know is untrue to life. Because at the moment it is more interesting or amusing to put something in, to forget the real sense of what we are doing in our amusement with the medium.

Amusement with the medium, encouraged by sophistication in its use, lies behind what is most deplorable in contemporary films. When fancy editing is confused with insight, and photography with characterization, then film, as an art, *has* reached a crisis. In varying degrees, even directors as independent as Fellini, Truffaut, Bergman and Antonioni cannot remain unaffected by the new bad taste. With enormous pressures on them to make money (consider the trouble Fellini had in financing *Satyricon*) and temptation to keep doing so once they have, even giants can be affected by lesser men—particularly when they form an audience.

Trained by critics who, having recently understood film technique, now confuse it with content, an audience, mostly young (and thus immature in thought and feeling) is being prepared to value films sheerly for their surface. Between this audience and the original film audience, which was thrilled simply to see a train enter a railroad station, there is no advance in aesthetic maturity. Instead, there is a decline, because the primitive audience knew it was watching a gadget and never mistook its appetite for taste.

In our present confusion of values, the first casualty is character. Anyone nowadays can invoke authorities, from Freud to Susan Sontag, against "that old-fashioned nineteenth-century idea of personality." Certainly, great films have sometimes questioned this idea (*Persona* being perhaps the greatest of them), or dispensed with it (one thinks, for example, of Bresson's *A Condemned Man Escaped*, whose hero is only the temporary manifestation of suprapersonal force). But when honorable skepticism or minority belief becomes fashion, the phony gets legitimized along with the truly experimental. There is a vast difference between a film like *Persona*, which questions the human, and *Fellini Satyricon*, which travesties it, just as there is a smaller but crucial difference, between the deliberate disintegration of personality in Bergman's *Persona* and his lazy failure to create it in *The Passion of Anna*. Filling in the hole with color does not conceal its depth.

Appropriately, each of the four films discussed was shot in color. Major films are seldom made now in black and white. When sound first came in, it did not heighten but rather reduced verisimilitude, and critics like Rudolph Arnheim were right to complain that indiscriminate use of the new dimension would ironically freeze film at the level of theater, depriving it of self-realization. How much more dangerous is the present moment when a panoply of techniques exists alongside an audience begging to be worked over by them. No wonder that MGM tried to sell *Zabriskie Point* as this year's *2001*. The wonder instead is that Antonioni could come so close to making a film whose actors might as well have been machines and whose principal virtues inhere only in the images. Few living directors possess both the technique and human understanding to make films that can compete with plays and novels as imitations (however stylized) of what it is like to be alive. If these men turn away from the person to worship the camera, confusing means with ends, they will not only reduce cinema but bring us all that much closer to the condition of characters in their latest films: that of puppets.

(1970)

BRESSON'S GENTLENESS

To be profitable, even "art" films must be entertaining; and although art and entertainment may coincide, the former is often starved because the latter is too narrowly defined. In literature, readers can enjoy Nabokov, whose difficulty is lightened by rococo language and sex, as well as Beckett, who is recondite even when funny. But in film, even cultivated spectators expect pleasure to require no personal exertion (you have to turn pages to read a book) and austerity is regarded almost as an affront.

Often, great directors reach their audience through sensational but artistically inferior efforts. Because it is a fine film one doesn't deplore the success of *Blow-Up*, although one wishes more attention were paid to *L'Avventura*; but a preference for *La Dolce Vita* over Fellini's early comedies, or for *The Seventh Seal* over *The Naked Night*, is deplorable. When a good film doesn't bathe the eye or gratify the emotions, it often sinks quickly into oblivion (I think, in recent years, of Henning Carlsen's *Hunger*, Alain Jessua's *Life Upside Down*, or Vittorio De Seta's *Bandits of Orgosolo*). Some directors are dismissed *in toto*—like the excellent Ermanno Olmi. When his film *The Job* was renamed *The Sound of Trumpets*, filmgoers still weren't blasted out of their houses, and even free tickets couldn't get them to the theater when *The Fiancés* played in New York City.

As we move up the scale from Olmi to Robert Bresson, the carnival mentality of most filmgoers does even greater damage to the cause of art. Except for Antonioni and Bergman, no other Western director possesses so original a style, although Bresson wouldn't welcome the comparison. He dismisses Antonioni as a mere photographer and Bergman as someone wrongly dependent on rhetoric. Accordingly, Bresson himself is linguistically concentrated and visually unadorned —so spare, in fact, that even admirers of the other directors (artists who are distinctly not crowd-pleasing) find Bresson too rarefied. This helps to explain why Bresson has been able to direct only nine films in thirty years. Nevertheless, he has become more and more appealing to producers without compromising his stubborn austerity. During his first decade, when he was forced to direct professional actors (although he hates their artificiality), he was able to find backing for only two films; during his latest, most Bressonian decade, he has found backing for five. This is especially remarkable because only one of his efforts (*A Man Escaped*) has been a hit—and this principally in France—and because his recent works have been pretty much restricted to film clubs and art cinemas and, in America, to one-night-stands at festivals.

By now, Bresson is slighted neither by producers nor by film scholars; audiences are what he requires. That his newest effort, *Une Femme Douce*, might provide them is evident from the admiring review it earned in *Time* (no proponent of the avant-garde) when it was shown at the 1969 Lincoln Center Film Festival. Perhaps sensing that Bresson's hour had come—since the new film is in lovely color, features a beautiful leading lady (the then nonprofessional Dominique Sanda) and treats a favored subject (unhappy marriage)—Paramount Pictures toyed with the idea of underwriting commercial distribution. Eventually, however, Paramount's courage receded, leaving the possibility of import to the more adventurous but less wealthy New Yorker Theater. Daniel Talbot, who manages that crucial showcase for neglected art, has every intention of bringing *Une Femme Douce* to this country; but, as he says, "I've discovered that young peoples' taste, . . . and they would be 95 percent of the audience for a film like *Une Femme Douce*, is hopelessly conservative." Therefore, in a time of economic jitters, Mr. Talbot may not be able to risk dependence on an audience—for all the cant about a "film generation"—whose taste remains uninstructed. Should this film not reach America, we will perhaps have missed our easiest entrance into Bresson's art; but, since at sixty-three the director shows no sign of slowing down, the loss will be entirely ours.

Unlike Bergman but like Antonioni, Bresson is even more distinguished for his method than for individual films (although like Antonioni, he has produced, with *A Man Escaped*, at least one cinematic landmark). His method is a relentless pursuit of inner truth. Because Bresson disdains acting, rhetoric and spectacle, he considers himself a realist, but viewers rightly contend that life is not so spare as it appears in his films. Bresson's "realism" is to be understood as a definition of intention, not as a description of style. In fact, he is the most rigid stylist in the history of cinema, and no one but Bresson himself would think to call his work "natural."

His realism produces a surface only in order to uncover its depths, as is revealed by the first crucial aspect of his technique. Alone among his peers, Bresson habitually films preexisting texts. Although he remains strictly faithful to them—retaining most of the action and dialogue and rarely adding or inventing anything—he arranges the details so as to release an insight that was only latent. For example, the Madame de la Pommeraye episode from Diderot's *Jacques le Fataliste*, which Bresson used in *Les Dames du Bois de Boulogne*, is only a clever anecdote, illustrating feminine wiles, about an aristocrat who avenges herself on a faithless lover by tricking him into marriage with a courtesan. Comically, her pot misfires: when the lover upbraids his wife for her cooperation in duping him, she is so contrite that she wins him over. By updating the story, Bresson diverts attention from specific social attitudes, which are prominent in the original, to uncover a deeper moral meaning. Filming Diderot's plot and dialogue in the emotionally compacted style of Racine, he shows how vengeance is emasculated by its own character. Locked in unforgiving rage, the mistress cannot even imagine the merciful love that makes her jealousy self-defeating.

Dostoevski's novella, "A Gentle Spirit," Bresson's source for *Une Femme Douce*, is, to begin with, richer in possibility than the Diderot episode. While his young wife lies on her bier, the narrator of Dostoevski's tale reviews his marriage in order to comprehend the girl's motive for suicide. He recalls how his infernal pride made him alienate her affection to test it. Because she had been poor, he flaunted the financial favor conferred on her by marriage. Because she was naturally loving, he responded coldly. It is not surprising that all this drove her to hatred and almost to adultery, but when the husband rented a room to spy on her, he had the triumph of hearing her repulse the other man. Nonetheless, his humiliation of his wife caused her to attempt murder. With her gun at his temple, he momentarily awakened and kept himself from flinching to impress on her his largeness of soul. This he did so effectively that the girl was crushed by guilt and, spiritual creature that she was, made atonement by leaping to her death while clutching an icon. Concluding his baleful story, the husband curses his own perversity and avers that all men live in unbreachable solitude.

This story required less alteration than Diderot's to make it suitable to Bresson's sensibility. Nonetheless, he made one major change that greatly enriches his source. Whereas in Dostoevski the wife is mainly an item in her husband's reminiscence, in Bresson she is a living presence. This is accomplished through the second important feature of Bresson's technique.

In half of his films, Bresson uses narrated commentary; a device, widely condemned as anticinematic, that is instead the director's most important formal contribution. Narration is obviously efficient because it elides time; in place of functional but undramatic scenes it permits speedy summation ("For six weeks she was feverish," *et cetera*). More important, it allows Bresson to present both objective and subjective views of the action.

Asynchronous relation of dialogue to image has long been standard cinematic technique, as in the classic example of a man murmuring love-words to a woman on whom he advances while the camera holds on a knife in his hands. But although this technique is normally put to such melodramatic uses, in Bresson it is employed to reveal the soul. Thus, in *Diary of a Country Priest*, the titular narrator frequently tells us through his commentary that he is doing exactly what we see him doing on the screen. Such duplication, so apparently wasteful, becomes functional through deviations, as rhyme becomes more than mere adornment when occasionally it goes "off." At one moment, for example, the priest tells us that he is feeling better and can even eat bread and wine (he is dying from cancer of the stomach), while the image tells us with what difficulty he eats and how sick he really is. By comparing his total accuracy when reporting priestly activities with his failure to register the state of his health, we comprehend his humility: he reports what he is doing but neglects to acknowledge the personal odds against doing it.

In *Une Femme Douce* this technique is even more essential to Bresson's meaning. Dostoevski's narrator fully understands his experience; Bresson's does not. As only cinema can, this film solves the long-standing literary problem of how to present a story through an unreliable narrator without confusing the audience about the plot or the character. Thus the film's dramatic sequences are not flashbacks; they are illustrations of past events accompanied by a commentary that exposes the husband's inability to cope with them.

Unlike Dostoevski, Bresson shows the wife independent of her husband's viewpoint, and this increases both our participation in the failure of their marriage and our comprehension of the complexity of its cause. Two minor alterations in detail point toward the latter intention. In Dostoevski, the husband hears his wife spurn her would-be lover through a door; in Bresson, he comes upon the couple by accident as they are sitting in an automobile. All we see is the wife moving away from the man; we do not hear, as the husband tells us he heard, her refusal. As a result, we are free to suspect his attribution to his wife of perfect innocence, a suspicion strengthened by the other change. Bresson's heroine does not die clutching an icon. Before her jump, she fingers but rejects an ivory Christ, leaving behind her only a shawl that floats to earth with ironic grace and is the only visible sign of her suicide. Because of these and many other indications in the film, both husband and wife become ambiguous figures. She is not merely the gentle victim of his egotism; he is not simply a monster trying her soul. The moral distinction between them is made rather clearly in Dostoevski, but Bresson constantly reminds us that responsibility for the failure of a relationship can never be simple.

Avoiding discursive dialogue, so essential in Bergman, or visual symbolism, as in Antonioni, Bresson makes things doubly difficult for his audience; but the power of the film depends on our awareness of mystery. Although he was referring to another artist, John Updike has nicely formulated what is also the essence of Bresson's appeal. We are held, Updike says, either by stories that offer basic "circumstantial suspense" or, more significantly, by those whose suspense is "gnostic." In the former we want to "know the outcome of an unresolved situation"; in the latter we read on "in the expectation that at any moment an illumination will occur." Most directors even more than most writers cater to the former interest: Bresson is preeminent among those who court the latter. For that reason, he always begins his films by telling us what will happen. The heroine of *Les Dames du Bois de Boulogne* says she will be avenged and immediately we see the medium of her vengeance; in *Diary of a Country Priest* the face of the priest tells us instantly that he will die; the very title gives the plot away in *A Man Escaped*. Just so, in *Une Femme Douce*, the film commences with the suicide. What draws us on, like the husband, is the desire to know why. But to know why in Bresson (as is not the case in Dostoevski), we have to watch intently everything that happens because nothing is explained and even the explainer is an item to be fathomed. Many viewers find Bresson cold and remote, but this coldness may be only a reflection of their own passivity. If you can be excited by the search for understanding, you can be excited by Bresson.

So Bresson forces total concentration. Actors are not permitted to act lest we be diverted by their excellence as performers from what they incarnate. Framing is constricted lest our eye wander to an irrelevant detail. Scenes are enacted and assembled without differing degrees of emphasis lest we strain forward for one and relax in another. Dialogue is held to a minimum lest we settle for abstractions in place of facts. Only at the very end of each film does Bresson release us from our hush of contemplation with a shock that sums up what we've seen, as when bubbles emerge from the river in which the heroine of Mouchette has drowned herself and a blast of the *Magnificat* admits that death alone is victory for such a life.

The last scene of *Une Femme Douce* is equally conclusive. Throughout the film, the husband has been pacing around the corpse of his wife, seeking but failing to breach this final barrier. Now he can only raise her bloodless face from its final repose and murmur hopelessly: "Oh. Open your eyes. A second—only for a second." Then her head is lowered, the screen momentarily darkens as his back passes in front of the camera, and we hold for several seconds while a coffin screw is fastened; the sound of its turning indicates the finality of his defeat.

Figuratively, the screw had always been turning on a separateness no more irrevocable in death than it was in life. Recalling their first real conversation on one of the girl's trips to his pawnshop, he comments that she was pleased to find him more educated than she might have expected, but we see on her face little more than sullen regard. Thus begins the husband's attempt to understand things only insofar as they can support his repeated desire for "a solid happiness."

"How voluptuous when one no longer doubts," he tells the impassive maid who must listen to his monologue. But, whereas he dotes on intellectual certainty, his wife is certain only that life is mean. Paleontology, she tells him, dictates that even men are structured like mice. When he buys her flowers as a sign of love, she wryly mocks the act's distinctiveness. Seeing a nearby woman receive an identical bouquet, she rids herself of hers, remarking, "We, too, form a couple, all based on the same model." But obscurely she searches for some higher satisfaction, although she cannot even specify the object of her search. In Dostoevski, the wife is an orphan, exploited by her relatives, who marries to better her position. In Bresson, her motives are deliberately enshrouded. All she reveals is that she comes from a sinister house, and she succumbs to the pawnbroker's entreaties for no apparent reason. When he tells her that she will help him by marrying him, she asks whether it would not be possible to do so without marriage. Then, when she finds herself tied to him, committed as she is to her obscure ideal, she tortures his bourgeois certitude.

He tells her that they must be frugal so as to improve their lot, and to mock him she offers prodigal sums to his customers. He asserts that marriage is a state desired by most women, but she expresses her contempt for this ideal through apparent infidelities. Because he is devoted to certainty, the infidelities torment him, the more so because his devotion to his wife makes it unthinkable that so gentle a creature should be heartless.

Is she gentle? The husband keeps saying so, but the action undermines his contention. He admires her passion for books and records, but we see her listening to jazz (the soundcuts to it are always accomplished with deafening volume) while munching fancy pastries, or leafing through books, only to extract the lesson that man is no more august than a mouse. Do these actions express intellectual passion or emptiness of spirit? Does her esteem for books accord with the careless way in which she tosses them about, as we recall the disarray of her dresser and the provocative lingerie found on her bed? When they go to a museum she disagrees with her husband that there is a gap between classic and modern art, but does she deny the gap out of catholicity of taste or because nothing means very much to her? Moreover, doesn't she express her denial simply to mock him? "Young birds are drawn to the same chant as their parents," she tells her husband, "and all birds sing the same way." Is her whole life a doomed attempt to break away from her "sinister" upbringing, her aspiration a baffled yearning toward what her imagination cannot conceive?

Yet the husband persists in regarding her as gentle, finer than he is, more intelligent, more compassionate, and, above all, faithful, that is to say, secure. When they go to a movie and a man next to her tries to make a pass, the husband forces her to change seats; and when they exit from the theater and she throws her arms about her husband, he comments that she obviously wants to love him. What he will not face is the possibility that she is incapable of this. He blames himself for accepting possession merely of her body, but that is all she offers him. Even in the midst of their alienation she turns toward his flesh.

In the dramatized sequences, the wife seems lost, perhaps more ferocious than gentle, but at least she is honest whereas the husband is sentimental, and, unlike him, she is not so stupid as to think that cash and marriage insure happiness. Desiring to educate her to his parochial values, the husband drives her to adultery. Desiring to free herself from his stifling conventionality, the wife awakens in him a terrible perturbation of spirit.

But worse lies ahead, ironically. During their first conversation (as in Dostoevski), the husband quotes Mephistopheles in Goethe's *Faust*, who proclaims himself one of those wishing to do evil who inadvertently does good. Although the line is here pronounced to impress the wife with the husband's learning, it should be recalled during the latter half of the film, where, out of their mutual enmity, a bizarre mutual improvement springs.

After the wife is driven to attempt murder, the husband makes use of her action to gain control. Refusing to admit what he saw, he nonetheless punishes her by banishing her from his bed. She, in turn, driven wild by her uncertainty about his motive and, as we later learn, by her fear that he will abandon her, falls into a fever from which she emerges transformed. Whereas all her energy had gone into combating her husband, now she seems to turn her criticism inward, at last attaining that gentleness in which her husband took such solace. Jazz is replaced on her phonograph by Bach and Purcell, she begins to serve her husband dutifully, and she promises to be a faithful wife. Watching all this, he feels torn between pity for her abasement and exultation at her new docility, but the change gives him hope for their future. She has indeed become more nearly the tender creature he has always sought and, out of gratitude, he confesses how badly he has sinned against her spirit and proceeds to show that he too can change. Committing acts of ostentatious kindness to his customers, he also literally abases himself to his wife in love.

Why, then, does his wife burst into sobs when he tells her how deeply she is adored? Because the new spirituality that he has released in her makes her intolerably guilty. But he cannot moderate his passion because the act of murder to which he nearly drove her has awakened in him an equal measure of guilt. They are as terribly isolated in their mutual regret as they were in their former enmity. The evil that they did to each other ironically produced good, freeing her from desolate negation and him from self-protective acquisitiveness. Now this good produces evil.

Lost between the self she was and the self she has promised to become, the wife cannot summon sufficient faith to believe in the permanency of her new dispensation. The husband wishes to sell the shop, move away, and devote his life simply to adoring her, but the more he affirms this plan the more unbearable becomes her sense that she is unfit for adoration. Before their marriage she had come to him to pawn a gold crucifix with an ivory Christ attached and had not wanted the Christ which he had offered to return. Now, in her perplexity, she fingers it in the drawer where it has lain, but when the maid comes in to inquire after her, she quickly hides what she is doing. Then, donning a shawl, she steps on a little iron table and leaps from her balcony into the traffic that has been resounding throughout the film.

The wife is not what her husband thinks her to be, yet when she almost embodies his erroneous image, her integrity is shattered and she can only die. The husband is brutal, not so much when he seeks to possess his hard-eyed wife as when he seeks to make amends for having sought possession. Watching their marriage progress, we feel a growing terror, because opposites merge and solutions turn out out to be worse than the problems they solve. The husband's story, in its ironic complexity, ridicules his very effort to understand it. He never comes closer to the mystery of his ineluctable misalliance than when he confesses that he cannot understand the impulse that made him leave his wife at their highest moment of intimacy, thus unintentionally facilitating her suicide.

The film's clear point is that tragedy can be comprehended as a process, while still evading our need to fathom motives and fix blame. Therefore, Bresson uses his cinematic means—framing, editing, dialogue, acting—to achieve an even emphasis that precludes abstract summation. Whatever inspires these people can only be inferred from their laconic utterances and meager gestures. But this very meagerness—which we are made to experience—comes as close as anything can to being the source of their solitude. Both Dostoevski's story and Bresson's film light up the distance between two human souls (although Bresson magnifies the distance by giving us a fuller portrayal of the wife). Dostoevski, however, attributes the distance to a fundamental human perversity; Bresson links it to a world without spiritual force.

Throughout the film we hear more traffic noises and footsteps than dialogue; we see more doors and empty stairways than people. Usually a frame is filled with objects; fragmentation even turns characters into things. In Nathanael West's novel *Miss Lonelyhearts* the Christ-hungry protagonist sees the world as "dead . . . a world of doorknobs"; this is also the world in which Bresson's tragedy transpires. The wife yearns obscurely beyond a universe in which all is matter; the husband tries to turn matter into might. "Why did we adopt silence from the beginning?" the husband laments, and as the couple is shown to us we are tempted to give an answer. Neither husband nor wife can rise above the world of things; as a result they can reach toward each other, even gaze into each other's eyes, but they can communicate nothing of their souls. In the midst of his agony the husband wishes he could pray but knows that he can only think. The wife can finger her Christ, but the tentative movement seems almost to shame her. The maid's silence makes her simulate the role of confessor, but when she pronounces her first line, late in the film, we learn how distant she has been from the husband's ordeal ("After the burial, I will leave for eight days, if you will let me.")

Une Femme Douce is distinguished from Bresson's other films by the absence of some principle of redemption. The courtesan in *Les Dames du Bois de Bologne* receives forgiveness; the hero of *A Man Escaped* is granted liberty. Even in those films where Bresson's heroes die, some promise of transfiguration is made; all the victims resemble that most Bressonian of characters, Joan of Arc, who loses the earth but achieves Heaven. *Une Femme Douce* is, however, the darkest of three recent films in which Bresson contemplates the modern world. Successively, in *Au Hasard, Balthazar* and *Mouchette* and this work, he portrays a spiritual wasteland, characterized by brutality and a self-punishing pursuit of pleasure. But even Balthazar dies amid a field of peacefully grazing sheep and Mouchette drowns to the *Magnificat*; the wife in *Une Femme Douce* falls to the cacaphony of screeching brakes.

It is this bleakness that will, I think, make the film seem more tenable to the uninitiated than the profound Christian certitude of Bresson's other works. But although the mood here is untypical, the technique is not. In *A Man Escaped* the mystery of human courage and of divine aid are illustrated through the most mundane details. A spoon is needed in Fontaine's escape; by chance he finds it, and we marvel at the concentration with which it is used. The contrasting spiritual aridity of *Une Femme Douce* is shown through the same close-in depiction of the ordinary.

The wedding sequence can serve as an example. In the scene immediately preceding, the husband begs the girl to say "yes," but although she looks at him before entering her apartment, she makes no answer. Rather we witness her assent in an immediate cut to the signing of the marriage register, an act itself quickly replaced by hands exchanging rings over a restaurant table. We then see reverse shots of the two gazing at each other and cut to an almost excessively detailed staging of their entrance into their new home. Again, there is no dialogue, only the sound of a key turning in the lock, of a door opening and closing, of footsteps and traffic. They embrace but we see her staring quizzically over his shoulder. They hesitate, but she finally pulls him forward. In quick cuts, we see her walk to the bathroom, throw a nightgown on the bed, while he watches television.

She comes to him, laughingly unbuttons his shirt, turns off the television (in the action dislodging a towel and giving us a glittering view of her lovely body), and then jumps into bed. They pull the covers over them, we hear the sound of laughter, and then only silence. Car noises come up on the sound track, followed by his voice commenting that he had to "throw water" on the "marvelous drunkenness" of his joy.

Each detail measures the paucity of their hopes. The marriage is not asssented to but only performed, and then not as a sacrament but as the signing of a register. Even the real marriage, at the restaurant, is only a series of movements and looks, and the consummation, initiated by the wife and excited by the mechanical noise of auto racing on the television set, is meager in its unseen joy. Yet the husband persists in regarding this uncommunicative, wholly material coming-together as something marvelous in its intoxication.

Many artists would depict a desolation of spirit so profound through more striking dramatization, but Bresson would think this a mistake; he includes in *Une Femme Douce* a scene that illustrates his aesthetic. When the couple see *Hamlet* at the theater the husband is impressed but the wife doesn't join in his applause. Returning home, she explains why, by running to a volume of Shakespeare to read lines that had been eliminated in the performance only so that the actors could get away with shouting and gesticulation. The lines come from Hamlet's advice to the players (in a French translation) and among them is the veritable motto of Bresson's art:

> in the torrent, the tempest, the whirlwind one must always be moderate and acquire even a certain gentleness.

Like the wife herself, Bresson shows that gentleness of manner does not deny inner ferocity. For the spectator who can match the film's concentration with his own, Bresson, by rigorously controlling passion, inspires it.

(1971)

THE CONTEXT OF
A CLOCKWORK ORANGE

FROM THE BEGINNING, most American filmmakers have been *idiots-savants*: technically brilliant but unintelligent about life. D.W. Griffith taught the world to join shots, but his mind contained only fragments of thinking, and the flow of his images was regularly muddied by trashy sentiments. His best followers either (like Hawks) bypassed depth for verve or (like Ford) made simplemindedness into a strategy. The first group, reveling in cynicism, concocted a fantasy world of "screwball comedies," gangster films or musicals; the second, opting for sentimentality, devised melodramas full of picturesque difficulties solved by rough justice or, when at their most romantic, Westerns. Neither may be said to have inspected anything real; both rendered life through the formulas of pulp fiction.

The one native talent who had seemed exceptional merely proves the rule. *Citizen Kane*, America's first contribution to film art, is important only as a contribution to the art of making films. Its script is little more than sturdy planks of plotting nailed together by wisecracks. Execution, not conception, wins applause: Toland's superb photography, with its monumental vistas and suggestive lighting; the expressionist sets and resourceful music; dazzling transitions between shots and scenes; bravura acting; endless devices. As insight, *Kane* is laughable. Indeed, admiration can be sustained only if we accept the final revelation—hence, retroactively, the film—as deliberate in its failure to explain because a man's motives can never be satisfactorily fathomed. No such convenient excuse is available for *The Magnificent Ambersons*, which, although more boldly propositional in treating mores, is hamstrung by the shallow Booth Tarkington novel that is its source. For the rest, Welles's career is a sad tale of craft in search of a subject; its few victories (the last scene of *The Lady from Shanghai* or the beginning of *Touch of Evil*) poignant in their excess of manner over matter. Little wonder that the one artist thriving in Hollywood has been Alfred Hitchcock, who regards reality as impertinent, emotion as something that happens to the spectator, and mind as a spoil-sport needing to be allayed.

Most American films share Hitchcock's disdain for common experience. As a result, they don't feature people but rather stars who inflate them. Chronically unable to contemplate the native culture, they rather represent it through their fixation on deeds. American film art has been influential by its action genres because only in these does the essentially technical genius of our filmmakers find a proper subject. Themselves masters of know-how, our directors are drawn to ingenuity and expertise in their characters. Possessing the world's most envied machinery for making motion pictures, they express themselves powerfully only when their subject is motion unencumbered by feeling, morals or contemplation. The rhythm of American films takes its cue from the racing pulse.

How easily this nonhuman emphasis on sheer skill might turn into something blatantly inhuman we see from the host of contemporary films that raise the level of kinetic excitement until it becomes arrant bloodlust. *Straw Dogs*, for example, is only more graphic in depicting violence and more wholehearted in advocating force than its countless predecessors. Peckinpah's film is remarkable for the honesty with which it declares its values, not for the values themselves: power-worship, anti-intellectualism, and a fear of femininity that, in less brazen times, simply dictated avoidance of sex.

Its hero is a parody thinker whose head in the stars blinds him to the ditch at his feet, into which he is thrown by his wife's libido. Childishly fixated on her own pleasure, when David insists that he must work as well as make love, Amy goads a former lover and one of his bestial friends into raping her. Meanwhile, a village girl also fixated on her own pleasure goads the town idiot (David without the disguise of learning) into a tryst that ends in her death. When David blunders upon the fleeing idiot and insists on caring for him, the couple is made vulnerable to a siege by the village toughs, but David vanquishes his enemies because he turns his intelligence— at last, we are made to feel—toward the production of force. Man the doer is most truly man.

Although Stanley Kubrick began his career within the artistic tradition I've sketched, he soon displayed signs of rejection. After two obviously apprentice films, which he currently deplores, Kubrick made a tightly plotted action movie that nevertheless subverts some of the genre's basic assumptions. So far from showing a meticulously planned heist as the expression of human adroitness, *The Killing* reveals how poignant an error it is to neglect needs and feelings in one's dependence on technique. Without departing from the crime-does-not-pay formula, *The Killing* humanizes its characters just enough to produce a modest critique of faceless organizational efficiency.

In his next film, *Paths of Glory*, Kubrick attacks one of American filmdom's most admired exponents of action. He depicts the army unheroically, as a vainglorious organism that thrives on the sacrifice of weaker members, adding vindictiveness to brutality when its methods fail. The particular army in question, however, is French rather than American; thus the native relevance of the criticism is somewhat qualified. Concern over this mitigation perhaps dictates Kubrick's casting of actors who patently hail from the less elocutionary boroughs of New York as French soldiers and inserting in their speeches argot unsuitable to the time and place. But anything thereby gained in relating the work to its American audience costs credibility. When one also notes the film's populist dichotomy between evil officers and good or at least guiltless draftess, he begins to think that *Paths of Glory* does not go so clearly against the American grain as its pacifist polemics might first suggest.

Paths of Glory muffles its pacifism by locating evil in a single class. The result is a tendentiousness never quite overcome by the graphic portrayal of war's horrors. Timidity also mars Kubrick's next film, *Lolita*. Heeding some internalized form of conventional sanctions (with Nabokov's collusion), Kubrick prettifies Humbert's sordid obsession and captures the novel's grotesque comedy only in the secondary roles of Mrs. Haze and Quilty. The result is neither the pathetic May-December romance that major casting and composer Nelson Riddle's arpeggios seem designed to achieve nor Nabokovian satire, but an incompatible mixture of the two.

Nevertheless, flawed as Kubrick's first films are, they clearly established him as more than an entertainer willing to adorn any project offered him with the standard quantity of kinetic thrills. His preeminence among American filmmakers was subsequently assured by a film consolidating all the best in its predecessors. *Dr. Strangelove* combines the critical plotting of *The Killing*, with the pacifist and anti-institutional themes expressed in *Paths of Glory*, by perfecting the comic style marginally evident in *Lolita*. As a result, *Dr. Strangelove* holds up to devastating ridicule values that a film like *Straw Dogs* deplorably celebrates.

Beginning with the shot of two bombers copulating in mid-air, *Dr. Strangelove* presents America's fascination with might as an absurd confusion of libido. The crew of the lethal American fighter plane read *Playboy* magazine (whose centerfold wears *Foreign Affairs* across her buttocks) and receive prophylactics in their survival kits; the general who orders their attack had formulated his insane scheme during intercourse, when, as he says, he realized that sex threatens his "vital essence"; the ex-Nazi scientist who advises the war machine looks forward to a postapocalypse eugenics program. We are meant ultimately to share the astonishment of General Turgidson when he is torn between chauvinistic pride in the bomber's invulnerability to Soviet intervention and his un-American discovery that it must be destroyed in order to save the world.

Dr. Strangelove is exceptional not only for placing this self-criticism before us but for doing so with an hilarious relentlessness that takes us laughing right through Armageddon. Moreover, while exposing the ultimate destructiveness of a culture perversely in love with machines, the film itself avoids mechanical flourishes, making direction reticently serve the content. Long scenes are enacted without camera movement (in a salient example, George C. Scott's room is outfitted with a mirrored wall so that no shifts need interrupt his performance); except for the simple crosscutting necessary during the climax, most of the editing contrives to point up lines (as in the war room sequences). So much less brilliant a piece of filmmaking than *Citizen Kane*, *Dr. Strangelove*, unlike Welles's masterpiece, can stand with works that interpret life.

With some of the critical alertness displayed in *Dr. Strangelove*, Kubrick's next film *2001* speculates about what life might become. Numerous details reveal the underside of futurist technology: the insipidity of cosmic cuisine, the colossally disproportionate effort and boring experience of space travel, the atavistically banal human behavior that makes the film's one colorful figure a computer programmed to feel. Yet, Kubrick's critical voice eventually seems to be crying in the wilderness, drowned out by the alluring special effects with which he fills up the vastness of space.

Thus, the last sequence suggests a faith that man will ultimately transcend whatever follies still cling to him as he enters the era of total mechanism. We are, however, never told why. Nor can we explain how an artist who distinguished himself by satirizing mindless, heartless mechanization can suddenly find it promising. Albeit with a residue of doubt, Kubrick seems to have embraced the subtitular message of *Dr. Strangelove*, stopped worrying, and learned to love the enemy.

Yet this turnabout is not completely evident unless we read comments Kubrick published after the film or the far clearer novel drawn by his collaborator, Arthur Clarke, from their screenplay. Suggesting some fundamental ambivalence, *2001* is so obscure that it has become a cult object for those who argue that a film should not mean but be. It doesn't signal a shift in Kubrick's thinking so much as a new fascination with the sheer joy of making images.

This fascination renders Kubrick's latest film "sensational" in both senses of the term: "outstanding" and also a work dependent on "exaggerated or lurid details." Some reviewers welcome the luridness and discount the exaggeration because they believe that a world of senseless violence is just around the corner and, hence, that Kubrick is sounding an essential alarm. Others, feeling no urgency behind the effects, charge Kubrick with secretly reveling in the violence he purports to expose.

But *A Clockwork Orange* is no *Straw Dogs*; love of violence is not its problem. Although detractors argue that Alex, the film's antihero, is too charming and clever, this charge is shortsighted. Alex must appeal to us or we won't care enough about him to comprehend the film's total situation. A thoroughly repulsive criminal raises no doubts about the proper response; he must simply be eradicated. Kubrick and Burgess want to make Alex sufficiently valuable, however, so that we can feel that the methods used to repress him may be as deplorable as Alex himself. Burgess makes the youth charming by endowing him with a charming language; Kubrick relies in part on this intriguing patois, but even more, since his work is a film rather than a novel, on the personal magnetism of the actor who plays the major role.

In *Straw Dogs* violence isn't charming; it is necessary. In *A Clockwork Orange* it lacks appeal because it is so manifestly unnecessary. From the beginning of the film, when we see Alex and his friends drugged in the Korova milk-bar, violence is never presented as a response to any threat that might justify it. Alex and his "droogs" beat and rape simply because they are bored. Moreover, they commit their mayhem with indiscriminate combinations of verve and fatuousness, unlike the hero of Peckinpah's film, who realizes his inventive powers only in the act of violence. We might, for example, admire a certain hideous showmanship when Alex rapes the writer's wife to the tempo of "Singin' in the Rain," but there is absolutely nothing to admire in the preceding scene when the gang amuses itself en route to its night's "entertainment" by running cars off the road. And if Alex is charming, his gang, including an aptly named Dim, fails to exhibit this or any other virtue. Through his association with them, we also understand that Alex, charming though he be, is far less intelligent than he thinks. Needing to assert dominance over his followers, he tosses Dim into a body of water and slashes his hand, vaunting himself on the brilliance of this inspiration but, as we learn later, ironically igniting a vengefulness that tries to destroy him. Kubrick emphasizes the casual connection between the two events, and thus Alex's ineptness as a leader, by shooting in identical slow motion both the water that splashes up when Dim falls and the milk that bursts from the bottle with which Alex is later hit.

Underneath Alex's apparent charm there is motiveless malignity just as there is lack of foresight underneath his apparent cleverness. The film clearly regards him sardonically. If we compare one of Kubrick's few transformations of the novel, we can see how critical Kubrick means us to feel.

In each version of the story, Alex pushes aggression to the point of murder, thus falling victim to the authorities. In the film, however, the murder is more gratuitous than in the novel and hence Alex is more foolish for having committed it. Burgess' cat-lady is an old woman who threatens the gang when, with larcenous intent, they try to enter her home; and she attacks Alex as his back is turned toward her after he succeeds in breaking in. Since he is also goaded by her yowling, scratching pets when he tries to defend himself, the crime is made partly instinctive. In the film, all of his actions are utterly deliberate—clear instances of overreaching.

Kubrick also increases the critical implications of the scene by making it less of a plot device than it is in his source. By turning the cat-lady from a rather undifferentiated old woman into a narcissist (devoted to making herself look younger than her years), a hypocrite (who talks unctuously to the police and profanely to Alex), and a poseur (who arrogates to herself the virtues of culture, although she is only a collector of pornography), Kubrick goes further than Burgess toward portraying a world where teen-age violence, if not produced by a lack of value in the adult culture, is at least facilitated by this lack.

The authorities who condition Alex into virtue use methods as violent as his own. The civil libertarian writer who deplores the boy's consequent loss of free will is actually motivated by opposition to the ruling party and—when he learns that Alex is his wife's assailant —by manic vengefulness. Even the priest, who preaches Christian values, is implicitly compromised by the violent and erotic elements in the Bible that Kubrick pictorializes and Alex takes such pleasure in. Like religion, art is shown to exert no restraining influence of civilization (in the scene where Alex is being conditioned, by scoring

Hitler and the Nazis with Beethoven, Kubrick reminds us that art doesn't even influence the society that produces it).

Kubrick's film, however, is itself artful for finding cinematic means to display Burgess' ironic equation between lawlessness and the presumed alternatives. Most strikingly, Kubrick signals a breakdown of value distinctions by accompanying the violence with musical and sometimes decorative elements that are ostentatiously benign. A gang rape takes place to the strains of Rossini in a baroque theater. While Alex lies on his bed masturbating to Beethoven and dreaming about what he calls "ultra-violence," the camera dances about his room, eventually panning across what appears to be a plaster statue of four randy satyrs; but, as the music becomes livelier, syncopated cuts reveal that the satyrs are Christs. Kubrick uses Burgess' ironic details, like the drunken tramp wallowing in filth as he spouts platitudes about law and order and the erosion of youth's respect for age, or Alex's father and mother, whose parental guidance is conspicuous by its absence. He also invents details to illustrate the widespread disappearance of legitimacy; in the final hospital scene, for example, the moans that signal Alex's return to consciousness serve to uncover a doctor and nurse fornicating in the next bed.

What Kubrick does not emphasize is the novel's theme; the unreality of goodness when not freely chosen. In Burgess, the victimized writer is writing a book on this subject and the priest delivers a speech that states the point directly. Kubrick underemphasizes the speech and totally eliminates the book. But before he is charged, as he has been, with desecrating a superior work of fiction, we must remember how localized the theme is in Burgess' novel, where it exists alongside far more striking details that articulate a nearly contradictory point: good and evil have become equivalent.

Burgess does not explain how this equivalence might come about. His novel is visionary in the narrowest sense of the term and convincing only if we already believe that the envisioned future is latent in our present. Redundant in plot (Alex commits mayhem, is rehabilitated, and then becomes the victim of mayhem), full of cartoon characters, it is striking only as a feat of construction. Kubrick finds brilliant cinematic equivalents for Burgess' gimmicks, but he is limited by the original's intellectual and emotional thinness. As a result, grand show that it is, *A Clockwork Orange* simply reminds us that Kubrick is a master visualizer. Visualization is, of course, the essence of cinema, but it is not the whole of the art. Even Hitchcock, who tells us as little about life as any director who matters, nonetheless directs his visual genius toward a human goal: evocation. Kubrick seems intent merely on showing us how to embody filmically a world first imagined in words. His expertise is undeniable, but it is also narrow and unedifying. If, as everyone claims, he is the best American film-maker, this fact merely reminds us of the terribly limited achievement of his native context. Once in his career Kubrick transcended his tradition; now, entertainingly but to our ultimate disappointment, he seems to be going the way of his predecessors.

(1972)

HYPHENS OF THE SELF

For many film critics the thumbprint of style signifies *auteurship*, whether left at the scene of a crime or upon a good achievement. For them, there is no qualitative distinction between serious films and entertainments or between directors who possess unique sensibilities and those who possess only recognizable trademarks.

Yet in correcting these critics, we musn't forget that facts always spill over neat distinctions. Occasionally a director, despite frivolous content, masters film form in a way that makes his technique significant. As I've argued, such is the case with Alfred Hitchcock. But if he earns *auteurship* despite conceptual vacancy and produces major though unserious films, he still lacks the coherence of sensibility. Artists continually refer to themselves, thus attaining self-realization; artisans attain only self-imitation, thus impressing their personalities on us.

Truffaut showed how inaccurately he perceived his colleague when, in his book on Hitchcock, he attempted to emphasize by means of an interview the American director's resemblance to Pascal rather than to Pavlov. The inaccuracy isn't evaluative, however, since Hitchcock is quite as expert a filmmaker as Truffaut believes. Yet if one compares their films, he will understand the superior interest attaching to film art over artisanship, even when the latter is masterly. As it happens, each man has a film currently in debut. The fact that neither is a success suits my purpose, for I want to demonstrate a distinction that pertains not to individual films but to different goals in making them.

Because it returns to his beloved London, his favorite situation (one man accused of a crime committed by another), and his artful mixture of comedy and horror, Hitchcock's *Frenzy* has been greeted by critics in much the same spirit as the audience displayed when I saw the film: it burst into applause twice—at "Alfred Hitchcock's *Frenzy*" and "directed by Alfred Hitchcock." But between the two phrases there is a shade of meaning which, in this case, is darkened by a failure in craft. *Frenzy*, although unquestionably Alfred Hitchcock's, is unevenly made by him.

What is good is very good; above all, the three best scenes. In one, the villain, a notorious but publicly unidentified psychopath, rapes the owner of a marriage bureau and then strangles her with his tie. Not quite so brilliant as the shower murder in *Psycho* (which is more unexpected), this is nonetheless a powerful display of editing and staging. While the assailant is heard reaching his climax—an uttered "lovely" matching each thrust—his poor victim is seen trying to cover her bare breast with the ruins of her brassiere, all the while reciting a prayer that counterpoints his groans. One frame is slashed by her arm reaching for a phone that must ring unanswered; another frame brings death to her eyes by suddenly, almost imperceptibly, freezing. Both are effects of a certain form of genius.

Because the rapist's victim was Blaney's ex-wife, he is wrongly accused of killing her. To make matters worse for Mr. Blaney (but thrilling for the audience), in the second and third of the film's outstanding scenes Rusk murders Blaney's girl friend.

After she exits from a pub, having just chucked her job there, the poor girl moves into jeopardy. Hitchcock literalizes this by cutting all street noises, thus establishing the girl's troubled self-absorption and allowing her future assailant to come up behind her in an ominous silence with, "Got a place to stay?" Since he had already illustrated Rusk's brutality, Hitchcock now reverts to his own versatility by placing the second murder at a brilliant remove. He does not take us to it but rather tracks back from Rusk's apartment in another unnatural silence and then, by bringing up only the street noises while we return to "normal life," achieves both a dramatic crescendo and an implicit defeat of the victim's inevitable scream.

Scene three adds typically ironic humor to the horror and technical bravado. While being strangled, the barmaid apparently grabbed her abuser's monogrammed diamond-studded toothpick; now he must get it back. But since he had placed her body in a potato sack and the sack in a truck, a certain awkwardness ensues. What is awkward for the villain is nonetheless opportune for his creator, allowing Hitchcock to mock death as one might when he has spent over thirty-five years making his living from it.

While Rusk is undoing the sack, the truck starts to move. Potatoes fall about (both inside and onto the road), the rigid feet sock his jaw, and he is nearly overcome by a fit of sneezing. When he finally locates the toothpick, he must break the corpse's fingers to dislodge it. All this time, the scene is turning comic because other cars, and ultimately the police, become involved in a sort of Mack Sennett chase with the driver.

Elsewhere, the film is comical without being macabre; Anthony Shaffer has supplied Hitchcock with more witty lines than he has had since *North by Northwest*. The minor characters are well drawn and skillfully acted. The horrors, equaled only by those in *The Birds* and *Psycho*, are better executed and less gimmicky.

Nonetheless, like pieces of fish in a soup offered the film's detective by his wife, *Frenzy's* ghastly goodies float in a mixture that can't be swallowed. Critics are right to applaud signs that the Master can still serve up a Grand Effect; they are wrong to ignore what robs it of tastiness.

Since belief (even though minimal) and empathy are crucial to Hitchcock's effects, the failings of Rusk and Blaney make *Frenzy* uninvolving. One man is meant to win us through wronged innocence and the other through charming kinks. Yet despite Hitchcock's repeated use of this pairing, only once—in *Strangers on a Train*—did he ever succeed in making his nut plausible and unrepellent, and his innocent troubling rather than insipid. Whereas *Strangers'* villain was charming, Rusk has only a few snappy lines with which to involve us in his crimes, and these are almost literally drowned out by the offensive sound of his teeth-sucking. More serious, *Frenzy's* hero, played by Jon Finch, is less interesting than his alter ego in *Strangers* and is also implausible.

Indeed, the whole film is so implausible that one hardly responds to its few excitements. Hitchcock is notoriously careless about probability, but what is acceptable license in a chase thriller becomes damaging in an intrigue directed by human motives. Among other things, this psychological melodrama asks us to believe that a notorious tie-murderer, who has been terrorizing London, would apply for victims at a marriage bureau, and that, having taken a fancy to its proprietress, he would bide his time so as to go at her only when most likely to cast suspicion on the hero. We are told that sex-nuts are otherwise normal. Why, then, should Rusk wish to implicate his friend? Does lust that is self-scourging enough to inspire contempt for its object also provoke vengefulness against a pal who failed in marriage and seemed appealing only to a homely lover? And what mass murderer confines himself, as it were, to killing *en famille*? (Both of Rusk's victims are Blaney ladies; the only other corpses we see are props to start and end the film.)

But all this is airtight compared to the evidence that exposes Rusk after the hero's indictment: a cleaning brush that he'd borrowed to tidy himself up after his truck ride is retrieved by the police. Despite the long period that had gone by between Rusk's murder and Blaney's capture, trial and incarceration, the brush is still saturated with potato dust (presumably its owner never used it).

Implausibility vitiates countless details (that coexist with an equal number of technical flourishes reminding us how little Hitchcock cares about the human dimension). Finch is too young to have been the R.A.F. hero dictated by the plot, and neither of his women is commensurate with him in age or beauty. But then one shouldn't be surprised by false casting in a film whose very title is a ruse: despite its big scenes, Hitchcock has rarely made a work so *unfrenzied*. Although he rightly stigmatizes most other films as "photographs of people talking," fully half of *Frenzy* falls under this description.

One series of such scenes shows how the film contrives to disguise the emptiness of its progress. Throughout *Frenzy* the detective recites details of the case to his wife while she is plying him with gourmet monstrosities. Hitchcock obviously means us to admire his skill in covering functional dialogue with comedy, but we can do so only if we forget that we have already witnessed what the detective relates. So far from being functional, the dialogue is merely an excuse for comedy that could not otherwise exist. What we see here is not Hitchcock's old magic but a rather newer variety that allows him to be called a magician when he isn't performing any trick.

A particular Hitchcock film warrants admiration on strictly instrumental grounds: because of numerous and various thrills, arresting transitions, characters just real enough to be audience surrogates, and plots sufficiently eventful to keep us from raising questions. Performances rather than statements, these films invite us to compare them on grounds of skill; as would not be true for a deeper artist, it makes sense to indicate that Hitchcock does national caricature better in *The Lady Vanishes* than in *Frenzy*, the will-his-friends-betray-the-hero? bit less well here than in *The Thirty-Nine Steps*, et cetera.

Instead, critics have been emphasizing continuities in theme (terror in the everyday, the inevitability of sexual antagonism, and so forth), forgetting that these aren't themes but rather patented excitements. Concentrating on sensibility rather than devices, such critics ignore signs of nonsense in *Frenzy*'s plot and characterization.

One mustn't forget that Hitchcock *has* been astonishingly fertile, that he knows better than anyone how to move an audience with movies, or that he has demonstrated his craft through several perfect examples. Nevertheless, no film of his can be more than the sum of its parts. Precisely the reverse is true of an artist like Truffaut, who rewards our interest even when he is not at his best. Truffaut's films are not more or less successful versions of a method of filmmaking, but rather more or less ample embodiments of a vision of life. They do not imitate each other; they all refer to Truffaut. Hitchcock displays techniques and fixations; Truffaut reveals his sensibility.

Sensibility isn't popular though; whereas *Frenzy* is chalking up an international success, *Two English Girls and the Continent* flopped so badly in France that Truffaut, out of desperate hopefulness, cut fourteen minutes after the initial run. Even so, it is doubtful that his effort will ever be shown here (although there has been some talk of a screening at the New York Film Festival). I, therefore, want to summarize this film so as to suggest how it adds to Truffaut's artistic presence and why it is more interesting than *Frenzy*.

It concerns a young Frenchman who becomes involved with two English sisters when one of them, intending him for the other, invites him to be their houseguest. Muriel fascinates Claude just as thoroughly as Anne had wished; but she will not give way to her growing passion for the man. Her hesitation is abetted by their parents, who decree a year's separation before any possible wedding.

During this period, Claude returns to France, where he frees his blocked libido through writing and chasing girls—one of whom is Anne, when she arrives in search of a life no less exciting. Back in England, Muriel suffers the torments of unsupportable passion, while in France Anne finds herself yielding to the easygoing continental mores. Partly because she knows that fidelity would chafe Claude, partly because she has caught his taste for sexual variety, Anne begins arrogating to herself masculine privilege just when she falls most deeply in love. Claude becomes jealous but cannot deny her right to live out his morality. Indeed, he is so reasonable that Anne finds herself unimpeded when she decides to marry another man.

Because this new liaison frees Claude for Muriel, Anne now confesses the affair to her, but this moral candor only produces a physical upheaval that shows how terribly Muriel has repressed passion. Coincidentally, Muriel had already sent to Claude her adolescent's confession of one night's quasi-lesbian experience that left unassuageable guilt in its wake. Now that she knows as much about Claude's "sins," however, as he about hers, Muriel decides to journey to France for the purpose of accepting sexuality. She gives herself to Claude. But then, proclaiming that he will never be a husband while she will remain *"une puritaine amoureuse,"* she departs.

Each of the principals comes to a richly ironic end. Anne, who adopted French freedom out of love for Claude, dies before her marriage, whereas Muriel, the repressed Englishwoman, marries and bears children. Claude reproduces himself only through a novel commemorating their affairs but translating the genders of all participants and spends his days cruising the boulevards in hope of chancing upon Muriel's daughter.

Toward the end of the fiction of the same name on which the film is based, Muriel sends Claude two letters. One concludes: "La vie est faite de pièces qui ne joignent pas," and the other asks "Qu'est-ce donc que l'amour, Claude?" The question is made rhetorical by the prior assertion: man's most precious adhesive only proves that things will not stick.

Intensely romantic and novelistic, *Two English Girls* seems, if not so implausible as *Frenzy*, at least as remote from our experience. And although more thoughtful, it thereby achieves no inherent superiority but only an obvious distinction in kind. For the sake of argument, let us also note that Truffaut's film shares crucial flaws with Hitchcock's. In both, the hero is uninteresting (Claude, until the end, is only appetite alternating between longing and bewilderment), and in both the blank in characterization is deepened by bad acting (excessive in the case of Jon Finch; subversive in the case of Jean-Pierre Léaud, who plays Claude with his special brand of wryness that invites us to regard the story with indulgence rather than sympathy). In both cases, as well, the antagonist threatens even that minimum of appeal requisite for involvement. No less than Rusk—with his toothpick and his ties—Muriel seems a boring exaggeration of the sexual impulse.

She is also less dramatic, for her anguish, unlike Rusk's, is stated rather than displayed. Yet having entered the Bressonian terrain of commentative style and spiritual subject, Truffaut largely shows himself a stranger to its required artistry. As Bresson's unique success makes clear, interiority is viable in this most exterior of mediums only when intense concentration turns all gestures and utterances into notes of a mental score. The invisible becomes dramatic only if it is incarnated with agonizing slowness but inexorable acceleration. Instead, Truffaut—the Mercury of great directors—pans, tracks, zooms away the contemplative hush in which his characters are meant to take on life. Distractingly mannered, the style of *Two English Girls* would be ruinous were it not internally defective. Luckily, Truffaut has outgrown his mercurial tendencies just enough to save his film from moving always on, rather than below, the surface.

The faults of *Two English Girls* prove that Truffaut is as inferior to Bresson in spiritual technique as Hitchcock is inferior to Truffaut in organic sensibility. But whereas a Hitchcock film is only as good as its technique, a Truffaut can triumph through sensibility even over technique that is unsuited to its subject. All Hitchcock films are about the director's skill in making them; Truffaut's are about a view of life variously embodied but always humane.

Like most of us, Truffaut finds the world unsteadying; like most of us, he hopes that love may prove a linchpin. Like those of us who remember that the linchpin is a person, he recognizes that love adds to the instability it is meant to mitigate but that what insures this problem is the source of everything valuable. Heretofore, neither Truffaut nor his characters allowed such comprehension to bleed off gusto. In *Two English Girls*, however, he enters upon a new sobriety. No longer does he joke about life's puzzling mixture of pleasure and pain; but being basically positive, he also doesn't become tragic. Pathos and irony result. Without changing his views or abandoning his subjects, he thoroughly revises his feelings about both.

He also revises his masterpiece. *Two English Girls* is taken from a book by Henri Pierre Roché in which the triangle disguised in Rochés earlier novel *Jules and Jim* is finally unveiled: hence, Truffaut's new film transforms the old film he had also drawn from Roché. But since Roché cast each autobiographical confession in a fictional rather than historical mode, and, since the two trios—Jim, Jules, Catherine and Anne, Muriel, Claude—are not strictly interchangeable, Truffaut was virtually invited to turn the second film into a meditation on the ambiguous relationship between truth and art. Indeed, this theme distinguishes his *Jules and Jim* (with its inset narratives and self-reflexive techniques) from Roché's. But in the manner of an authentic artist, Truffaut has grown into a deeper concern for his material. In *Two English Girls*, we see his youthful style, with its New Wave scintillations, receding. What remains is sheer insight.

Yet just as Roché sought the bedrock truth of self through a fictive overlay, so does Truffaut. Just as Roché understood life more deeply by recollecting his earlier version of it, so Truffaut, in order to reach deeper understanding, recalls the earlier versions of his own theme that are his previous films.

Some allusions simply parallel Roché's: just as the later Roché novel refers to the earlier, so Truffaut's *English Girls* refers to his own *Jules and Jim*. Hence, Claude takes Anne to the cafe to which Jules and Jim went; Anne lives in Catherine's studio; in both films Picasso's lovers hang on the walls. Sometimes, Truffaut alludes to non-Roché films. Early on in *Two English Girls*, Claude's voice "thinks" on the sound track that he ought to make a pass at Anne, just as Charlie did while walking with Lena in *Shoot the Piano Player*. In Truffaut's previous films such allusions were a game—much like Hitchcock's signature appearances—designed by a master entertainer to amuse watchful spectators. But they were also—as was never the case with Hitchcock's—self-conscious signs of continuity. Here—appropriately for a film that in its entirety alludes to an earlier work—they become systematized into a chart of growth.

Miraculously, this personal growth coincides with that of another person. For the allusion to Lena and Charlie—to take the cited example—was made possible in the scene between Claude and Anne because Roché had written into it a corresponding division between Claude's thinking and his behavior. Also authorized by Roché is the allusion to Balzac, who also figures in *The Four Hundred Blows* and *The Soft Skin* (which have no connection with him) and the pervasive literariness that reflects not only Claude and his creator but also a director who confesses to loving books as much as films and both more than people.

This miracle—that by being Roché, Truffaut can be more himself—underlies the newly serious assumption of a spokesman's role, which is the first thing one hears in *Two English Girls*. Truffaut's *Jules and Jim* begins with a voice reciting in total darkness before the credits:

"You said to me: I love you. I said to you: wait. I was going to say: take me. You said to me: go away."

The new film also begins with a disembodied voice, but it speaks after the credits and sounds like this:

"This night I relived our story in detail. One day I will write a book. Muriel thinks that an account of our troubles might help others." [my translation]

This parallel clarifies Truffaut's new goal. The speech from *Jules and Jim* is artfully disorienting. We know neither speaker nor occasion; the words themselves are puzzling, and since they occur before the credits we aren't even sure they belong to a film. By contrast, Claude speaks after we know where we are. He defines both the style and function of the film we are now witnessing and even says something about its subject. Earlier in his career, Truffaut replicated life's puzzlement in a style meant to arm us with pleasure against any pain implied in the vision—and we often thought less about the message than about the ingenuity of the messenger. Now he moves beyond entertainment (although some of the old habits cling), seeking use and thus aspiring to clarity, directness, relevance. Now old enough to put behind him the high jinks of prodigy, Truffaut is also experienced enough in life to take a more candid and unmitigated look at it.

This is evident from the film's presentation of lovemaking. Because Truffaut usually keeps sex distant, he has earned a reputation for tenderness; but the modesty is sometimes less tender than soft. In *Two English Girls* the tenderness shows itself and then turns tough, acknowledging the harshness of love as well as its loveliness.

Midway in the film, Claude takes Anne to an island where they consummate their passion in idyllic circumstances. Although the scenes show more nudity and erotic pulsation than had been typical, they are characteristically witty and oblique. But in the later lovemaking with Muriel, Truffaut strips back completely. Muriel's loss of virginity is reflected in her eyes, which are first seen holding their serenity and then yielding to voluptuousness. Then Truffaut tracks "tenderly" over her bare legs until he reaches a pool of blood into which the lens zooms, astonished. Earlier, we had seen Muriel vomit after hearing Anne's confession; now there is blood. Trauffaut is at last ready to show the mixture of fluids that is love: the pain mixed with delight, the self-transcendence that threatens both safety and integrity and so inspires an impulse toward separation no less powerful than the desire to remain linked.

Coincidentally, *Frenzy* is also franker sexually than Hitchcock's previous films. Never before had he shown bare breasts or come so close to showing intercourse. But these departures are profoundly impersonal, responses to the audience's new tolerance. Janet Leigh wore a bra while pressing up against John Gavin's bare chest in *Psycho* because Hitchcock needed to be sexy in this scene, but breasts were not then public performers. By contrast, Truffaut was covering breasts when his compatriots were scrambling to discover what else might be shown. Hitchcock uses sexual pain because the audience is ready for it and because it increases his store of thrills; Truffaut, because he is ready for it and because it is true.

Hitchcock has said often that he would never make films to please only himself and critics because he doesn't possess the self-indulgence that might throw colleagues out of work. He indulges himself with technique, leaving other choices to effective consensus. For this reason, he can never surprise us. His method is essential to the art of film, but once you have understood it—although local manifestations of inventiveness may newly crop up—you have lost its fundamental novelty.

With Truffaut, the situation is different. Starting with self—to which he continually cleaves via personal references—he indulges himself in every choice. Although what pleases him often pleases others, often—as with *Two English Girls*—it does not. Yet it is always surprising—in the manner of any growing thing.

As a result, despite the fact, *mutatis mutandis*, that *Two English Girls* is almost as defective as *Frenzy*, even unmoving, a moment's reflection—which only disintegrates the Hitchcock film—serves to make it seem astonishing. Who would have thought that so archaic a story had such contemporary application? Who would have thought that what we now needed—even in an imperfect version—was a work announcing the dominance of belief over libido and of sentiment over both?

At the very moment when men spell love with three letters or turn mating into a form of incorporation, Truffaut goes back to a novel that mocks such oversimplifications with its own—faintly ludicrous— refinements. Heedless of fashion and contemporary mores, Truffaut reminds us that every revolution enthrones a tyrant. The Freudian repressed no longer returns disruptively; rather, we long for its return so as to free ourselves from new disruptions. Having seen that the penis makes a ludicrous monarch, swingers long for the return of firmer standards. Long ago, trembling on the brink of an age of freedom, Roché's characters forecast this coming bondage. When Anne and Muriel tried to inhabit the freer world of Europe, they only taught the continent to regret the restraint it had thrown off. To fathom the startling relevance of their story, we have only to change its geographical antinomies into temporal ones, since those among us who are most ferociously modern seem most to need the old verities. For such people, sex has lost the power to thrill; as the film shows, naked bodies can be shocking only when they aren't taken for granted. And as we see outside the film, those who do take them for granted often end up, like Claude, cruising the urban landscape in search of a child who can save them. In strict violation of his common practice, Truffaut alters the novel to make it seem more archaic. In Roché, Anne marries and bears children; Claude sees Muriel's child. Truffaut makes the ending more baleful, whether in behalf of implications I sketch here it is impossible to tell. But I take it as a sign of the artistic independence I am exploring that he made these

188

changes despite all apparent risk and his long-asserted principle of strict fidelity to a source. It seems also a sign that Truffaut has used Roché to become himself, since Truffaut is literally responsible for the ending.

That Truffaut wishes us to ruminate in this manner, the film clearly shows: underneath its credits, we see piles of Roché's novel, and then only a single copy, annotated in Truffaut's hand. His film meditates upon its source, using the selves contained in it as a means toward his own maturation. This is the way of art, which, even when unartful, beckons us toward growth. No amount of skill can simulate it, and skill alone can never compete with it in interest.

(1972)

HOW NOT TO FILM A NOVEL

PARTLY because it is easier to borrow than to devise narrative material, partly because producers like to invest in what has already proven itself, partly because the forms are similar, movies have often been adapted from fiction. Unless a fictional source is reconceived for the screen, however, bringing it there involves little more art than is demonstrated when one arranges a harpsichord piece to be played on the guitar.

Distributed rather than translated by filming, most fiction is also thereby reduced. Our culture is strewn with the flesh of great novels rotting away as nonreaders march to local movie houses to see the narrative bones reassembled. But even lesser books are disintegrated. The venality that sends filmmakers to fiction is usually accompanied by laziness. Books are exploited not only for a story line on which to hang visuals or as a known commodity to attract ticket-buyers but also as a substitute for all art save the technical one of transcription.

Such parasitism has lately been encouraged. Commercial novelists now write in hopes of movie sales, since few people buy books anymore; more serious writers, influenced by the fashionable aesthetic of the *nouveau roman*, avoid interpretation and analysis as being falsely anthropomorphic. Yet even novels that emulate cinematic objectivity are saturated with interpretation, because words, in which fiction must be written, are discursive mental constructs. Pictures, on the other hand, can be wholly representational, and if a filmmaker expresses meaning principally through language, he is violating the genius of the medium. Only by means of eloquent images and expressive visual or aural transitions (with words in an ancillary role), can a film be both meaningful and cinematic.

But since fiction is adapted from motives of ease and security, visual eloquence, which requires effort, is rarely attempted. Most filmed novels are illustrated paraphrases, with setting and characters pictured, and theme rendered through dialogue. *Fat City* exemplifies both this method and its cost.

A flatly circumstantial story of two boxers—one, near thirty and oblivion; the other, young and starting his career—Leonard Gardner's novel intercuts these lives as if by parallel editing. Also cinematic is its emphasis on physical detail, its action milieu, and the sort of banal dialogue that can be spoken unobtrusively.

Furthermore, since the novel fails to show how or why its principal characters wind up in "fat city" (argot for "out of condition" as well as for a loser's vain dreams), it appeared destined to benefit from filming, because documentation is an effect more convincing in film than in fiction, as well as being more appropriate to the form. But while Gardner, who adapted his book, and John Huston, the director, have reproduced much of the original, they haven't taken pains to include what gave the novel its effectiveness.

Accretion of detail makes the book's points. *Fat City* depicts not only Billy Tully and the newcomer, Ernie Munger, but a host of lesser characters, some evident for no more than a sentence or paragraph. The heroes' squalid situations are thus made parts of a general condition. As a result, the absence of explanation is less bothersome: if everyone we see is down and out, why wonder about what ruined Billy or Ernie? Mistakenly, the film thins out this dense human backdrop.

The resulting loss of significance is clearest in the depiction of love. In the novel, Billy constantly compares his affair with the barfly, Oma, to his unsuccessful marriage, which, in turn, is compared to the affair, ending in marriage, of Ernie and Faye. The men's manager, Ruben Luna, is also a marital casualty, as we see when he muses about the "thick, wide, fierce lips that had once excited him" and the "plump cheeks creased where there had once been dimples," belonging to his now old and unresponsive wife. The film eliminates Luna's unhappiness, reduces Tully's past to a few references, and drastically cuts the tormented progress of Ernie's courtship and marriage. The emphasis on disappointment in love, which is one of the chief elements of the condition "fat city," almost disappears.

Yet the book's meaning depends on facts like the following: Ernie "had begun taking [Faye] out because for a time she had gone with Steve Bonomo, whose success with a previous girl Ernie had read about on the wall of a high school lavatory." Women as a conventionalized symbol of status and their unfitness for so emblematic a role go far toward explaining the malaise shared by all the novel's male characters. The loss of some filmic equivalent for a passage like the following is a loss not only of atmosphere but of Gardner's vision of his subject:

Then the man began to sing, repeating a single phrase, his voice rising from bass moans and bellows to falsetto wails. *Earth Angel, Earth Angel, will you be mine?* The song went on in the locker room, the singer, as he put on his clothes, shifting to an interlude of improvisation: *Baby, baaaby, baaaaby, uh baby, uuh, oh yeauh, BAAAAAAABY, I WANT you,* while naked figures walked to and from the showers and steam drifted through the doorway. Drawing on his pants, Ernie, bruised, fatigued and elated, felt he had joined the company of men.

The laconic distillation evident in such a passage is what allows Gardner's novel to be naturalistically circumstantial without the boring superabundance of naturalism. Yet what the book sketches through its background is so diminished by the film that speechifying must often make the author's points. One sees this in the single major alteration of the novel: a final scene invented by Gardner (and by Huston?) to replace the novel's more suggestive ending.

Leaving Tully in total dereliction, the novel fades out on Ernie, who is hitching back to Stockton after a successful bout in Salt Lake City, which has filled him with elation despite his meager fifty-dollar winnings. One of the two girls who picks him up seems potentially responsive when he begins to nuzzle her cheek. Suddenly, however, she gets angry and tells him to get out. Ernie protests being dumped in the desert, but the girl insists. Getting another ride takes some time, and he is forced to make the last lap of his journey by bus. Arriving in Stockton, "feeling in himself the potent allegiance of fate," he passes through a lobby, "where unkempt sleepers slumped upright on the benches."

This scene exemplifies Gardner's representational style. Ernie's consciousness doesn't register the portents suggested either by the woman's rejection or by the bums' presence, although events in the novel make us certain that they, not pugilistic triumph, are the fate that dogs him. But the film, whose atmosphere is much sparser, must spell things out. Thus a final meeting is contrived in which Tully accuses Ernie of being "soft at the center." Then the men go to a poolroom-bar, where they order coffee from an ancient oriental, whose appearance provides Tully with an occasion to talk about the tragedy of it all. Turning to look at some cardplayers, Tully's image freezes, while silence abruptly descends. He has, we are meant to feel, seen God knows what horror! Shaken, he asks Ernie to stick around, and the film ends.

Embarrassingly blatant, this is also false to the characters. Essential to Tully is the unreflectiveness that makes one vulnerable to circumstance. Nor does his attack on Ernie fit either his or the young man's behavior. The freeze frames pictorialize some epiphany, but what can he have learned? Tully's condition is qualitatively constant throughout the film. Indeed, unalterability is the essence of his misfortune.

The film duplicates structure, setting, and dialogue; but with a frugal presentation of background, it also needs rhetoric to convey meaning and thus betrays the book's spirit. Rare instances in which Huston tries to be visually expressive are equally traitorous.

Two examples: Tully accidentally meets Oma, who drunkenly chronicles her misspent life. She confesses that her second husband had "unnatural desires," as Huston keeps the camera on Tully. Visibly, the man is excited by lust, but the point of his affair in the novel is that Tully drifted into it because Oma's scolding reminded him of his wife. What the novel shows as another example of the trapping repetitiveness of loser psychology is turned by the film into a cute—but irrelevant—randiness.

A more disruptive error occurs in the otherwise well-staged fight scene between Tully and Lucero. Prior to the bout, we learned that the Mexican is also a wounded man; in his case, literally: he urinates blood. Hence the fight becomes graphic proof of the ubiquity of "fat city." Nor can defeat really be vanquished. Tully wins only through a т.к.о., which, in his dazed condition, he can barely understand, and he gets only one hundred dollars for his ordeal in the ring. When he goes to Lucero to offer consolation, they appear not as victor and loser but as battered men hugging one another in pain.

Midway in this scene, however, Huston focuses on Tully's eyes, when the man sits being tended in his corner. As in the ending, this moment implies a portentous realization, but we cannot imagine what Tully is thinking; and, in any case, it is false to imply that his problem is visibly distinct. (If in this shot Huston meant to show that Tully is dazed, he may be accused of blatancy inappropriate to his film's more prevalent style of understatement.) In this and other moments of adventitious drama Huston is shouting or winking at the audience because he doesn't know how to command our attention through eloquent detail.

Eloquence is only present—occasionally—in photographer Conrad Hall's lighting: a long shot that shows Ernie crossing before the dazzling clapboard of Luna's gym—the novice entering "the big time"; or the green gray haze of the boxing arena abruptly vanishing when incandescent bulbs come on to expose the spectacle's sordid sweatiness; or the image of Tully entering a bar that shows as livid black and white against the sun and so instantly makes us feel the interior deadness.

Paucity of detail, erroneous visualization and obtrusive rhetoric also mar the cinematic translation of James Dickey's *Deliverance* (like *Fat City*, adapted by its author). But since Dickey's book is richer and more ambitious than Gardner's, this story is made to seem even more underdeveloped.

Like its source, the film version of *Deliverance* mixes psychological and ethical speculation with a barely credible adventure from the world of pulp fiction. Three middle-class, middle-aged men, drawn by the superman mystique of a fourth, take a canoe trip down a wild stretch of river that is soon due for taming into an artificial lake. In passage, they encounter challenges from nature (raging rapids, capsizing torrents, unscalable cliffs that must be scaled) and from man (sodomy and the need to commit self-defensive murder). One voyager loses his life, another his dignity, and the leader his leg; but the hero gains in skill and cunning, although he forfeits some of his morality.

The first problem with *Deliverance* is the plot, which Dickey recognized to be preposterous, so that the novel, to disarm criticism, repeatedly acknowledges that its action is as incredible as what one finds in movies. The movie, ironically, takes everything straight, with the result that events become doubly incredible. Chief among them is the rape scene. Sodomy hardly seems the most likely threat awaiting Sunday woodsmen, but it is even less believable to see than to read about. Why hillbillies should seek pelt rather than pelf is a question made all the more clamorous by director John Boorman's lengthening of the scene in his adaptation. Moreover, by casting the role of middle-aged average Ed Gentry with the too-young, too-handsome Jon Voight and the rapist's victim with the too-fat, too-vulgar Ned Beatty, Boorman adds puzzlement about the hillbilly's taste to wonderment about his behavior.

Equally destructive of credibility is the manner in which Boorman stages the threat posed by the landscape (it is also boring: repeated shots of canoes running the rapids). In the crucial scene where Voight scales the cliff, for example, Boorman elects to compress and shorten the ordeal by means of interior dissolves. Unfortunately, this reminds us that no human could perform this feat without interruption, hence it could not be photographed in a long take. But this also throws away the suspense (brilliantly evoked by Dickey's prose in the relevant passage) that only a long, continuous climb could inspire.

But the film's errors in visualization are nothing compared to its failure to represent Dickey's meaning. As I argued in the *New Republic* (April 18, 1970), *Deliverance* makes sense only if we regard its narrator-hero as someone afraid to understand what has happened to him. Ample evidence in the novel indicates suppressed homosexual longing on Gentry's part for the muscular, risk-taking Lewis Medlock. What the hillbillies do to their victim, Gentry would do to his idol, were he not prevented by psychological inhibition. Without the presumption that males fear latent homosexuality, the novel's events seem unmotivated. Why else does Medlock conclude that the hillbilly is bent on rape even though he can't see him? Why else is Gentry so willing to hide Bobby's shame and bury his attacker? Fear of homosexual desire also explains Gentry's developing hatred of the victim, a hatred that ultimately becomes almost murderous. Saved by surrogates from having to act out his dangerous passion, Gentry nonetheless assuages the envy of Medlock's masculinity that inspired desire. Delivered from perversion, he delivers the others from danger, thus proving himself even more manly than Medlock. The latter loses his leg in their ordeal, so that Gentry's final triumph includes Medlock's symbolic castration.

One could hardly expect producer-director John Boorman to capture this theme in a film aimed at an audience whose tolerance for man's homosexual component is likely to be no less troubled than Gentry's. Unsurprisingly, then, he cuts out the pre-trip section, which makes the book's erotic orientation unmistakable. Similarly, he eliminates the eroticizing of apparently neutral actions (in the book, even scaling the cliff is compared to intercourse). But since Dickey's novel is comprehensible only in terms of its sexual nuances, Boorman's attempt to pitch things at the book's more public level was perhaps doomed from the outset.

Nonetheless, the film bowdlerizes more than it needed to. Gone, along with the erotic descriptions of man merging with nature, are even such innocent details as the heat of the sun, the way in which canoe seats cut civilized flesh, and such brilliant episodes—all eminently cinematic—as the horrible chicken's head, refuse from a factory, which the men find floating in the river, or the owl that invades Gentry's tent. As a result, the trip is made more monotonous and less frightening than in the novel. Replacing Dickey's portents, Boorman invents visual clichés (like the full moon in an angry sky before the rape scene) or facile ironies (like the rainbow after it).

Far worse is the film's attempt to render Dickey's apparent message about man against the wilderness. As in the novel, this seems imposed rhetoric, although it is even more disjunctive here. The script is full of inflated dialogue, made doubly ludicrous when spoken by the muscle-bound Burt Reynolds, as Medlock: "Machines are gonna fail and the system is gonna fail. Then survival. Who has the ability to survive. That's the name of the game: survival." Or: "Sometimes you have to lose yourself before you can find anything." As in *Fat City*, such dialogue indicates a failure to make events speak for themselves. But, as I've said, unless taken as a censored fantasy, the events in *Deliverance* are both incredible and obscure.

Medlock planned the journey because he believes that man is himself only when meeting the challenge of the wilderness. Thus the damming of the river is one more sign that modern society threatens man with emasculation. But, contradictorily, emasculation takes place because the characters leave civilization; and nature, although the occasion for tests of strength, only becomes so because the hillbillies have turned the trip into an invitation to lawlessness. We might take *Deliverance* as a critique of Medlock's code, but the action puts us wholly on the side of an understandable will to survive horrors. Hence we can't tell whether the tenderfeet have been improved or brutalized by their experience. Moreover, the relationship between hillbillies and nature is obscure: savage and unmodern though they are, the country people are not natural phenomena.

Instead of clearing up such contradictions or ambiguities, the film emphasizes them. For example, the movie begins with shots of bulldozers while Medlock is heard philosophizing about the majesty of nature. Near the end, when Gentry is lying his way out of the crime, Boorman makes him and us see the pathetic image of a church being moved to make way for the lake, its bell tolling as if in judgment. Both details suggest that progress is culpable and that a valuable heritage is being destroyed. But the hill people haven't been shown in an admirable light, and civilization has scarcely been shown at all. All we've witnessed are two lustful and cretinous backwoodsmen and some men like ourselves with whom we are in total sympathy in their desire for deliverance.

As in *Fat City*, the book's ending is altered for greater drama, but the result only adds further confusion. At fade-out Gentry is seen in bed, awakened by a nightmare vision of the dead hillbilly rising from the lake. If we are to take Gentry's success in murdering with impunity as a sign of moral deterioration, what are we to make of this manifestation of troubled conscience? But if we claim that conscience sets civilized man above nature and the savages, what are we to make of all those nasty bulldozers and the raped church?

Clearly, Boorman was no more concerned about clearing up the plot's significance than Huston was interested in finding a style appropriate to the laconic and representational prose of *Fat City*. Neither man was translating a vision from one medium to another; both were exploiting narrative material so as to be able to make a movie. This practice is as old as Hollywood. Something new has been added, however. The current willingness to regard film as the greatest form of narrative art springs from illiteracy and an avoidance of distinctions, for if the form has done astonishingly well in its short life, time (to say nothing of financial pressure) has kept it from equaling the older art. Yet men who reduce the work of others are not only uncriticized by those ignorant of anything not on celluloid: they are credited almost as if theirs were original achievements. Although John Huston manifestly thinned out what was already a thin (though affecting) novel, *Fat City* is being hailed as his return to the ranks of great directors. In the case of *Deliverance*, John Boorman has even been congratulated for having improved on Dickey's book (see Stephen Farber in the *New York Times*, August 20, 1972).

It is not as if we lacked relevant comparisons. Great films have been made from fiction: one thinks of the Bresson versions of Bernanos, of Truffaut's best work, or of the Joseph Heifetz adaptation of Chekhov's *Lady with the Dog*. Occasionally an indifferent novel becomes a brilliant film: think of what Stanley Kubrick did by turning Peter George's conventional thriller *Red Alert* into *Dr. Strangelove* or of how Carol Reed made his version of Conrad's *Outcast of the Islands* more masterly than the original. In such films, the book is reseen, its essentials translated into specifically cinematic terms. Far more frequent, unfortunately, are movies like *Fat City* and *Deliverance*, which cut their sources down to the length and expressive dimensions of a mere movie.

(1972–73)

197

TAMPERING WITH REALITY

By COMMON CONSENT, the most interesting films of the season (I write in the time warp peculiar to quarterlies) are Luis Buñuel's *The Discreet Charm of the Bourgeoisie*, which won the National Society of Film Critics' top prize, and Ingmar Bergman's *Cries and Whispers*, favored by the New York Film Critics. In my judgment, the Buñuel is silly and the Bergman hollow (although brilliantly acted and photographed). Yet both films are interesting because they shed light on a central choice between fantasy and realism.

Owing to its photographic medium, the essence of cinema seems to be verisimilitude. The Lumière brothers, who startled late-nineteenth-century Parisians with moving pictures of trains, crowds and so on, are generally credited with having set the form's aesthetic identity. No sooner had they proven the camera's documentary genius, however, than another Frenchman, Georges Méliès, showed it to be an equally good tool for actualizing fantasy.

For the most part, Méliès's fantasy films were a trivial combination of vaudeville and circus; but when commercial interests began to dictate that realistic films contain narrative and that they arrange their stories according to contrived stage formulas, fantastications like those of Méliès became, arguably, no falser to life. Materializing imaginary worlds isn't any more artificial than representing human behavior through the conventions of melodrama. Nor is it necessarily more honorable. Most realistic films resemble literary best sellers, which adopt the style of realism in order to lend daydreams a comforting credibility. Fantasy films may seem to offer an alternative, sacrificing reality in the interest of truth, but most works in this mode try only to be exciting and spectacular. Between plausible daydreams and sensational fantasies, there is little difference in seriousness.

Faced with the fact that most films carry false messages or none at all, critics often shift their attention to the envelopes; commerce may cause a filmmaker to lie, but art can still express itself as invention. Audiences are also drawn toward a brilliant surface because, notoriously, most of them go to movies as an escape from life. Therefore, it is no accident that even among the handful of films that are serious, only the exotic prove widely popular. Hence directors like Fellini, Buñuel or Bergman (when he is mystical) enchant even those who don't understand their films, whereas a realist like Antonioni doesn't pull crowds until he flirts (in *Blow-Up*) with expressionism. Reality, in movies, at least, is what critics and the *hoi polloi* make common cause in shunning.

I do not want to say that movies shouldn't be diverting or that reality equals realism. Purely diverting films are pleasant, and realism (which is one style among many) is not the only way to represent truth. I do want to say that our desire to clothe a taste for thrills in some dignity shouldn't make us ascribe truthfulness to methods aimed primarily at excitement.

In special ways, Buñuel's and Bergman's films are exciting. *The Discreet Charm* has some good comic premises, titillating shocks, and beautiful women wearing lovely gowns; Bergman's film is visually ravishing, dramatically sensational, and its women are even better to look at. The Buñuel also lays claim to being a serious, although comically articulated, comment on the middle class, while the Bergman purports to treat human isolation. In this, each film is pretentious.

The Discreet Charm commences as a plausible lampoon. A smartly dressed couple, the wife's sister, and their ambassador friend arrive for dinner at the house of a third couple. As might well occur, they have come a night too soon; but being urbane as well as pleasure loving, they cover their embarrassment and assuage their disappointment by insisting that the hostess accompany them to an inn. Their refusal to wait until she changes into street clothes believably marks them as oversophisticated, as does the condescension with which they choose a meal (finding the inn unfashionable, inexpensive and empty of customers, they fear that the food will be contaminated). While the men are ordering, the women wander off to a nearby room, where they discover a funeral being held for the previous owner, who had died that afternoon. This surprise is amusing but barely credible; since it comments on the greed of merchants rather than on the privileged class (the new manager explains that this restaurant is always *à service*), it is irrelevant to the film's announced subject. Henceforth, credibility and relevance fade away.

Midway in the film, a lieutenant, who has been staring at the three women from a distant table at a cafe, comes over, asks if they had a happy childhood, and, without further ado, recounts his own. The following memory scene, since it includes ghosts, is acceptable only as fantasy. Later, the interrupted meals that give the film a narrative motif are ever more bizarrely managed. In one, another soldier gratuitously describes a dream. Subsequent scenes turn out to be dreams by a given character or by one character about another who is also dreaming. The whole film eventually disclaims realistic status through intercuts of the six characters walking aimlessly on a road—a device that presumably symbolizes the bourgeois aimlessness of which prior scenes are the symptoms.

Buñuel's gradual erosion of reality is itself aimless, however. The dreamlike arbitrariness cannot imply, as one might suppose, that middle-class reality is as senseless as a dream. For that point to be made, Buñuel would first have to convince us that he is presenting middle-class life accurately and only exposing its fundamental illogic. Instead, the film's absurdity is Buñuel's style, not an inference about the middle class; the gradual erosion of reality is only an excuse for the preposterousness of the film's details. A true absurdist like Ionesco distorts reality to uncover some underlying truth; Buñuel, on the other hand, denies reality so as to buffer us against the pain of taking anything he shows as a judgment. This, I think, explains why middle-class moviegoers find so charming a film that consists of unrelieved and irresponsible slander against them. Since it is all a fantasy, why worry?

Critics, on the other hand, have taken the film seriously. The male half of the film's three principal couples deals in cocaine; one of the husbands easily leaves his wife in the apartment of the ambassador after discovering that she had been hiding in the man's bedroom; neither fact is a likely representation of middle-class behavior, yet the film is called an incisive satire. Many of the details aren't even this plausible. For example, the ambassador, on discovering a terrorist pretending to sell stuffed animals outside his window, obtains a carbine and shoots one; and a cafe, established as existing in the real world and not in a dream, runs out of both coffee and tea. Neither surprise has the remotest relationship to satire, but both induce a laugh that greets the unexpected.

The Discreet Charm is little more than a succession of switcheroos, some of which are not only unexpected but contradictory. A scene in which the original host and hostess insist on making love despite their maid's announcement of luncheon guests suggests a vitality, impulsiveness and disdain for social forms that are exactly contrary to the traits elsewhere ascribed to the middle class. In another scene, when an army invades the couple's dinner party and begins smoking pot, one of the three female protagonists, on learning that pot is also favored by Americans in Vietnam, steps out of character to raise the cogent objection that as a result they bomb their own troops.

But, of course, this disorderly and opportunistic little film has no consistent characters, just as it has no consistent meaning. The repeatedly interrupted dinner party lends a specious air of unity, but this plot device does not support the implication that the middle class is successfully rapacious. Several elements in the film don't even seem to belong to that subject. For instance, Buñuel introduces the character of a bishop whose parents were killed by the family gardener. For no apparent reason, the bishop applies for such a post at the house of one of the couples and is later, coincidentally, asked to confess the dying murderer. This he does, only to turn around and shoot the man. Such a sequence we owe not to the film's announced subject but to Buñuel's obsessive anticlericalism. Similarly, the long subplot about the mythical dictatorship of Miranda is not an attack against the bourgeoisie but rather, with embarrassing circumspection, a sidelong gibe at Buñuel's native Spain. As if in recognition that he had stopped dramatizing his announced subject long before the film's conclusion, Buñuel resorts to flat-out assertions in the last scene, where, for example, one of the guests reports that the traffic through which they hurried to reach their meal forced them to run over about 150 cyclists.

Half the film is neither satire nor farce. The lieutenant's memory scene, in which his dead mother advises him to murder the father who's killed his true sire, would be horrifying were Buñuel not as inept at picturing corpses as he is fond of devising irrelevant occasions for doing so. Similarly horrific—at least by intention—is a scene in which the French police torture a suspect by placing him in a wired piano where his writhings draw music from the strings and—in a final Buñuelian touch—red cockroaches that fall on the keys as a substitute for blood.

These scenes, oddly neglected in the ecstatic notices for Buñuel's "comedy," are disjunctive in meaning as well as effect. The lieutenant's dream is slightly relevant since it ends with his assertion that the crime was never punished and so supports the presentation of a blithely criminal middle class. Even so, it goes on too long, and when we hear the second soldier's dream, we understand that both episodes contribute not to Buñuel's satire of the bourgeoisie but to his preeningly outrageous disdain for motherhood (the lieutenant's mother makes him a murderer and the soldier's mother frustrates the longing that she had gratuitously inspired).

Buñuel's film doesn't deserve to be called surrealistic because its dislocation of reality isn't dictated by theme but by narrative opportunism. Nor is it absurdist, because the details are too silly and incoherent to be taken as cogently interpretive. Rather *The Discreet Charm* is yet another sign of Buñuel's commitment to incongruity. For people in search of titillating diversion from their daily lives, switcheroos may seem exciting; but such trifling doesn't deserve to be taken as a reflection of anything significant, unless—owing to its successful reception—it reflects a middle class whose most salient fault may turn out to be a tolerance for insult.

Bergman's film is also unflattering to the middle class, which is represented by two sisters—one, vain, hypocritical, adulterous; the other, harsh, unloving, self-destructive—and their husbands, who torture or are tortured. Only a third, dying sister has any attractive qualities, but even she is less impressive than the one nonbourgeois character, a saintly maid.

Within this ambience, as always, Bergman explores human isolation, which is here ironically and temporarily mitigated by the even greater horror of death. *Cries and Whispers* is so much more artful than *The Discreet Charm* that, were I aiming at comprehensive criticism, I should have to explain how the acting, camera movements, lighting and sound track in Bergman stand as a reproach to the nonperformances, arbitrary tracking, garish colors and contradictorily naturalistic background noises in Buñuel. But I am more interested in the tampering with reality found in both films and so must neglect their wide disparity in skill.

Like Buñuel's film, *Cries and Whispers* begins realistically and gradually becomes dreamlike. Through Harriet Andersson's superb enactment, the early scenes powerfully dramatize the ordeal of dying: the yellowing skin, cadaverous cheeks, stertorous breath and pain that sets one to howling. Nothing is spared us; not the last dry retching, heartbreaking final peace, or the laying out of a corpse whose hands have already become too rigid for easy placement on its breast. But this intensely real death occurs in a context of insulting artificiality. With its limited palette of red, black and white, the physical production seems, under the circumstances, obscenely chic. And although one might argue in Bergman's defense that it is meant as a calming influence, the sensationalism of the film's events makes it seem more nearly an elegant background designed to set off horrors.

During the deathwatch the two sisters characterize themselves by remembering episodes from their past. What they recall is too sketchy for explanation and too violent for credibility. About Maria (Liv Ullmann), we learn that she has had an affair with the doctor who tended the maid's daughter and then added to this offense against marriage and motherhood a refusal to aid her husband when, immediately and melodramatically after divining her betrayal, he plunged a letter opener into his chest. Karin (Ingrid Thulin) is also badly married, although her ordeal leads to self-destruction. After a stagy scene of silent hostility while dining with her husband, she mutilates her genitals with the shard from a broken wineglass, then marches into his bedroom to offer her violated self in reproach. Credibility is even more obviously sacrificed to sensationalism here than in Maria's reminiscence. Because Bergman means us to take Karin's deed as an extreme reaction to long-standing anguish rather than as a sign of aberration, he cannot show it as clearly planned by her. But it is difficult to believe that she would have taken the shard from dining room to bedroom if she had no idea what she would do with it.

Falseness for effect overwhelms the film, when, as in Buñuel, memory gives way to dream. In the climax of Cries and Whispers, the dead woman comes back to life begging for comfort, only to be rejected by her sisters. Karin's refusal is complete; Maria, pliant and hypocritical, initially ministers to the ghost but bolts in terror when it grasps her. The scene ends when the maid, who had earlier taken the dying woman to her breast, similarly comforts the corpse.

This scene, fundamentally preposterous, is also redundant. What it tells us about the three women, we have already learned. Only if we take it as the maid's self-aggrandizing fantasy—it is presented as her vision—does it have any possible excuse for existing, outside of effect. The rest of the film, however, shows that the maid is a figure of pure selflessness. Were the dream ironic, it would save Bergman from the charge of class sentimentality as well as redundancy, but, obviously, we are meant to take it straight.

The pretty idea of the all-giving servant is no easier to swallow than the miracle because Kari Sylwan performs her part so badly. Physically, she is perfect—comforting girth and blankly innocent eyes —but she remains an abstraction given body without soul, since her eyes barely register emotion. The emptiness of her performance— unique in the whole range of Bergman's films—exposes the willful tendentiousness from which the role springs. As in Buñuel's film, the supernatural is invoked only to excuse the unbelievable. We conclude that the vision is assigned to the maid not as a means of characterization but only to permit a scene that Bergman wants for its shocking effect; since the maid is simple-mindedly pious, we can accept the fact that she might imagine such a thing.

Nonetheless, Bergman needs the scene to be more than a hallucination; he has the corpse call it a dream for the maid but not for herself. Yet the staging maintains a stylization that emphasizes unreality; for example, when, having heard the corpse moan, the maid tries to rouse the sisters, they are shown as soundlessly muttering statues.

This sort of noncooperation between image and dialogue occurs frequently in the film, even when we are not meant to think ourselves in some ambiguous twilight zone between reality and dreams. Exemplary of this flaw is the long critique of Maria's character that her lover delivers while both peer into a mirror. He comments on the "discomfort and hunger" in the once-soft mouth, on the telltale wrinkles above her eyebrows, and so on. But when the woman quite properly asks, "Can you really see all that in my face?" (he had already admitted that the wrinkles are visible only by daylight) he replies, "No, I feel it when you kiss me." This remark is like excusing the miracle by assigning it to the vision of a superstitious peasant. Bergman needs to convey this information about Maria and the nature of her affair, and he wants the effect of two actors talking directly to the audience. Intensity created by the close-up masks the clumsiness of the exposition; but the intensity is denied by the invisibility of what is "seen," so Bergman simply asks that we take the scene as a metaphor.

Bergman often permits his characters to make speeches in which they act as their own interpreters; but, at his best, he makes these part of the action (the great confession in *Persona*, for example, is extorted from the nurse by the actress's silence). In *Cries and Whispers*, the characters' revelations are inadequately motivated. Through much of the film, the crisis of death is used the way bad playwrights use alcohol—to loosen tongues. But in a scene like the lover's critique not even an atmosphere of tension is invoked to excuse the loquaciousness.

Rarely has Bergman made a film in which drama and rhetoric seem so independent. Without such devices as the blasphemous speech of the priest who delivers Agnes's eulogy, the film would even lack a theme, and its painstaking dramatization of dying might seem only clinical. Yet even that would be better than surrounding the clinical with rhetoric and sensationalism. Although Bergman wants not only to show the horror of death but to say that life is scarcely less terrible, death alone is real in *Cries and Whispers*.

Despite the vastly greater skill with which it is executed, *Cries and Whispers* is as ill-conceived as *The Discreet Charm*. Each film fails to convince us of its theme. *Cries and Whispers* implies that the anguish of death differs only from that of life in being terminal (among other indications, Karin, at one point, howls exactly as Agnes had just before her death). Yet death is recreated with recognizable accuracy whereas life is reduced to a series of attitudinizing speeches and poorly motivated outrages. Most husbands don't attempt suicide as a simple consequence of (unseen) adultery; most women, even after years of speechless meals and marital derision, don't mutilate themselves; most clergymen don't speak of living "on the dark, dirty earth under an empty and cruel sky." A dour view of life can be represented through exceptional cases, but we must be permitted to see an element of common humanity. For all its immediate power, *Cries and Whispers* can seem persuasive only to those already convinced that life is rotten, just as *The Discreet Charm* can only seem more than a vaudeville show to someone who believes that the middle class is, by definition, a pack of monsters interested only in self-gratification and suavely impervious to crime, war, or revolution.

Since I now want to argue that the season's best film is Jan Troell's realistic *The Emigrants*, let me reiterate my awareness that realism is not the only valid film mode. I have previously celebrated in these pages examples of rigorous stylization (*Une Femme Douce*) and expressionism (*Deep End*) because those films used intensification or exaggeration without losing credibility. Furthermore, as I have argued when discussing Hitchcock, dedication to emotional effect is a valid aim by itself so long as no pretense is made to being truthful.

Nonetheless, by capturing the look and movement of the physical universe—of which, of course, man is a central part—film expresses its formal uniqueness. If we needed reminders not only of the potential beauty in such replication but of its power to inspire and enlighten, *The Emigrants* provides them. Troell's is not only a good but a great film.

This greatness is, however, difficult to describe. Recounting events from Bergman's or Buñuel's film or quoting some of their dialogue conveys a good idea of what each film means to say and of how it does or does not move us. Physical imagery is frequently disjunctive in *Cries and Whispers* (although the actresses' faces are crucial and superb), and in *Discreet Charm* one can nearly close his eyes after a first view of the characters' studied elegance, so redundant and visually inept is Buñuel, so inattentive to what is neither verbal nor conceptual. *The Emigrants*, on the other hand, lives in its images. Everything is said by golden sails against a blue sky above green water, by the weary, worried faces of the travelers, by the serpentine water oozing like oil after a storm, by the dazzling flash of a red waterwheel in intense close-up when the emigrants reach the promised land and see their first steamboat. For a film that lasts three hours and ten minutes, less than fifty triple-spaced typescript pages are necessary to record the dialogue.

Unfortunately, the film's greatness has almost been put beyond American audiences. Fearing commercial failure with what has been ballyhooed as the first recent gamble by a major American distributor on a foreign film, Warner Brothers cut Troell's original from 190 minutes to some 140. The film's favorable but unpassionate press may, in part, be explained by this fact (but, Warner Brothers would argue, so would its decent showing at the box office). The result, nonetheless, disfigures a masterpiece because the corporate butchers cut frames and trimmed scenes virtually everywhere.

Someday, some lucky scholar, by comparing prints of the original and cut *Emigrants*, will be able to document the apparently instinctive Hollywood conviction that life is a well-made play. In films that are conventionally plotted, this instinct inspires efficiency and conciseness—virtues typical even of unimpressive American films. But Troell wants to approximate the randomness and lack of emphasis in real life. Warner Brothers, instead, brought his film (which I was able to see uncut in Stockholm) as close to slick narrative practice as it could.

Troell's adaptation of Vilhelm Moberg's four-volume novel shows why the Swedes came to America, documents the ordeal of their migration, and ends with the settlers' arrival in Minnesota (a second film, *The New Land*, will trace their subsequent experience). To encapsulate a complex historical phenomenon without lessening its dimensions, Troell disclaims all abstracting or nondocumentary intentions. As I presume the novel does, the film exemplifies the migration through a small group of characters with whom we can easily identify. Prominent among these are a young couple, Karl Oskar and Kristina, Karl Oskar's younger brother, Robert, and a priest uncle named Danjel. We see how poverty, agricultural failures and family tragedy impel the couple, how Robert is attracted away from his apprenticeship to a cruel farmer by the promise of freedom, and how religious persecution drove out men like Danjel. Troell transcends the efficient limits of paradigm implied by this conventional use of representative figures (although his means are interfered with in the reediting).

Most apparent are quick brushstrokes in the background of the canvas. For example, when the protagonists' ship nears America, Troell, for this once, shows another ship alongside, startling us with a fact obscured by our emotional investment in the principals: what we have been witnessing was, in the actuality, multiplied many times over. This could not be altered but throughout the film Warner Brothers cut similar reminders of the protagonists' surroundings: starving children hovering around the kitchen where Kristina cooks, for example, or the appearance of an old man on crutches when she and Karl Oskar are walking away from their burned barn. By such brief details, often unremarked even by the characters, Troell lets us infer social conditions that help to explain the migration. Warner Brothers, in the manner of most American producers, will not risk asking their customers to infer anything and so tightens scenes for the very blatancy of explanation that Troell has labored to avoid.

The Emigrants disavows explanation precisely so as to immerse us in what seems a bare chronicle of daily life. Although Troell is, artfully, giving us data pertinent to comprehension, in order to draw us into the process of comprehending, he forswears narrative highlighting, interpretive emphasis, explanatory dialogue, symbolism— all discursive devices that abstract or distill.

Essential to this effect is the peculiar way in which he intercuts events from the lives of Karl Oskar, Robert and Danjel. Narrative intercutting is conventionally used to link spatially or temporally separated units and thus to diminish our sense of the distance between them. A director interested in narrative thrust, will, therefore, move us along quickly through visual connectives or analogies between scenes that increase tempo or establish narrative causality. Troell, on the other hand, wishes to avoid obvious manipulation or interpretive signals and to maintain our sense of large stretches of time even though he is showing only a small part of what happened; hence, he uses transitional bridges sparingly and does not try to link all his scenes. Sometimes, he will even confuse us about which of the stories we have entered; often, he will delay the narrative point of an episode so that we believe we are witnessing a vignette from daily life when we are really seeing a fact that will later be recalled as having helped to explain the characters' motives. This seeming neglect of pertinence and consequence allows each moment to stand out in itself, thereby focusing our attention on its actuality rather than on its contribution to narrative meaning. Troell's calculated jaggedness has been polished by Warner Brothers into the smooth turning of a historical saga (although certain sequences have been ground down too far, so that they seem not jagged but incoherent). Several untouched sequences remain, fortunately, to indicate how Troell, by arranging narrative eddies, simulates the actual flow of time.

One sequence in particular serves to exemplify both this and Troell's determination that no event achieve more emphasis than it would have for his stoical characters, even if such determination forces him to neglect a seductive opportunity for spectacle: Karl Oskar's barn burns, ruining a crop that he had brought in after a year of drought. The flames are beautiful and dramatic, but Troell shows only enough of them to establish that they happened. We next have a brief scene of the couple's reaction to the devastation and then immediately cut to a hat seen above a wall, so that it takes us moments to understand that we have been brought into Robert's story again, leaving Karl Oskar and Kristina to deal with their problems beyond our view. Instead of conventionally dramatizing the causal relations between one big moment and another, Troell lets some of them develop offscreen; the first part of *The Emigrants* creates a sense of ongoing lives, which we are privileged to witness from time to time.

The vividness of life and ubiquity of death are also exemplified by one of the few sequences entirely cut from this version. Very early in the original film, Robert drowns an ailing cat, pelting the animal with stones in order to put it out of its misery. This poignant scene is abruptly terminated; only about two hours of playing time later does it assume any importance—when Robert is sick on the way to America and thinks that he is being made to repent for the cat.

Death is the constant that both qualifies the film's essential optimism and adds poignance to the dream about America through which this optimism is expressed. Hardship, including the death of a child and the continued threat of starvation that is implicit in Kristina's fecundity, is the principal motive for Kristina and Karl Oskar's emigration. En route, Danjel's wife dies and, later, his child; Kristina nearly dies as well; funerals of minor characters punctuate the journey, which is also bedeviled by bad food, seasickness, lice. When they reach America, they learn that an even longer journey awaits them, for they must cross a vast land.

The second part of the film, which records the hardships of the trip, provides vicarious experience as vividly as anything ever filmed. Even more brilliant, because its immediacy is also so economical and so illuminating about the characters, is the superb docking sequence.

Troell's photography and construction convey the moment's excitement without inflation or sentimentality. We see both the setting foot on shore and the teeming life of the dock, both subjective shots of what the emigrants see and reaction shots of the Americans (even shots of one crowd seen through the other crowd); Troell does not let us forget that the thrill of arrival must have been qualified by logistical confusion and the fear of being a stranger. With a tactfulness that seems breathtaking, Troell also permits us to note—very briefly—blacks in chains, wastrels and harlots. No visual underlying is given; we are only expected to remember that very early in the film Robert had read from a book proclaiming America a land exclusively composed of free men and successes. Troell even achieves here a moment of visual poetry. From Kristina's vantage as she is lolling on the grass, he cuts to a blinding shot of the sun, then tracks quickly down to her as she clutches the grass as if in terror, only to realize that she is not under attack but rather basking in dazzlement.

Visual dazzlement is, indeed, the style of the film; but, unlike the pretty *Cries and Whispers, The Emigrants* makes gorgeousness discursive. Central to its meaning is the natural beauty that makes leaving Sweden a plan thinkable only in extremity and arriving in America a solace because it, too, is beautiful. Dazzling as well is the acting in this film—above all, by Max von Sydow and Liv Ullmann (as Karl Oskar and Kristina), who perform the miracle of making you forget that they are stars, not peasants, and stars trained by Bergman in a style as far from Troell's understated naturalism as could be imagined.

In addition to being an extraordinarily beautiful film and one of the few that deserves to be called epic, *The Emigrants* is free from false drama, from sentimentality and manipulation. It captures a historical experience with the intimacy required for identification and the scope required for understanding, and every frame is shot, lighted, staged and conceived as if it were the last. Not intellectually complex or emotionally various, it nonetheless provides food enough for thought and feeling through the amplitude of its representation and the artfulness of its means. "Reverence for life" is a grandiose phrase, but *The Emigrants* makes you understand what it can mean. By contrast, Buñuel's and Bergman's films express little more than reverence for their creators' dreams. Dreams may be this season's winners, but reality will remain our champion.

(1973)

NOTES

CAROL REED AND THE NOVELISTIC FILM

1. The best-known and fullest accounts of this subject in English are: George Bluestone, *Novels into Film* (Baltimore, 1957), Allardyce Nicoll, *Film and Theater* (New York, 1936), and Robert Richardson, Jr., *Literature and Film* (Bloomington, 1969).

2. For further discussion of this issue see the essay by Arnold Hauser entitled "The Film Age." As Erwin Panofsky indicates in his classic "Style and Medium in the Motion Pictures," film narrative springs from melodrama and the penny dreadful. Both of these pieces are available in my *Casebook on Film* (New York, 1970).

3. Among the deplorable are films of unredeemed staginess and literary frivolity like *Midshipman Easy* (1935), *Penny Paradise* (1938), *The Girl in the News* (1940), and *Kipps* (1941),—although this last has a good story, adapted from H.G. Wells's novel, good performances (especially by Michael Redgrave in the title role), and the charming authenticity of background Reed sometimes achieves even when forced to use sets. Less worthy is a group doomed by awful scripts: *The Running Man* (1963), *The Agony and the Ecstasy* (1965), *Flap* (1970) and *The Public Eye* (1972).

All Reed's trivial films have some merit: *A Girl Must Live* (1939) is a sort of *Stage Door* musical comedy, ruined by its plot but full of tangy details about show business and beautifully acted and staged. *Night Train to Munich* (1940), made in blatant imitation of *The Lady Vanishes*, is wholly inferior to the original, though it does display Rex Harrison to good advantage. *Young Mr. Pitt* (1942) is an intelligent historical film subtly designed to make contemporary audiences spot an analogy between Pitt trying to rouse England against the threat of Napoleon and Churchill doing the same against Hitler, but the film is trivialized by a silly romantic subplot and by a physical production that fails to make models and process photography create a bygone era. Here, negatively, is a good example of the crucial importance of setting in Reed's best films. On the other hand, story is important too, as one sees from *The Man Between* (1953), in which Reed tried to repeat his success with *The Third Man* by revisiting an occupied post-war setting (East Germany this time) and the theme of disillusioned innocence. However, *The Third Man*'s script is a masterpiece by Graham Greene, but Harry Kurnitz's for *The Man Between* is pabulum. *A Kid for Two Farthings* (1955) and *Trapeze* (1956) are the most poignant near-misses in Reed's career. The former tells a charming story, but is made with so uncharacteristic a neglect of authenticity (sets alternating with locations, and an ill-assorted cast speaking in incompatible accents) that its delicate blend of fantasy and versimilitude never jells. *Trapeze* is, so far as I know, the best example of an artistic use of Cinemascope, which suits its circus subject and which permits Reed to offer his most dazzling examples of multiple actions simultaneously occuring on several visual planes (see page oo for a discussion of this technique in *The Third Man*); but it is hampered by a hackneyed and tawdry script. *The Key* (1958) is similarly authentic in background and phony dramatically, although it is one of Reed's best-performed films (by William Holden, Sophia Loren, and Trevor Howard). *Oliver!*, Reed's first musical, is a triumph of craftsmanship, but the show isn't very good. (See Pauline Kael's fine tribute to this film in *Going Steady*, New York, 1970.)

Three of Reed's films are officially listed as lost: *Talk of the Devil, Who Was That Lady?* and *Climbing High. Laburnum Grove* exists, but I have been unable to see it. I have omitted *Odd Man Out* (1947) because, although I do not share the general opinion that it is one of Reed's best efforts, the film presents too complex a case for the brief treatment I have given the other films in the interest of comprehensiveness.

4. See Reed's account of the filming in my *Encountering Directors* (New York, 1972), pp. 169–72. Hereafter cited as *ED*.

5. Reed is right to say that Baines mustn't die for Philip's error (see *ED*, p. 165), but he is wrong to shift our attention so fully. More important than Baines's fate is Philip's discovery of his false bravado. Had Reed not been restrained by his instinctive commercialism, he might have ended the film, without putting us at ease about the valet, at the moment when Philip realizes the extent of his childish error and thus begins the process of maturation. The treatment of Jenny in *The Stars Look Down* provides a precedent, but presumably Reed was less willing to leave the audience in doubt about a character whose life was in danger than about one whose future was wholly undetermined.

6. This issue will first be broached in the discussion of theatrical vs. cinematic dramaturgy in Jean Renoir, but the realistic essence of screenwriting will not become a fundamental issue until the chapters on De Sica and Olmi.

7. See *ED*, p. 170.

8. See *ED*, p. 177.

9. Before leaving this tantalizing near-success, we ought to note one last sign of Reed's crucial and cinematic improvement of Greene's conception. Much of the tale's comedy involves Wormold's efforts to recruit his agents, but since the joke comes from the repeated discrepancy between what Wormold tells the Foreign Office and what he actually does, repetition diminishes the humor. Reed turns the process into a nearly silent montage and pictorializes the discrepancy by using a split screen. As a result, he speeds things up, thus minimizing the anti-comic effect of Greene's redundancy. Moreover, since Wormold's activities go by almost literally too fast for us to think about them, the subsequent contradiction between the Foreign Office's stupidity and its presumably dangerous wickedness is rendered less blatant in the film than in the book.

10. Reed decided to keep Kerima (Aissa) mute because she had no acting experience and he was afraid she might miss her cues. Art springs from strange causes. See *ED*, p. 167.

11. Although the details are discussed in behalf of a somewhat different view of the film, the alter-ego motif is fully treated in Joseph A. Gomez, "The Theme of the Double in *The Third Man*," *Film Heritage*, VI (Summer, 1971).

12. Apparently, the murder-betrayal was to have been clearer than it is in the film, but censors insisted that Martins appear to be acting under orders. See *ED*, p. 175.

13. Reed and Greene are agreed on this point. See *ED*, p. 170, and Greene's introduction to the novella he later drew from the script of the film.

14. Reed always keeps us aware of the real world in which the action is taking place, even when it would be simpler to shoot on a set rather than on location. For example, during the early scene at a cafe in which Calloway has his first talk with Martins, Reed places Calloway against a window through which we can see the legs of passers-by. Here and elsewhere through the film, street noises are realistically rendered. This is a small detail, but one can distinguish between cinematically inclined directors and those who think only of dramatic action by noticing whether or not outdoor noises are heard in their indoor scenes.

15. The film abounds in examples of brilliant compression, most of which are less dazzlingly clear. For example, when Calloway asks an aide to take Martins to a hotel, the aide begins telling the writer how much he admires Westerns and when both enter the lobby after a cut, the conversation has just reached its conclusion. Smooth transitions, with such elisions neatly covered, are crucial to the film's propulsiveness.

16. Reed, quite properly, took full credit for these decisions in our interview. See *ED*, p. 171.

17. The script misquotes this line, as well as several others. It also gets some details wrong. I have never yet seen a printed script that is accurate to the film in all details. This remains one of the chief problems in the bedeviled area of film criticism.

18. The significant decision that we never actually see Harry doing something criminal inspires two of Reed's best cinematic inventions. In one, the porter offers to give Holly information, then turns back into his room and, with the zither going mad on the soundtrack, looks offscreen in astonishment. The shot is held very long; only its duration and the music evoke the impending murder. In the second example, when Calloway takes Martins to a hospital where he hopes that the spectacle of Lime's penicillin victims will persuade Martins to cooperate, we are made to infer the suffering caused by Harry from the reaction on Holly's face.

We do see Harry shooting an M.P. in the sewer chase, but our censure of this is qualified by the knowledge that it was self-defense and that it was partly caused by Holly, whose childish bravado put his life in jeopardy and caused Paine to lose his trying to defend the amateur.

19. *ED*, p. 169.

JEAN RENOIR AND THE THEATRICAL FILM

1. *Jean Renoir* (New York, 1973), p. 22. Both because Bazin is perhaps the most admired film critic here and in his native country and because he regarded Renoir as "his favorite director" (*op. cit.*, p. 8), it is important to find him admitting that Renoir's silent films aren't distinguished works of art. But neither Bazin nor François Truffaut, who edited the cited volume, will say just how bad Renoir's silent films are. For the record, I see some merit in the first of Renoir's eight works in the silent era. *The Water Girl* (1924) has some realistically staged and lovely outdoor scenes, but the others show how limited is

Renoir's visual sense. *Nana* (1926) also contains some striking shots, but these are mostly due to Claude Autant-Lara's ingenious sets.

2. Outdoor scenes, particularly those containing rivers, are misconstrued by Renoir's admirers. Facts are turned into symbols and thence into mere figures of speech. Andrew Sarris, the American master of the *auteurist* school which keeps people from understanding Renoir by submitting him to unquestioning adulation, regards the master's career as "a river of personal expression." See *Confessions of a Cultist: On the Cinema, 1955/1969* (New York, 1970).

3. Accidentally, for production difficulties kept Renoir from completing the project. Renoir's troubles with this film are recounted in many places. A convenient source is Bazin's book, already cited. The unphotographed scene, together with another that had been designed to start the film, can be read in Pierre Leprohon, *Jean Renoir* (New York, 1971), pp. 178–181.

4. All quotes from "Une Partie de Campagne," *L'Avent–Scene,* XXI (December, 1962). My translations.

5. "A Picnic in the Country," in *The Mountain Inn* and *Other Stories,* translated by H.M.P. Sloman (Penguin, 1955), p. 142.

6. This, of course, is not true of farce or slapstick, which helps to account for the prevalence of these forms in silent film.

7. "The Surfaces of Reality," *A Casebook on Film,* p. 40.

8. (Cambridge, 1949).

9. To a certain extent, accident makes Renoir's version seem less plotted than Maupassant's. The scene that Renoir could not shoot contains a line, as in the story, that more or less tells us Henriette *was* impregnated and therefore had to marry Anatole. The omission is a happy accident. Since the story's irony is evident even without the baby and since the baby seems a triumph of narrative neatness over biological probability, the loss of this detail is not to be regretted. Furthermore, although we also lose the important implication that Mme. Dufour suffered from sadness unforseen when she set out to enjoy herself, the baby thrown out with this bathwater would have upset Renoir's treatment of the love scene, which is markedly more lyrical than Maupassant's. Both versions give us a nice day that turns stormy, but Maupassant's is also nasty whereas Renoir's is bittersweet.

10. Andrew Sarris, Pauline Kael, Penelope Gilliatt, William Pechter—American critics who can't agree about anything—join in praise whenever the subject is Renoir. Probably no other major filmmaker is so uneven, but few of Renoir's admirers will utter even respectful questions about his work. This odd lack of discrimination, together with the near unanimity with which it is expressed, is a subject worthy of investigation. However, it has barely been noticed here. In France, Clément Cartier has pointed out the existence of a Renoir cult. See "Le Jouet de Jean Renoir" in the Premier Plan volume on Renoir (Lyon, 1962).

11. Cf. Pierre Leprohon, *op. cit.,* p. 160; ". . . the natural loveliness of the setting grates badly against the schematized characters . . . And what can be said about the outdoor comedy scenes which are played in the worst theatrical tradition . . . ?"

12. The first line is quoted from my notes, the second from Leprohon, p. 189.

13. Many such examples of inept visual symbolism disfigure Renoir's films. In *The Human Beast,* for another instance, Renoir cuts from the lovers sinking to the floor in a passionate embrace and shows a barrel filling up with sluice-

water. But see the discussions below of the geranium in *Grand Illusion* and various symbols in *The Rules of the Game*.

14. Renoir has often proclaimed a hortatory motive behind this film. See, for example, the interview with Robert Hughes, quoted in Leprohon, p. 167 and *ED*, p. 215.

15. Cf. Leprohon's similar discussion of the film in his book already cited, pp. 108–109.

16. At his best, as in this film, Renoir is relentless in avoiding theatrical clichés. In our interview, he analyzes very accurately both his motive and the effect of the film's depiction of prison life:

> I always try to fight clichés. For example, movies always pretend that everything leads to drama. Instead, in *Grand Illusion*, when one of the soldiers is told that his wife is sleeping with another man, we would normally expect him to agree when another soldier tells him to forget her. "There's more than one woman in the world," the other soldier says. And the prisoner replies, "Yes, but I have only one." In the same scene, there is a teacher-prisoner who believes in cliché. When he hears they are going to Holland, he says, "Ah, Holland, the tulips, the flowers," and another replies, "Holland, the cheese." (*E.D.*, p. 244.)

See the script (Simon & Schuster; New York, n.d.) for the actual lines. Renoir seems to have forgotten that the betrayed husband is also the teacher, so there is an additional avoidance of cliché, because the man of fidelity and unexpected stoicism is later revealed, as Boeldieu says, to have "the taste of a parlour-maid" (pp. 52–54; all citations to this edition).

17. Cf. Otis Ferguson, "War and Other Pieces," *The Film Criticism of Otis Ferguson* (Philadelphia, 1971).

18. *Theory of Film* (New York, 1965), pp. 109ff.

19. Occasionally, Renoir states his ironic theme. Thus Maréchal and Rosenthal, before making for neutral Switzerland, discuss the meaning of what they do:

> MARÉCHAL: . . . German snow and Swiss snow look pretty much the same!
>
> ROSENTHAL: Don't worry, there's a genuine man-made frontier right there, even though nature doesn't give a damn.
>
> MARÉCHAL: I don't give a damn either . . . And when the war's over, I'll come and get Elsa. . . . We've got to finish this bloody war . . . let's hope it's the last.
>
> ROSENTHAL: That's all an illusion!

But, like Henriette's speech, such lines are rare enough to point up the finely symptomatic quality of most of the film's dialogue.

20. Renoir's original treatment would have underlined the ironic fact that war creates more fraternity than peace. There was to have been an epilogue in which Maréchal and Rosenthal, who had foreseen celebrating the armistice with Christmas at Maxim's, would manifestly not meet there. The empty table would have symbolized the grand illusion of fraternity in peacetime. See Bazin, p. 182.

21. *Theory of Film*, p. 73.

22. Leo Braudy makes the same point in his *Jean Renoir: The World of His Films* (New York, 1972), p. 126. His book also treats extensively—albeit with an

emphasis different from my own—the combination of theatrical artifice and realism in Renoir's films.

23. The best example of this strategy in Renoir's work is *Boudu Saved from Drowning* (1932). But this charming film, distinguished by Michel Simon's brilliant performance of the title role, remains too nearly a play to require extensive treatment here. Other films almost equally noteworthy, and for the same reason negligible in this context, are *The Crime of M. Lange* (1935) and *The Golden Coach* (1953). Both contains a single brilliant performance (by Jules Berry in *Lange*, Anna Magnani in *Coach*). Moreover, the former is based on an original script by Jacques Prévert (in collaboration with the director) that is one of the best Renoir ever used. However, as André Bazin says, "the dialogue is considerably more obtrusive in *M. Lange* than in Renoir's other films. It often asks you to listen to it for its own sake." (*Op. cit.*, p. 43.)

24. Films in this category include *Toni* (1934), *The Human Beast* (1938), *Swamp Water* (1941),, *The Southerner* (1945) and *The River* (1950). The first two present melodramatic crimes of passion in proletarian milieux that do not adequately influence events and thus merely make the plots seem less natural than their contexts. The other three fail because Renoir doesn't seem on intimate terms with the relevant foreign settings. James Agee discusses this issue pointedly in the case of *The Southerner* (see *Agee on Film*, volume I [New York, 1958], pp. 166–168).

The other Renoir films not treated here are either "theatrical" in the worst sense of the term (*Chotard and Company*—1932, *Madame Bovary*—1933, *The Lower Depths*—1936, *This Land Is Mine*—1943, *Diary of a Chambermaid*—1946) or simply lacking in sufficient weight or interest: *Purging Baby* (1931), a silly Feydeau farce done simply to prove that Renoir could shoot it quickly. *The Bitch* (1931), a pointless *crime passionel* story with a few good moments and Michel Simon. *Night at the Crossroads* (1932), a notoriously confused attempt at a mystery film. *Woman on the Beach* (1946), melodrama, badly performed and worsened by studio interference. *French CanCan* (1954), a Vincente Minelli musical executed without comparable skill. *Elena and the Men* (1956), a leaden farce performed by actors with absolutely no talent for this genre (Ingrid Bergman, Mel Ferrer and Jean Marais). *The Will of Dr. Cordelier* (1959), a trivialization of *Dr. Jekyll and Mr. Hyde*. *The Elusive Corporal* (1962), the very entertaining prison break film that *Grand Illusion* isn't. *The Little Theater of Jean Renoir* (1969), a revue made for television.

La Marseillaise (1938) is a sport in the Renoir canon: a nearly documentary film about the French Revolution that contains many finely realistic scenes but never rises much above the level of an historical pageant. A more comprehensive treatment of the director than I attempt here would pay close attention to this film, which, like *Boudu*, *M. Lange*, and *The Golden Coach*, belongs to Renoir's second level of achievement.

25. All quotes from *Rules of the Game* (New York: Simon and Schuster, n.d.).

26. Like everything about the film, this is the most successful expression of a common device in Renoir's work. By playing a character whose life function resembles that of a director but who fails where his alter-ego must succeed, Renoir jokingly reminds us of the necessarily approximate parallel between life

and any artistic representation of it. This, in turn, reflects a modesty that is Renoir's most attractive feature. (See the passage in our interview [*E.D.*, p. 218] in which Renoir explains that he started *The Bitch* with a Punch 'n Judy show to remind the audience that it was watching a spectacle and not life itself.) Like many modern artists, Renoir is half-ashamed about the pretentious claim of art to be telling the truth, but he prefers gentle mockery on this point to, say, the brooding investigation that Bergman undertakes in *Persona*.

27. Introductory material in *Rules of the Game*, p. 14.

28. Introductory material in *Rules of the Game*, p. 5.

29. Even Lisette, who, like Marceau, represents an animality that contrasts with romanticism (Christine and Jurieu) and social compromise (Robert and Geneviève), shows herself less willing than any of the men to play the game continuously. When Octave says he will go off with Christine, she asks him to take her too, and perhaps even instead.

30. Numerous details hint that La Chesnaye has long been paying this price in his marriage. Even before he almost loses her to Jurieu, he shows how the rules have kept her distant. Separate bedrooms, the knock before entering, decorous handkissing, are all poignantly *comme il faut*. By contrast, Octave, who is sentimentally rather than sexually involved with Christine, is shown rolling on a bed with her. Robert's rules almost permit one peaceful maintenance of a harem, but they don't allow too obvious a display to the favorite.

31. The parallel is mostly established through visualization, but occasionally the script underlines it rhetorically. For example, Marceau tells Octave that Jurieu "rolled over like an animal, when you're hunting" (p. 165). The cinematic superiority of *Rules* to Renoir's other films is indicated by the superfluousness of such underlining, but so is Renoir's inveterate theatricalism.

32. Introductory material to *Rules of the Game*, p. 17.

33. Like all distinctions between theater and film, this is quantitative and historical, rather than essential. Until very recently, few plays exemplified "mixed media" methods; although, of course, one need go no further than Greek drama to show that theater has always had room for other arts within its own domain. Nonetheless, the theatrical mode is so nearly synonymous with stylization that contrast between stylization and actuality is almost impossible in a play. David Belasco in America and the *Theatre Antoine* in France are exceptions that famously prove this rule. The recent vogue for "happenings," "mixed media performances," etc. is partly to be understood, I think, as the theater's attempt to incorporate effects that are relatively easier and more appropriate in film.

34. Here we touch upon one of the most self-serving evasions in film criticism. Except to clarify the meaning of a given film by showing how it altered its source, few critics are in the habit of comparing films with novels, plays, etc. from which they are—usually—drawn. But surely, one of the first questions to ask of a film adaptation is whether or by what means it is artistically justified as an independent creation. However, we have become so accustomed to the parasitic practice of most filmmakers and are—evidently—so partial to the medium that the question, "is this trip necessary," rarely gets asked.

I propose a rule-of-thumb: all adaptations are guilty of superfluousness until proven innocent, and any original script, at least initially, deserves the respect we bring to books, plays, poems, symphonies, etc. So far from being analogous to a symphony—or even a little song—the average film exhibits the arranger's craft rather than the composer's art.

An Outcast of the Islands is aesthetically valid because, in ways I have tried to describe, it improves on Conrad. Instead, most films merely exploit what they adapt. Nonetheless, Reed's film no more represents the most cinematic method of adaptation than the most cinematic method of anything else. The aesthetics of adaptation will be increasingly spelled out in the following chapters.

35. Cf. the excellent article by Dina Dreyfus, "Cinéma et Langage," *Diogène* (July, 1961), pp. 26–36.

FEDERICO FELLINI: JUXTAPOSITION

1. Philosophy and symbolism have been the chief subjects in most longer studies of Fellini. Among these—to me, misguided efforts—the most solemnly portentous and over-intellectual in Geneviève Agel's *Les chemins de Fellini* (Paris, 1956). Gilbert Salachas' book, scrappy though it be, is subtitled "An investigation into Fellini's films and philosophy." Supposed symbolism of setting is featured in the Fellini chapter of John Russell Taylor's *Cinema Eye, Cinema Ear* (New York, 1964). The other available works are either chatty or mystical or both. Examples are Deena Boyer, *Two Hundred Days of "8½"* (New York, 1964) and Eileen Lanouette Hughes, *On the Set of "Fellini Satyricon"* (New York, 1971). The best general study—although superficial—is Angelo Solmi's *Fellini* (New York, 1968).

2. Fellini uses collaborators—principally Tullio Pinelli and Ennio Flaiano—for his scripts, but he usually writes the original story and disdains adaptation. Nonetheless, the central importance of scripting in his films and the coincidence between his decline in quality and a new partnership with Bernardino Zapponi indicates that Pinelli and Flaiano share a good deal of the responsibility for Fellini's achievement. As always with cinema, the precise limits of this responsibility are unlikely to be known, but it is important to note that Fellini isn't quite the self-contained *auteur*.

3. *ED*, p. 126.

4. "I vitelloni," *Three Screenplays* (New York, 1970), p. 110.

5. "The White Sheik," *Early Screenplays* (New York, 1971), p. 197.

6. *Variety Lights* also has its seemingly digressive but significant scene, which shows that Fellini was hostile to conventional dramaturgy from the beginning and would subvert its rules even when working within an alien tradition (this first directorial assignment was a collaboration with the conventional filmmaker, Alberto Lattuada). The scene begins as the hero, Checco, stumbles upon two performers, whom he subsequently hires for his troupe, at a time when the piazza in which the gypsy plays would be empty of activity were it not for her performance. Her singing literally maintains joy and sociability after they have supposedly ceased, a point Fellini demonstrates by bringing on a night watchman who upbraids her for making noise after hours. When some roused neighbors shout complaints, however, the watchman is sufficiently caught by her appeal to merely beg that she lower her volume. As the scene fades, we see not only Checco, his jazzman, and the watchman delightedly listening, but a fat old woman whom the music dances into grace. This scene contributes little to the

plot but achieves a moving image of man's need for gaiety to hold back the night.

7. *Private Screenings* (New York, 1967), p. 24.

8. Like virtually everything else about him, this too was clear in *Variety Lights*. So long as the film is content to show the vaudevillians in action and to make the point that Liliana is pursuing a phantom by seeking success, *Variety Lights* is one of Fellini's successes. In the second half, however, as in the second halves of *La Strada* and *The Swindle*, plot takes over and credibility (to say nothing of pertinence) vanishes. Checco falls for the girl, becomes vulnerable to humiliation, and opens the film to an imitation of *The Blue Angel*, which, even if it were better executed, would be totally inappropriate to the prior context.

9. See *ED*, p. 128.

10. This point along with much else that should be said against this film can be found in John Simon, *Movies into Film* (New York, 1971) and Robert Brustein, "La Dolce Spumoni," *New York Review of Books*, V (December 23, 1965), pp. 22–24.

11. *Fellini Satyricon* (New York, 1970), p. 26.

12. *ED*, p. 137.

13. "Fellini Finds 'an Unknown Planet for me to Populate.' "

14. *Fellini Satyricon*, p. 38.

15. *Fellini Satyricon*, p. 8.

16. *New York Times, op. cit.*

17. *ED*, p. 31.

18. This account agrees with the analysis of Norman Holland in "The Follies Fellini," *Hudson Review*, XIV (Autumn, 1961).

19. *La Dolce Vita* (New York, 1961), p. 79.

20. *A World on Film* (New York, 1966), p. 321.

21. This suspicion receives support in my interview with Fellini, who avers that the title was intended to mean "the sweetness of life" and that *"la dolce vita* is very fascinating." See *ED*, pp. 131–132.

22. See Camilla Cederna's account of the filming in her edition of the original screenplay (*Modena*, 1965).

23. "Huit et Demi," *L'Avant-Scene*, LXIII (1966), p. 62.

24. Interestingly, Fellini responded to my question about the illogic of this scene with a defense that makes the flaw even more obvious: "I show what would happen if his dream were fulfilled. Since he is not an oriental caliph but rather an Italian Catholic, his dream isn't spontaneous but only a response to frustrations built up in him by his Jesuit upbringing. Therefore, his dream carries its own punishment. For that reason, the sequence quickly changes from joy to sorrow." (*ED*, p. 134.) But, of course, sorrow is ultimately banished in the scene: the revolt remains odd.

THE BLOW-UP: SORTING THINGS OUT

1. The Julio Cortázar short story on which *Blow-Up* is loosely based considers a question only hinted at in the film: does art have metaphysical and moral power over reality? Cortázar's hero is an amateur photographer but a professional translator, and the first part of his story is a characteristic dissertation on the difficulty of representing life in words.

The main event is the hero's encounter with a young boy and an older, blond woman in the square of an island in the Seine. Thinking he witnesses an act of sexual initiation, he takes a photograph. But when the woman asks that it be returned, an older man, who had been watching the scene from a car, interrupts their altercation. During the argument, the boy escapes, convincing the translator that, despite his meddling, "taking the photo had been a good act." When he returns home and blows up the photograph, however, he concludes that the older woman was apparently seducing the boy for the man. Revolted by what he has witnessed, the photographer now imaginatively relives the experience, trying to release the boy from the imagined horror just as he had released him from the actual scene.

Antonioni's transformations are nearly total: the ages of the couple are reversed, she becomes dark-haired, the scene takes place in a garden rather than a square, seduction becomes murder. More important, the art theme is made peripheral (by introducing a literal artist as a foil to the commercial, mechanical photographer), while Antonioni focuses on the social context that he invents for the episode. I can think of no better way to illustrate the profoundly social orientation of Antonioni.

Notice, too, that whereas Cortázar's hero never discovers whether his "good act" was really effectual, Antonioni's photographer learns that he accomplished nothing. Cortázar's territory is the imagination, where fabulous victories match equally fabulous defeats; Antonioni's world is sadly unconquerably real.

2. This detail is perhaps a shade too audacious, but there is precedent for it in *L'Avventura*. When Anna disappears, she leaves two books behind her: the *Bible* and *Tender is the Night*. We get a brief glimpse of the latter, which I presume was meant to hint at Anna's relationship with her father and thus help establish a motive for her disappearance. Thus we have the father's response when Claudia gives him both volumes: "This looks like a good sign. Don't you think so? As far as I'm concerned, anyone who reads the Bible could not have committed an act of impropriety." (This, like all passages from the first three films, is quoted from *Screenplays of Michelangelo Antonioni*. New York, 1963.)

3. The dialogue at the "pot" party is equally clear. After great difficulty, the photographer succeeds in getting Ron to listen to his problem:

P: "Someone's been killed."
R: "O.K."
P: "Listen, those pictures I took in the park—[No response] I want you to see the corpse. We've got to get a shot of it."
R: [Bewildered] "I'm not a photographer."
P: [Bitterly] "I am."
R: [Nonplussed] "What did you see in that park?"
P: [Resignedly] "Nothing." [Ron, who can't focus his eyes well, motions the photographer to follow him. The photographer does. Next scene shows him waking up from the debauch.]

4. Space limits prevent me from detailing Miss Kael's other vagaries, but I should like to draw attention to her one valid point. Miss Kael accuses Antonioni of secretly loving the mod life he exposes. This brings me to *Red Desert*.

Antonioni's first color film is in most respects identical to its predecessors, although it is less successful. More even than *La Notte*, it employs rather embarrassing dialogue. Also, whereas we can accept the representational function of normal people without needing to know much about them, a sick soul inevitably raises questions of causality which Antonioni is characteristically unable to answer.

More seriously, *Red Desert* is spoiled by a confusion in perspective, and it is here that Pauline Kael's point about *Blow-Up* is relevant. Much of the film seems to indicate that the camera is essentially inseparable from Giuliana's twisted viewpoint. That presumably explains why we see things change color or lose definition as she looks at them. But in addition to several scenes in which she does not appear, there are examples of contradictory focus: in one scene, objects are in soft focus before and behind her, while she is sharp. This technical confusion reveals a deeper thematic uncertainty. Much of the film suggests that Giuliana is sickened by an actually terrifying culture, full of slag heaps, loneliness and exploitation. But since Antonioni is at pains to show that industrial Ravenna is also beautiful (he even paints steam pipes in gay colors), we begin to suspect that Giuliana's inability to adjust is culpable. This would support the apparent optimism of the ending.

Blow-Up suggests, for some people, a similar ambivalence. Isn't Antonioni fascinated by the mod scene, which, although empty, is certainly colorful? So far as I can see, people who answer "yes" are confusing their own response to the undeniably exciting materials with the film's theme. (Could Antonioni have convinced us that a film was set in mod London if he had photographed London the way he photographed the Lipari Islands or Milan?) Nevertheless, I think this is an arguable and important question. Were it possible here, I should like to consider the nostalgia for answers that Antonioni shares with most great modern chroniclers of the wasteland.

INDEX

Kovacs, Ernie, 21
Kracauer, Siegfried, 3, 54, 56, 143
Kubrick, Stanley, 8, 14, 171–178, 197.
 Films: *A Clockwork Orange*, 171–178; *Dr. Strangelove*, 173, 174; *The Killing*, 172; *Lolita*, 173; *Paths of Glory*, 173, 2001, 174
Kurnitz, Harry, 211 n.3
Kurosawa, Akira, 6, 7, 8, 120

Laburnum Grove (Carol Reed), 212 n.3
La Dolce Vita (Federico Fellini), 104–107, 146, 160
Lady from Shanghai, The (Orson Welles), 171
Lady Vanishes, The (Alfred Hitchcock), 76–77, 182, 211 n.3
Lady with the Dog, The (Joseph Heifetz), 6, 197
Landis, Jessie Royce, 71
Landscape After Battle (Andrzej Wajda), 6
La Notte (Michelangelo Antonioni), 120, 123–124, 128
La Strada (Federico Fellini), 100–101, 104, 146
Last Year at Marienbad (Alain Resnais), 9
L'Avventura (Michelangelo Antonioni), 120, 121–123, 128, 130, 160, 220, n.2
Léaud, Jean-Pierre, 184
Leigh, Janet, 121, 187
Lemmon, Jack, 144
Leprohon, Pierre, 214 n.3, n.11, n.12
Les Dames du Bois de Boulogne (Robert Bresson), 162, 164, 169
Life Upside Down (Alain Jessua), 160
Lockwood, Margaret, 17, 76
Lodger, The (Alfred Hitchcock), 70, 80
Lolita (Stanley Kubrick), 173
Lumière brothers, 198

M (Fritz Lang), 6
Macdonald, Dwight, 120, 133, 135
Magician, The (Ingmar Bergman), 151
Magic Mountain, The (Thomas Mann), 122
Magnificent Ambersons, The (Orson Welles), 171
Mailer, Norman, 132
Maltese Falcon, The (John Huston), 6

Man Between, The (Carol Reed), 211 n.3
Manchurian Candidate, The (John Frankenheimer), 141
Man Escaped, A (Robert Bresson), 159, 161, 164, 169
Mankiewicz, Joseph, 14
Marnie (Alfred Hitchcock), 69
*M*A*S*H* (Robert Altman), 144–145
Masina, Giulietta, 98
Maupassant, Guy de ("A Day in the Country"), 43–49, 214 n.9
Méliès, Georges, 198
Meurisse, Paul, 50
Midshipman Easy (Carol Reed), 211 n.3
Miles, Sarah, 131
Mississippi Mermaid (François Truffaut), 148–150, 153
Miss Lonelyhearts (Nathanael West), 168
Moberg, Vilhelm, 206
Moravia, Alberto, 103, 146
Morgenstern, Joseph, 131, 136, 142
Mouchette (Robert Bresson), 165, 169
Musset, Alfred de, 57–58

Nabokov, Vladimir, 173
Naked Night, The (Ingmar Bergman), 150–151, 160
Newman, David, 137, 141
New Land, The (Jan Troell), 206
Nicoll, Allardyce, 211
Night Train to Munich (Carol Reed), 211 n.3
Nights of Cabiria (Federico Fellini), 87, 97–99, 101, 104, 106
North by Northwest (Alfred Hitchcock), 77–80, 81
Notorious (Alfred Hitchcock), 78
Novak, Kim, 71
Novels and films, 12–14, 31, 40–41, 190–197, 211 n.1
Nykvist, Sven, 154

Odd Man Out (Carol Reed), 212 n.3
Odyssey, The (Homer), 122
Oliver! (Carol Reed), 212 n.3
Olmi, Ermanno, 86, 160, 212 n.6.
 Films: *The Fiancés*, 160; *The Sound of Trumpets* (*The Job*), 160
Our Man in Havana (Carol Reed), 21–23, 24, 27

226